LIFE ON THE RUN

LIFE ON THE RUN
One Family's Search for Peace in War-Torn Ukraine

SERGEY MAIDUKOV

ROWMAN & LITTLEFIELD
Lanham • Boulder • New York • London

Published by Rowman & Littlefield
An imprint of The Rowman & Littlefield Publishing Group, Inc.
4501 Forbes Boulevard, Suite 200, Lanham, Maryland 20706
www.rowman.com
86-90 Paul Street, London EC2A 4NE, United Kingdom

British Library Cataloguing in Publication Information Available

Library of Congress Cataloging-in-Publication Data available
ISBN 978-1-5381-8573-5 (cloth: alk. paper)
ISBN 978-1-5381-8575-9 (electronic)

∞™ The paper used in this publication meets the minimum requirements of American National Standard for Information Sciences—Permanence of Paper for Printed Library Materials, ANSI/ NISO Z39.48-1992.

For my sweet granddaughters, Severine and Erica

Contents

Acknowledgments

There would be no book without my editor, agent, and friend, Claire Gerus, who worked diligently and patiently with me on this book. She made me feel comfortable, despite my unpolished English, for which I thank her with all my heart. I am also extremely grateful to executive editor Ashley Dodge at Rowman & Littlefield, who opened the doors for me to enter the US book market. I will never forget this, Claire and Ashley.

And Svitlana, my beloved and loving daughter, special thanks to you for your talented illustrations of our common history.

The weight of this sad time we must obey,
Speak what we feel, not what we ought to say.

—Shakespeare, *King Lear*, 1605–1606

Introduction

This book was initiated in February 2022, when my family and I shared the fate of millions of Ukrainian refugees driven out of their cities and villages by the Russian invasion. More than a year has passed since then, and now I am grateful that my memoir was not published earlier. It took a while for my initial fiery feelings to cool down. Events are often best seen from a distance, and then they can emerge with crystal clarity.

Moreover, I would not want this to be a bitter recounting of our experiences—although, in all honesty, vestiges of anger still linger within me. I prefer to focus on the moments of love, friendship, unity, courage, and faith that we Ukrainians experienced during this terrible year. While war can be experienced as an out-of-control fire, it can also bring forward the healing warmth of kinship.

I began working on this book in an atmosphere of overwhelming panic and despair as the roar of Russian missile explosions hit our country. Soon, I would join the millions of refugees who fled Ukraine. I finished writing it after my return to my homeland a year later, hunched over my computer in the darkness of blackouts punctuated by the howl of air sirens.

As the year passed, my attitude toward the war changed. It was no longer an "imminent disaster." Now, the war was a reality, forcing us to move forward into the unknown. Death, blood, destruction—we have had to accept their presence as part of our daily existence. Only by acceptance can we hang onto our sanity.

This does not mean that we've become reconciled to this scenario—far from it! We now realize that this war must be experienced and ultimately won—much like an illness to be survived before we can return to health and wholeness. Our goal is clear: to survive—despite daily threats of extinction as individuals, families, and a nation.

Who can predict what trials we will have to endure and where we will be when the war ends? Truly, it will take a miracle to keep us all safe as long as we have a hostile, aggressive neighbor with a nuclear arsenal on our troubled eastern border. Is there a force in the world that can stop this madness?

I think about these things now, and I thought about them at the very beginning of the war when my mind was reeling with more pressing questions. Can I protect my family? What will we eat tomorrow? Where will we sleep? How can we survive with no money?

Many of these questions are still unanswered. However, the one clear reality that emerged was this: We will not give up! We must resist a ruthless enemy whose primary goal is to capture our land, destroy our future, and reduce us to a faint memory. *This will never happen.* A free Ukraine *does* exist and will *continue* to exist. My people, my country, my beautiful family—all will continue to exist.

I am beyond grateful that I have been granted this opportunity to share my experiences with you, the reader, wherever you reside on this planet. At a time of challenges to our political, moral, and physical well-being, I offer this book as a testament to the power of tenacity, courage, and resilience.

Divided, we will fall, but connected, we can survive any challenges sent our way.

PART ONE
THE RUSSIANS ARRIVE

SVITLANA MAYDUKOVA

The Russians are coming!
—US SECRETARY OF DEFENSE, JAMES FORRESTAL, 1949

CHAPTER 1

Like Migratory Birds

MARCH 2022: THE SMALL RESORT TOWN OF TRUSKAVETS ON THE Ukrainian western border has never seen such a crowd, even in its prime. There are parents with whining children, married couples with their leashed pets, teenagers eager for entertainment, seniors barely holding up, youth gleaming with health, youngish women treasuring their passing beauty, loners and cliques, close-knit families, and motley crews.

These are not tourists, by the way. Since Putin declared war on Ukraine, several hundred thousand refugees have arrived here in western Ukraine, and this small town has become a hub for people seeking to escape to Poland, Slovakia, Hungary, or elsewhere. We have arrived here in Truskavets along with other refugees. No one truly knows where the roads they choose will take them. Therefore, many linger here for days or even weeks, gathering their courage before leaping into the unknown. It is almost impossible to rent apartments or houses, and sanitoriums and tourist hotels are packed to capacity.

The water is healing and crystal clear here in Truskavets and there are plenty of restaurants, bars, and shops. However, they are always packed, with long lines to endure if you're hungry or thirsty. This is only one of many frustrations. If you realize you're low on cash, even minimal purchases, like a bar of soap or a box of bandages, are exorbitant. And these inconveniences are only the tip of the iceberg, believe me.

Since everyone here is temporarily homeless, we are called "internally displaced persons" and can no longer receive assistance from the state. Volunteers help those who find themselves in hopeless situations and provide them with warm clothes, hot tea, soup, and shelter. The rest of us are on our own, but no one grumbles. Our communal misfortune has united us and made us more resilient and cooperative—for the most part!

Ukraine has become a battlefield with its own lines of defense, fronts, and rears. A once-distant war is now omnipresent. Armed minefields are made invisible by a sprinkling of soil. Nobody knows how many Russian mines are lurking in the fields and on the roads in this country. They sit there in the soil, biding their time. Some of them will be found by bomb squads, and some will remain unseen, a death sentence reserved for a future encounter. Whose child or which workman will find them? Will the mine be noticed before the fatal step is taken?

This is, indeed, war, and there was no more logic for its presence than there would be for the arrival of a tsunami, a fatal illness, or a serial killer with mass murder on his mind. Its time is now, its place is here in every corner of Ukraine, even in this town—Truskavets—a town with no newspaper.

War has a long reach: from the Kremlin's offices to the last miserable mountain hut in the Ukrainian Carpathians, and we are destined to feel its menacing presence. Will it be a dead relative, a lost friend, a broken home, a mental breakdown, job loss, devaluation, or something else? Everyone touched by war will pay the personal price that accompanies it.

Who'd have thought that one day the world would be completely dependent on the ill will of a short, pale man with a retreating chin settled into an underground bunker eyeing his red push-button messenger of death? Thousands of miles may separate you from him, and yet, he's everywhere. One can't even turn on the television or open a newspaper without seeing his round face with small, narrow eyes. He's even here in Truskavets. Billboards at the entrance to the small town are covered with graffiti saying "Putin *huilo*," which roughly translates as "Putin is a dickhead." The message is partly childish bravado, partly grounds for serious punishment. What has the world come to if someone like this can shake it to its foundations?

Each morning when I wake up in our hotel room, my first thought is of Putin. How many years, days, or minutes will pass before he dies?

Tonight, it is quiet and dark. An overnight curfew has been imposed on the entire country. Not a single light burns anywhere, not a single sound can be heard except the drip, drip, drip of the faucet. The only light comes from the digital clock by my bed. It glows green, flashing 4:00 a.m. So I just lie here with my eyes open, my mind racing from one thought to another.

Outside, the sound of an air raid siren begins. There is nothing human in that piercing howl. If I were a kid, I'd picture it as a giant beast howling at the moon. But I'm no longer a youth, haven't been for years now, and the moon is not visible. Outside the window, the stars shine down from above, cold and distant. The sound of the wailing siren fades, and dead silence reigns again as the water drips, drips, drips. It's almost time for the Russian bombers and missiles, and one can only guess where they are now and when they will appear.

I turn to my wife sleeping beside me. Luba's face, illuminated faintly, is calm. Looking at her, I reflect on how many beds we have occupied together. We met in 1978 and first slept together in her dormitory. It was so long ago, but I still remember that bed more clearly than the dozens of others since then—it was a narrow single bed that sagged in the middle. When we made love, the steel box springs counted our movements.

Modern hotel beds don't creak, so Luba can sleep peacefully even when I turn from side to side. Now she no longer wakes up at the sound of an air raid siren. We have stopped going to bomb shelters while here, and I hope I never have to regret this. The nearest bomb shelter is a ten-minute walk from our hotel, but getting there with our small grandchild would take twice as long. Baby Erica would need to be awakened, calmed down, and dressed. When all this was done, the air raid would be over.

Yawning, I wish I could sleep more, but I can't. My dream is over because you can't go back to sleep and get to where you left off, just as you can't go back to your former existence and start over. Life goes on. The war goes on. Hopefully, we go on . . .

At half past five in the morning, I leave the room with my laptop bag over my shoulder. You could call it my "money-making machine." Today, it's my most valuable possession. When we move from place to place, my laptop is always within arm's reach. I keep watch over it because I must guard it—the apple of my eye.

The soft carpet mutes my steps as I enter the dimly lit hallway. It is quiet and empty, the closed doors stretched into an even line. Everyone in the hotel who was awakened by the last siren has left their rooms to go down to the basement, where they feel safer. The rest continue to sleep as if nothing were wrong. The war is already changing our habits—and if it goes on long enough, it will also change our attitudes toward the war itself.

As time goes on, one begins to recall life in peacetime as if it were a favorite movie, full of color and often unrealistic. Now, we are learning to live in a completely different environment, as if we're occupying a documentary film with a powerful sense of needing to be present and participate in it. After all, live broadcasts leave no room for error.

I avoid using the elevator at night because I don't want to get stuck somewhere between floors if the power goes out. Instead, I walk softly down the stairs using the light of my cell phone to guide me. At the same time, I scan the news. Never have I read as much news as I do now. My phone has only ten hours of life before it goes dead, but I'm hardly shielded from the flow of information. Everything is War! War! War! To my ear, it sounds like *vor*, which means "thief." It's a suitable simile, as war steals literally everything we have.

The lobby is still in darkness. Only the reception desk is illuminated, like the command post of a submarine. The night porter never sleeps, and I greet him in Ukrainian.

"*Dobry ranok*," I say, which means "Good morning."

Nobody has anything against the Russian language, but we increasingly speak Ukrainian now. This reinforces that we and the Russians are *not* brothers. Our "brotherhood" was an invention of Kremlin ideologues to justify their claim to our lands, our history, and our identity. The lies were based on linguistic similarities between the two Slavic languages, and the policies of both tsarist and Soviet governments were intent on a violent Russification of Ukraine.

On February 24, 2022, however, the masks were dropped—finally and irrevocably—revealing Russia's true ruthless nature: one of cunning and total disregard for human life behind nearly all of their malevolent deeds.

On that day, Putin launched a large-scale military operation in Ukraine, announcing that one of his goals was to "de-Nazify" the country. This was his term for "de-nationalization" in the Orwellian language often adopted by the Kremlin.

Since then, we have no more "brothers" in Russia. There are only sworn enemies. Should some consider this too radical a statement, I invite them to imagine that the Russians have attacked *their* country and are now killing *their* compatriots. When one is facing cruelty, the heart may begin to harden.

Now I see that my "Good morning," both friendly and well-meaning, does not elicit a return smile from the night porter.

"Not so good," he scowls. "A couple of minutes ago, a Muscovite rocket was fired at Lviv again. It was shot down, but there were casualties. The bloody pieces fell on a residential building."

"Oh, no!" I shake my head, saddened by the images that appear in my mind.

"These bastards are aiming closer and closer to us," the porter continues.

Truskavets and Lviv are separated by only fifty miles—a mere trifle for an earth-to-air missile. Somewhere nearby, right now, flames are blazing and newly crippled people are screaming, being buried alive. Yes, this is happening in the twenty-first century, here in my country, here in Europe.

The night porter shares some more of his reflections. In his opinion, there are too many healthy young men living in the hotel who could be protecting Kyiv instead—or any other Ukrainian city.

I say nothing. My daughter's husband, Alexander, is also a healthy young man and he is here because Svitlana has insisted on it. She believes that a man must first take care of his family, and then he can think about protecting his homeland. I don't know what's right for anyone else. It's a personal choice for each one of us.

Truskavets is full of people who recently looked with compassion at Afghan and Syrian refugees, never imagining that they could find themselves in the same role. There is no starvation here yet, but the choice of products is extremely limited. And if you're on medication, you might have to visit every pharmacy in the area to find the right medicine—if you're lucky!

There is a long line at the ATM to get a thousand *hryvnia*—the equivalent of $30. How much can you buy for thirty bucks? And how much money is still in your bank account? How long can you last if a hotel room for four people costs you $100 daily?

As for me, my main savings are kept on deposit, which is tied up now. Everyone hopes for cash. Alexander and I carry small rolls of dollar bills stuffed in every pocket, which can be extremely uncomfortable. There are only three currency exchange offices in the whole city, and all of them have long queues. Nobody keeps a safe distance, and people no longer wear face masks. They cluster in elevators, and one might conclude that the pandemic spread of germs and viruses has suddenly dried up. In fact, the pressures of the war have caused COVID-19 precautions to become a thing of the past.

"You come here every morning with your computer," says the night porter, changing the subject. "On business?"

"Something like that," I say vaguely.

"Are you gonna fight?"

I think I know where this is going. "I'm sixty-six," I reply.

"I'm seventy, but I'll still go to war, if necessary," he says meaningfully.

"Then I'll go with you," I say, and walk away to avoid more questions.

The lobby of the hotel is a vast space filled with massive deep-blue armchairs placed at random. Coffee cups, plates of leftovers, and plastic cups are scattered on low glass tables. All day long, the place is filled with people waiting for vacant rooms. Now, it's empty.

I clear an end table beside one of the armchairs and put my laptop on it. As I sit down, an old air raid alarm sounds outside. You can't tell from the tone whether it's at the beginning or the end. Why hasn't anyone created a pitch difference? I'll tell you why: it's because no one expected such ancient devices to be used again in modern warfare.

Up from the basement comes a group of people with bags and pillows. They look rumpled and a little guilty. Sleeping children are curved into their parents' arms. A small dog is peeing on the floor near the eleva-tors. Its master makes a "Sorry, what can I do?" gesture, addressed to me.

I smile back at him, "It's not your fault, buddy." As we are on a night-time curfew, it is forbidden for anyone to leave the hotel until six in the morning. People and their pets will have to be patient. We *all* have to be patient.

I turn on my laptop. While it's loading, I browse the news again. It's not good. Apparently, the enemy is rushing toward Kyiv, trying to encircle it. Almost the entire coast of the Black Sea has been taken by the Russians. Now their army is confidently advancing from the north, east, and south. Only the west of Ukraine is relatively secure for now, but Belarus may soon join the battle.

Ukrainians are now living like hunted animals. We do not have enough weapons, armored vehicles, aviation, or air defense. In some sec-tors of the front, we have nothing with which to shoot the enemy. But we will surely win. How do I know? I cannot put it into words. And yet, this is my chosen field—words. But I have learned over time that a future truth cannot always be put into words.

At six a.m., workers begin to arrive at the hotel, one by one, in pairs and in small groups. I can see them through the long camouflage nets stretched across the lobby woven by women who live in the hotel. Every day these nets are rolled up and taken away to a hidden location. I always hope they will save someone's life, eyesight, or limbs.

My laptop's white screen is clean and untouched. I type two or three sentences about camouflage nets on it and delete them. As a writer, I can't stop writing, but I don't know what to write and for whom. The publish-ing house that released my books is located in Kharkiv. Today, there are no areas left in that region that escaped the damage of artillery shells.

When you look at photographs of Kharkiv, you might recall those that were taken in the long-suffering city of Aleppo, wiped off the map by Russians in the service of Syrian President Assad. This tactic was first used by Russian army general Pavel Grachev, in the days of the battle for the Chechen capital, Grozny, in 1995. The general was angry that his troops could not take the city by storm. His subordinates complained that the Chechens were shooting from behind their windows.

"Then make sure that there are no windows left!" ordered Grachev. I guess Putin gave similar orders during the sieges of Kharkiv, Mariupol, and other Ukrainian cities. He called it "demilitarization." George Orwell was able to see much farther into the future than he could have imagined when he wrote his novel *1984*.

I'm used to being a writer, but maybe it's time to get used to being a refugee. Ukraine has far more to worry about than books. At the same time, one of my ongoing frustrations is that I can't seem to break into the global book market. It's foolish to hope that a small fish like me will be noticed by HarperCollins or Penguin, Elliot & Thompson, or other major publishers.

So what is left for me to do? The answer is . . . NOTHING.

An hour later, the future doesn't look quite as hopeless as it did earlier. I remember how, eight years ago, I started from scratch when Luba and I arrived in Kyiv with two suitcases and no idea how, where, and what we would live on—and we made it! Humankind can overcome just about everything—except death.

It is for this reason that Putin is killing us. He knows that by staying alive, we will win. Well, I have some bad news for you, President Vladimir Putin. *We are not going to die. We will live as long as we can.*

The lobby gradually fills with sunlight. Muffled voices soon follow as people sit on chairs, their eyes glued to their gleaming cell phones. Everyone wants to know how the night went. Did the Russians manage to advance further? Which Ukrainian cities were captured, and which were subjected to night bombardments? How many Ukrainians did not live to see the morning sun again? How many invaders were killed?

Not all the faces around me are dejected or upset. This is a grab bag of ordinary human beings displaying emotions from indifference to cheerfulness. At eight a.m., the lobby bar will open, and soon the long-anticipated aroma of coffee will fill the air. Every single person, including two teenagers, calls friends and relatives to "check in" and get updates.

I learn that my neighbors seated beside me have made a long journey from Kherson and are happy to be here. As if by magic, the TV on the wall shows a picture of their hometown. A reporter's urgent voice on their phone says, "A counterattack by Ukrainian troops has pushed Russian forces back toward the port city of Kherson, our only big city to have been captured so far. Several thousands of people are marching through the city center, waving flags and singing the Ukrainian national anthem."

This report has the energy of a rap song dedicated to the tenth day of the invasion. We can hear automatic bursts—Russian soldiers firing into the air to deter the approaching crowd. We see a man in red trousers that resemble Cossack bloomers. The soldiers back away slowly, looking at each other. None of them dares to shoot the man. They look confused. But these are the same soldiers who recently stormed Kherson and killed the city defenders. They can open fire at any moment. What else can you expect from people who continued to shell Mariupol, despite agreeing to a ceasefire to let civilians leave the city?

My worst questions are confirmed by the next report. As the TV news reveals, Russians opened fire on a civilian car in the Bucha district near Kyiv. Two people were killed, including a seventeen-year-old girl, and four others were injured.

"Fascists," one man mutters tightly. His fingers are clenched into fists, his knuckles white.

The letter Z spotted on the side of Russian tanks and stylized in a thick brushstroke is a direct allusion to the stylized lightning bolt logo of Nazi Germany's SS. President Vladimir Putin is an apt pupil, quickly learning and adopting everything he can steal from his predecessors.

The collective unconscious memory of Western countries is paralyzed when Putin warns NATO *not* to impose a no-fly zone over tormented Ukraine. Politicians and military leaders remember the years 1939 and 1940 very well. It is a pity that their recollections of the Allies' victory over Hitler in 1945 are not as fresh. Putin is fully aware of this and takes advantage of the West's timidity.

The nearest Russian troops have advanced toward Kyiv by about fifteen miles. Meanwhile, the staff of the Chernobyl nuclear power plant remain trapped after the facility was captured by Eastern invaders. Many cities in Ukraine are under heavy fire or were destroyed by Russian artillery. The flame of war flares up more violently. Watching news bulletins can make you *feel* the heat emanating from the screen. TV channels broadcast scenes of death, chaos, and destruction. At this point, hundreds of thousands of refugees have fled Ukraine, babies in arms, suitcases dragged behind. The sides of the border roads are strewn with abandoned cars that lacked the fuel to go farther.

Before each of us lies a long and winding path through trials and hardships that have no end. We are at the very beginning of this journey, like migratory birds, with one important difference. We don't know where we are going . . . or if we can ever return.

However, this is a familiar situation for me. Eight years earlier, I had—for the first time—lost both my home and my homeland. I never expected to repeat the experience. . . .

CHAPTER 2

How It All Began

MARCH 2014: WHEN CAR TIRES BURN, THE AIR RETAINS THAT ODOR for a long time. I remember reacting to that odor on the first day of March 2014, when I arrived in Kyiv to visit my son Sergiy. Naturally, the first thing I did was to go to Independence Square. In Ukrainian, it is *Maidan Nezalezhnosti*. Maidan means "square" or "open space."

Throughout the previous winter, this area had been a citadel to the biggest, longest-lasting Ukrainian protest movement, known as "Euro-Maidan." It was provoked by the actions of then-Ukrainian president Victor Yanukovych when he broke a promise to sign far-reaching agreements with the European Union. Ukrainians protested vehemently and in great numbers because their president had been tempted to accept a $15 billion bailout from Vladimir Putin. It was the largest bribe in history aimed at keeping Ukraine in the Kremlin's sphere of influence. The protestors demanded that their country be oriented toward the West, rather than the East.

The riots had been going on for thirteen weeks during a brutally cold winter. There were 400,000 to 800,000 protestors in Kyiv alone! Elite units of the police, called the *Berkut* (Golden Eagle) opposed them. To keep the police at bay, protesters set tire walls on fire with bottled gasoline. This created a giant smokescreen to protect the public from the police and their weapons. That fire was constantly fed by more and more tires. The ground level of the square had risen over the month to three feet from the ash, and frozen pools of water were created by the police fire hoses.

Realizing that this fire could not be defeated—or even constrained—former President Yanukovych fled to Russia. The battle of Ukrainians with the pro-Kremlin government ended in a complete victory for the people! For three months, Maidan was the epicenter of a political hurricane, but so far, I'd seen it only on TV. The time had come to look at this glorious place with my own eyes. I liked to think that the two names—Maidan and Maidukov—had the same origin.

A quarter-mile parcel of central Kyiv around Independence Square looked like a deserted battlefield. Pictures of the fallen warriors were tacked onto impromptu shrines. There were mostly male faces, old and young, wrinkled and smooth, cheerful and grave, intriguing and plain—one hundred and seven of whom had received the title, "the Heavenly Hundred." Candles flickered under the silent portraits of the dead heroes. An Orthodox cleric, his robe black as burnt rubber, was chanting at the improvised memorial, raising his face to the gray, empty sky. Respectfully slowing down, I passed by as dozens of still eyes watched me from the photographs. I shivered.

Maidan was foggy with drizzle. The Revolution of Dignity was over, though the barricades were still blocking traffic, forcing me to make my way between high-heaped piles of trunks, shields, and burnt tires. Bottles of Molotov cocktails, stoppered with rags, lay forgotten among the trash. Two or three times, I had to step over drops of clotted blood on cobblestone pavements. They were like incompletely healed wounds. In truth, there are no bloodless revolutions.

I stopped near a frayed tent to talk to the scruffy men in camouflage. They said they were guarding the revolution, but they looked as if they didn't know what to do with their victory, or how to find a new goal worth fighting for. I stopped to put some money in a donation box at the tent's opening and asked the scruffy men what they were going to do next. They replied that they were not sure. "We'll see."

"We don't trust the new government," one of them said. "These guys are all from the old political stall. If they try to betray the revolution, we'll replace them with new ones. That's the reason we're here."

"Don't you know that Russians are eager to absorb our lands and our lives?" the other asked. "Who will stop it?"

"But how are you going to stop them by sitting here?" I asked in turn.

"It's enough for us to stop those shitty hypocrites in government who still look toward the Kremlin," they said. "The conversation with them will be very short. A suitcase, a station, then Russia."

Which meant: "Take your things, board a train, and roll on out of there."

I felt that arguing with them was a waste of time. "You win," I said at parting. "Now you can go home with lighter hearts. Everything's over."

"None of this is over," they replied to my retreating back. "It's only the beginning."

They were right, of course, although I didn't realize it at the time. Nobody knew. For the most part, we were drunk with our victory. We regarded ourselves as full-fledged Europeans now, and not citizens of a seedy Russian colony. The double-headed Russian eagle had opened its claws and allowed Ukraine to get away. We were happy to know that we were no longer a nation of caught birds and could fly wherever we wanted, rejoicing in the freedom of our own flight. The world seemed open and anything was attainable. It was a magical feeling.

Every word I heard and every scene I recalled that day in the center of Kyiv filled me with impressions, just as a freshly opened bottle of champagne is filled with bubbles.

"Wow, that was something!" I exclaimed at the dinner table at my son's Kyiv home. "You know, Sergiy, I envy you. You've been in the thick of things."

"If you'd been here, you'd have seen it with your own eyes," Sergiy said. "Dad, you and Mom should have moved here long ago. This is truly the time for you to change your place of residence—and your entire life."

He had been living in Kyiv for several years, working his way up as an illustrator. His rented apartment, its walls covered with paintings and sketches, looked more like an artist's studio or workshop than a family home.

"We're thinking about it," I mumbled.

"You shouldn't just think, but *act*," Sergiy insisted.

He spoke in Ukrainian, which only remotely resembled Russian. I tried to follow his example, but with limited success, since we all came from Donbas, historically the most Russified region of Ukraine. It was a bastion of Soviet nostalgia in the shadow of the Kremlin towers.

Sergiy was the first in our family who had shifted away from the country's old, rotten roots and plunged deeply into Ukrainian culture. As a rule, residents of capital cities are more progressive and creative than provincials. In Kyiv, the Ukrainian language had become not only a trend but a symbol of the modern way of life, a symbolic rejection of the past. The snipers who were killing unarmed protesters at Maidan spoke Russian, and since then, more and more Ukrainians considered it the language of the enemy.

One by one, Russian books, movies, and songs were being erased from my mind forever, but I still hesitated about moving out of my hometown to build a new life. Sergiy continued to insist on the advantages of doing so, but I admitted that although I didn't care for the people I'd met in Donetsk, I liked my home there.

"There are no good or bad people," Sergiy's wife, Tanya, pointed out. "There are only people who do good or bad."

Tanya was an actress at the Black Square Theatre in Kyiv. She was a tall, slender young woman who exuded intelligence behind her large, long-lashed eyes. She had recently given birth to their baby daughter, Severine, and now breastfed her at the table, covering herself with a shawl.

Because I thought this was not the proper time for a discussion, all I said was, "Well, I don't like people who do bad things, like the overwhelming majority of people in Donetsk."

"Nevertheless, they're still Ukrainians," Tanya said.

"I'm afraid they hardly recall that they are," I said.

"If so, Dad, then why are you going back there again and again?" Sergiy asked.

I don't remember what I replied, but I do remember thinking, "Everyone needs to return to where they came from." Whatever the city was like today, I had been born and raised in Donetsk and all my previous life had been spent there.

My wife and daughter lived there, too, and we had a very nice, recently renovated ground-floor apartment. Luba ran her ladies' fashion store most of the day, while thirty-year-old Svitlana (pronounced like "sweet Lana") was preparing for her PhD. She was busily writing scientific articles on ecology and hoped to submit them for publication.

On my desk stood my high-quality, reliable PC containing old manuscripts and improved drafts of my latest novels. Although I was eager to return to our home, I stayed for a couple of days and babysat my first granddaughter to give her parents a bit of a break. Then, I boarded a train from Kyiv to the southeast, heading toward Donetsk, my hometown.

Donetsk is easily recognizable from afar, thanks to its jagged line of black "slug mountains"—piles of solid waste that remained after coal mining. Some are so high they have been compared to the pyramids. Labyrinths stretched across the city itself, built mostly in the previous century for coal miners and steel workers—a good half of whom were former prisoners and war veterans. Their fates had left an indelible imprint on their descendants, whose body image, appearance, mentality, and habits were fully consistent with the nondescript architecture of Donetsk. Compared to Kyiv, it looked particularly unattractive. Never before had I sensed so keenly the difference between the two cities.

I had to admit it—postrevolutionary Kyiv had made an indelible impression on me. How could it have been otherwise? Every single Ukrainian had been impacted by the Euromaidan demonstrations of 2013. Some were inspired; others were disappointed, frightened, or even enraged, but there were no indifferent responses. The protests served as a national awakening, setting Ukraine on a path that diverged sharply from the increasing "Stalinization" of Putin's Russia with its rigidly constructed vertical of power.

This path turned out to be much longer, more difficult, and bloodier than it had seemed when we Ukrainians took the first steps.

On March 11, 2014, a few days after my return home, the Supreme Council of Crimea proclaimed the Crimean Peninsula a "sovereign state." This was the de facto continuation of the Russian occupation of Ukraine's territory. The internet was flooded with photographs and videos showing armed men in Crimea whose weapons and lorries were the same as those used by the Russian army. The men even spoke with Russian accents, though according to President Putin, they had bought all their uniforms and hardware in a shop. The media described them as the "little green men," which referred both to the color of their uniforms and their unconfirmed origins. The majority of journalists of the world, however, had little doubt about the true identity of those invaders.

Almost simultaneously, the cities of Donetsk and Luhansk became the capitals of the self-proclaimed "People's Republics." In the last days of that ill-fated March, another massive pro-Russian demonstration took place in Donetsk's main square. A huge, dark gray sculpture of Lenin over twenty-five feet high looked down approvingly at the sea of tricolor Russian flags swaying at his granite square-toed shoes.

My son and I visited the sculpture when he came to the city to visit us. It would be his last trip to Donetsk.

While walking through the downtown area, we came across Lenin's Square by chance. Here, a grand spectacle began to unfold before our eyes. Dark columns of people flocked to the square from all sides. The clear spring air was saturated with alcohol fumes and cigarette smoke. Speakers yelled militant slogans at the top of their voices through their megaphones. They urged people to seize administrative buildings and demanded that Putin bring his troops into the country. The square was surrounded by buses and cars with Russian license plates.

I was stunned when my son suddenly moved into the crowd and shouted the slogan, "Glory to Ukraine!" All eyes turned to him. I froze, shock and fear racing through me. Not so long ago, in this very square, several Ukrainian patriots had been beaten to death by a similar rowdy crowd. My son was only thirty-four, a young man with a hot heart and not-cool-enough head who refused to hide his feelings.

It was a miracle we weren't torn to pieces by these fanatics waving their Russian flags. They clearly couldn't believe their ears. Sergiy's escapade was almost too reckless to be real, so they probably thought he had shouted "Death to Ukraine" or something similar. To my relief, they just passed us by and marched on.

The next day, I took Sergiy to the railway station and promised him that Luba and I would soon move to Kyiv. It was a white lie. We couldn't muster up enough of an incentive to leave our city and our home, filled with so many personal belongings and memories. We had decided to sit tight for now.

Oddly, we hadn't seen the usual arrival of swifts and swallows outside our windows because the birds had not flown into Donetsk that terrible spring. They knew better.

Daily, I felt tensions grow. There was now, indisputably, a palpable sense of hatred and menace in the air. I tried to write, but something was blocking me. The previous week, I had finished my last novel for the Moscow publishing house, Eksmo, and had already been paid. Now I was blocked. Times had changed, and I had changed, too. After everything that had happened, I just couldn't cooperate with Russians, even if they did publish my books.

Instead, I wrote a series of articles for an American magazine, *American Thinker*, comparing Vladimir Putin to Adolf Hitler and describing the rise of fascism in Russia. For distant American readers, my warnings may have seemed exaggerated. However, in Donetsk, they came across as logical and inevitable. I knew I was risking my life by telling a truth that the world was slow to accept. I knew that my impassioned articles could lead me to imprisonment and even, possibly, the death penalty, but I couldn't let that stop me.

Meanwhile, here at home, our neighbors were obsessed with the Russian world. They were ready to kill for a single careless word spoken against them, or for a combination of yellow and blue clothing, considering it a reference to the colors of the Ukrainian national flag. Televisions blared behind every door, filling people's heads with lies and angry propaganda. Hosts of political talk shows were sounding like mad witch-hunters, frothing at the mouth.

In the intervals between these "five *hours* of hatred," a modern Big Brother would appear on television screens. He was a small balding man in shoes fitted with extended heels. His voice was soothing, and his posture lazy and relaxed. He wore mostly dark red ties and black suits and tended to perform against a blue background. This was the man who was once nicknamed "Pale Moth" by his KGB colleagues and is now known to the rest of the world as "President Vladimir Putin." He and he alone was the director of the drama now unfolding in the vastness of Ukraine.

In 2008, he bit off a piece of Georgia, and six years later he was here to tear Ukraine apart. After all, a predator cannot live long without flesh and blood.

In May 2014, with the start of the Ukrainian antiterrorist operation against armed separatists, Putin unleashed a "hybrid war" in the east of Ukraine, deploying a combination of local mercenaries and disguised regular troops. "We are not there," Kremlin officials kept saying, grinning brazenly.

They were.

To my dismay, my parents were absolutely delighted with this development. They spent their days in front of the TV watching only Russian programs. Ukraine had met its complete defeat on the information battlefield. The Kremlin was now investing billions of dollars in propaganda, and citizens who had learned the news in a general way from TV knew only what the Russian channels told them. The television tower in Donetsk was like a giant syringe filled with a drug to directly inject propaganda into millions of Ukrainian brains. I could see that my parents were becoming addicted to their TV and its nonstop messages of loyalty to Russia.

The last time I saw them was on May 13. It was my father's eighty-fifth birthday. I came to congratulate him with flowers and gifts from my family. The three of us sat at the festive table on which several delicious dishes were steaming, freshly cooked by my mother. It was like the good old days when I was the only beloved child in the family. Now, however, I was very upset about the indications of an information war. The subject came up over salmon steaks and continued to dominate the better part of our dinner conversation. To my dismay, my parents believed that Russia had the right to punish Ukraine for its willfulness.

"The Ukrainian nationalists in Kyiv staged a takeover of power," my mother said. "These scoundrels pushed our country into a quarrel with Russia."

"Putin will put everything back in order, you'll see," my father said. "There is no one in politics today who can be compared to him. His goals are clear and he knows how to achieve them. He will turn Russia into the most powerful and influential state of the world."

My parents had held fairly high administrative positions in Soviet science. The collapse of the USSR was, for them, the same tragedy as it was for Putin, who once called it "the greatest geopolitical catastrophe of the century." Until the end of the last century, Ukraine had been part of the Soviet—that is, *Russian*—empire. The imperial mindset did not allow my parents to see Ukraine as separate and independent from Russia.

My firm and somewhat disrespectful attitude infuriated them. In a fit of temper, Mom called me a "Nazi," and Dad said that I was as obstinate as a mule. As he slammed his fist on the table, a bottle of wine tipped over, a dark red stain spreading over the white tablecloth. I remember looking down at it and asking my parents if their admiration for Putin was worth the blood that was about to be spilled in the coming war.

In response, my mother shouted that I had ruined the celebration of my father's jubilee, that I was not their son anymore, and that she didn't want to see me again. The door of their home slammed behind me—and my mother's words turned out to be prophetic. Since then, we have not seen each other in person, and we probably will never again in our lifetime.

This demonstration of the power of Russian propaganda to separate me, a loving son, from my propaganda-addicted parents, was devastating. Even today, the depth of pain from this unwanted, unnecessary separation from my parents, now in their final years, haunts me.

Compounding this loss was my sense of separation from our neighbors. Donetsk had become a military city, a dangerous city. You could be heading to the market and run into men with weapons who seemed ready to shoot at the least provocation. There was something calculating about the way they looked at you. Or you might be driving down the street and see squads of bearded Chechen fighters in armored personnel carriers. Even when you were at home, you couldn't feel safe because someone could easily break in and arrest you or harm your family.

I was greatly relieved when my daughter, Svitlana, decided to leave this accursed city for Kyiv. Luba and I remained at home for a few more weeks, waiting for things to settle. Many would call it "being in a rut." People tend to continue in a certain direction out of inertia, which is correctly described as "inertness of mind." They might be challenged by unexpected circumstances and decide that change isn't worth the trouble.

Meanwhile, our life at home was getting worse with every passing day. The constant roar of the distant cannonade became the chaotic background against which we played out our lives. It was both frightening and exhausting. To top it off, my wife lost her shop. Armed men burst in one day and informed Luba that approximately $50,000's worth of her goods had been confiscated.

Why? Apparently, there had been a brief delay in paying rent. The mall administrator had discovered an easy way to get rich by using the services of Donetsk militants. It was useless to appeal to the court, as legal norms were no longer valid in Donetsk. The military laws of war were now in force.

From then on, a bitter, confused Luba spent all her days at home, not knowing what to do with herself. Both of us were left without work and without income. We were both moody and preoccupied with our separate anxieties. To relieve the stress, I returned to my old habit of secretly smoking cigarettes. I'd cover the odor with mints, which not only catered to my needs but also allowed me some time to be alone.

Early on a July morning, I was walking by my children's old school when a strange vision in the distance caught my eye. It was a dark green truck with its dump section poised in the raised position. One word pulsed through my brain: *Grad!* I saw before me not an ordinary truck, but a military truck that had served as a wheeled platform for the Grad rocket launcher. It was named after the Russian word for "hail" because it was created to spray fiery missiles over long distances in the vague direction of enemy territory. As far as I knew from the news reports, these monstrous military machines could not be used in populated cities. With this in mind, I couldn't help but wonder what they were doing here in a schoolyard in the middle of residential blocks.

A group of men in camouflage uniforms was standing next to the truck with machine guns across their shoulders. They noticed me and one of them signaled me to approach. He wore spotted green-brown pants and a blue-and-white striped undershirt under his military jacket.

"Are you spying?" he demanded harshly.

I told him that I was just walking by, and he asked why here and not somewhere else.

"Why not be here?" I asked in my turn.

The men exchanged glances. Then one of them said: "Why don't you just shoot him down, Kolyan? I don't like him."

"Me, neither," the guy in the striped undershirt said, and told me to keep moving and not to look back.

As he pointed in the direction that I should go with the machine gun, I realized that I could die in a few seconds, right here near the school where my children had studied and about three hundred steps from my house. What I felt was both real and unreal at the same time. One thing was certain: these men wouldn't hesitate to kill any passerby who caught their eye. I took another step, and my knees became weak.

"Wait, Kolyan," a voice said behind me. "I know him from my childhood. The old geezer lives nearby."

Looking over my shoulder, I said, "Yes, I do."

"Then why the hell are you standing here like a fool?" Kolyan yelled. "Get out of my sight!"

As I walked away, I kept anticipating a bullet hitting me in the back. In those days, citizens of Donetsk were often shot in the streets. Afterward, their corpses were shown on local TV with comments that they had been murdered by some mysterious Ukrainian Nazis.

Shakily, I arrived back home and told Luba about what happened with the *Grads* men.

"I'm scared, Sergey," she said. There was nothing unusual about this. Fear had long become the norm of our lives. We went to bed alarmed and for a long time, we lay in the dark, listening to the distant cannonade.

"Don't be afraid, it's far away," I told Luba.

"I hope," she whispered.

Later that night, we heard a sudden grinding, a rumble that made both of us jump out of bed and run straight to the window. Over the roof of our house and up into the darkness in front of us passed a flight of flaming arrows. We couldn't hear each other over a loud drone whistling and roaring overhead. The walls were shaking, the floor was shaking, and then, silence. I heard Luba shouting, "Don't, don't, don't!"

"Calm down," I reassured her, rushing to hold her. "It's over now."

"I will never be able to calm down," she said, shaking her head. "Never."

The next morning, the local media trumpeted the news of the vile shelling of Donetsk's civilians. They claimed it had been arranged by Ukrainian terrorists using rocket launchers disguised as garbage trucks that were driving around the city at night. Russian TV hosts went completely mad and were calling to destroy Ukraine.

On that hot July day in 2014, Luba and I left Donetsk for good. The train we caught proved to be the last train out of our now-occupied hometown. We were on our way to Kyiv and ready to begin a new chapter of our lives.

CHAPTER 3

From Russia . . . with Weapons

OUR OVERNIGHT TRAIN JOURNEY FROM DONETSK TO KYIV LASTED thirteen hours, though it seemed endless. Most readers have not experienced being onboard an ancient Soviet train car in the summer heat: The windows do not open because it is prohibited.

Each car is divided into nine 6 x 9 foot locked two-set bunkbed compartments called "coupes."

Food is usually laid out on a small plastic table below the sealed window, its odor strong in the stale air.

Men and women take turns undressing in a very narrow space, and at night their bare hands and feet hang over the sides of the bunks.

The toilets located at opposite ends of the car are usually occupied, so one has to wait somewhere close by with a towel, soap, and a toothbrush at the ready.

Does the above sound . . . uncomfortable? Well, compared with what Luba and I experienced, it was the lap of luxury! Our spontaneous decision to leave Donetsk and the rush to pack made us late to arrive at the station. There, we learned that there were no more seats on the train. We had to bribe the conductor to let us into her own tiny service compartment half the size of the cramped passenger compartment. She herself slept above us in the upper bunk while Luba and I huddled below. The toilet behind the thin wall was noisy and in frequent use.

Our entire life together had been packed into two suitcases and one bag. At the time, we believed that the Ukrainian army would take Donetsk back in a month or two. Then, we could return if we wished.

Hah! Those were the days of innocence when we had no idea what the war—and Russia—would hold for our future.

The conductor of our train was a stout woman with a fondness for chewing sunflower seeds. Her jaws were constantly in motion. During train stops, which were frequent, she would leave the compartment to open the doors for passengers. At the beginning of the journey, while we were passing through the eastern territories, she spoke Russian, but before arriving in Kyiv, she switched to Ukrainian.

In the morning, I was standing in a narrow carriage corridor when she approached me to ask if we were going to return to Donetsk. I confirmed that yes, we were.

"Well, when you get back, don't tell anyone that I spoke Ukrainian," she said. "I don't want any trouble."

Luba and I set foot on the Kyiv platform the morning of July 18, and Sergiy was there to meet us. He looked both excited and anxious.

"Have you heard the Boeing news?" he asked.

Puzzled, we shook our heads. Sergiy told us that the day before, Malaysia Airlines' flight MH17 had been shot down over Ukraine by a Russian missile. It had been en route from Amsterdam to Kuala Lumpur and crashed not far from Donetsk. There had been 283 passengers aboard, including 80 children. Of the victims, 189 were Dutch nationals, 44 were Malaysian, and 27 were Australian.

There were also passengers from Indonesia, Great Britain, Belgium, Germany, the Philippines, the United States, Ireland, Canada, New Zealand, and Hong Kong. Investigators believed it was between sixty and ninety seconds after the cockpit came off that the rest of the aircraft hit the ground.

It was impossible to even imagine what those parents experienced, holding their children on their knees while their plane fell from a great height, slowly turning upside down. When I tried to visualize it, my breath caught in my chest, but the images stayed with me for weeks afterward.

Soon the news stations were showing terrifying footage from the crash site, and one couldn't look at it without tearing up. Scattered among the wreckage were picture books, children's toys, and dolls. But I remember most vividly the photo of a boozy Russian mercenary holding up a little stuffed monkey that he found among the debris. After posing for the reporters, waving the toy around as if it were a prize from a carnival game, he pulled off the military cap from his bald head and crossed himself. Can anybody imagine what kind of "God" he was praying to?

In Ukraine, we all naively believed that after such a tragedy a great punishment would follow, and that Putin's Russia would soon be overturned. Surely the civilized world would not forgive terrorists! Surely, this time, Putin and his henchmen had gone too far! The Hague was about to deliver justice to these monsters!

Coincidentally, I had recently read Nassim Taleb's bestseller, *The Black Swan*, and its message was powerful in view of this recent disaster. The Black Swan theory describes an event that comes as a surprise, has a major effect, and is often rationalized later with the benefit of hindsight. I had actually viewed the Malaysian Boeing disaster as a predictable "black swan" that would break the neck of the evil nestled behind Kremlin walls. I soon realized that I was not the only one who had, once again, naively underestimated Russia. When Putin began invading Ukraine in 2014, it was impossible to imagine that this war would drag on for years with no end in sight.

For the most part, the plane crash (Do you remember when people called such tragedies "disasters" instead of "incidents?") seemed not to have affected the attitude of the Western countries toward Russia. Australia's prime minister, the Secretary-General of the United Nations, the Committee of the Red Cross, and other leading politicians expressed deep concern, and that was where it ended.

In 2016, the Dutch-led Joint Investigation Team concluded that Flight MH17 had been shot down by a missile launched by a BUK-TELAR. It had been brought into Ukraine from the territory of the Russian Federation. Subsequently, after having hit the target, the launcher was taken back across the border. And then what?

Nothing. The world cringed, shuddered, paused for a moment, and then continued to spin on its axis.

We can remember the most terrible tragedies, but we cannot recreate them in our minds so that the pain and shock are as fresh as they were when it actually happened. This is ultimately how we guarantee our sanity. All things pass away. All things *must* pass away.

When we arrived in Kyiv, Luba and I settled into an apartment Svitlana had rented for us. It had one room and a tiny kitchen overlooking a typical Kyiv courtyard, with big, lush chestnuts spreading over dumpsters. I slept in a folding chair below the window, and at first, every loud noise below our window woke me up. But gradually, the war faded into the background, and I began to have normal, peaceful dreams. I didn't miss Donetsk—not at all.

Kyiv fascinated me. It's an amazing city built on hills, very green, with lots of squares and parks. On the street, you can see a hundred-year-old oak tree sticking out of the sidewalk. Between the roofs, church domes are visible, resembling golden onions. The pavements are littered with spiky green balls dropped down from thousands of horse chestnuts.

Perhaps this is the only European capital that is almost provincial and homey, despite possessing the facade of a modern megapolis. I could walk around Kyiv for hours, either alone or with baby Severine in the stroller, and enjoy every moment. After I deserted Donetsk, this city resembled a modern-day Babylon. I avidly watched the streams of expensive cars, noisy tourists, and small islands of brightly colored cafes, enjoying the aura of wealth and prosperity.

At the same time, I felt twinges of resentment and bewilderment. How could all these people be enjoying themselves while my hometown and all of Donbas were on fire? Were these people really so indifferent to the deaths of our soldiers on the eastern borders? Why did I constantly hear Russian being spoken in the streets?

Kyiv was full of cars with Donetsk license plates. About a million of my countrymen had moved to the capital to save their families, their businesses, and their lives. After everything they had experienced, one could expect that they would have become fanatical patriots of Ukraine.

But this was not to be. Mentally and spiritually, the vast majority appeared firmly aligned with Russia, and this tendency in the territories of the former empire was widely used by the Kremlin propagandists. The shared language was the glue that held the project known as the "Russian world" together. In fact, Russia has proclaimed that every Russian speaker is its citizen. Thus, Ukrainian society was split at a roughly fifty-to-fifty ratio.

Russian military aggression had planted a deepening wedge into our common lives and weakened our solidarity. With every military strike, the entire country shook like an old hut in a fierce storm, ready to burst at the seams. Every day, we recognized that we owed our survival to the desperate courage of Ukrainian heroes who sacrificed their lives on the Eastern front.

Now, it seemed as if their strength was about to run out. The world watched the beating taken by Ukraine the way viewers watch a fight in the schoolyard when a hefty bully kicks a child and is unpunished. The economic sanctions were no more than pinpricks that increased the bully's fury.

The main battles were fought around my hometown. Gunfire and explosions from the area of Donetsk airport boomed from all districts of the city. I could clearly hear the rattling and roaring through the phone when I called my parents. I couldn't hold a grudge against them and tried to act as if nothing had happened. They were lonely old people at the epicenter of the war's hurricane. And they *were* my parents—Mom and Dad—who had given me a happy childhood and carefree youth. My heart was heavy every time I thought of them.

During daily phone calls, I did my best to persuade them to move to Kyiv, but all my attempts failed. They kept saying they were not going to live among the Nazis whose dream was to destroy their beloved Mother Russia. Their view was reinforced by the round-the-clock news channels broadcasting from Moscow, supplying false information that was contrary to anyone with common sense.

Unfortunately, my parents weren't seeking logic or common sense. They believed everything they had seen and heard on TV. In their eyes, Russia was striving for peace, NATO was a fiend, and Ukraine danced to the tune of the Pentagon war hawks. Nothing could be done about this informational poisoning. My eighty-year-old mother considered Putin to be the savior of the world, and she meant it.

Today it may sound like a huge exaggeration, particularly in light of the attack on Ukraine, but if you search through the internet archives, you'll find that not so long ago, Putin's personal rating surpassed that of every other celebrity of the time, including Daniel Craig as 007 in *Skyfall*, and Lady Gaga with her third album, *Artpop!*

In October 2013, he was named "The Most Powerful Person on the Planet" by *Forbes*. In December, he was named "International Person of the Year" by Britain's *The Times*. When former Secretary of State Hillary Clinton compared Putin's aggression in Ukraine to actions taken by Hitler's Germany leading up to World War II, it stirred up a media frenzy. However, her words failed to make the slightest impact on the political life of the United States. Like Bush before him, Obama didn't dare confront Putin. As for the rest of the Western politicians, they preferred to stay loyal, because too many European countries were heated by Siberian gas and too much of Russia's money circulated through their banking systems.

Because, in the eyes of Vladimir Putin, the West was rotten to the core, he not only became convinced of his impunity, but he also believed in his own greatness. He allowed himself to be late for meetings with world leaders and puzzled them with questionable jokes. At international summits, he behaved condescendingly, if not arrogantly.

The Russians applauded him. From the poorest families on the icy outskirts of the country to the richest oligarchs in the Moscow suburbs, everyone suddenly felt like a winner! President Putin had rid them of the inferiority complex they inherited from their Cold War defeat. Now he had become their idol, famous for his bare-chested horseback riding, triumphant hockey playing, taming of wild animals, and scuba diving on the sea bed.

The combination of carefully rehearsed made-for-TV stunts with multihour interviews and a steady stream of foreign leaders visiting the Kremlin had a particularly strong effect on impressionable women of an advanced age. One of them was my mother.

Sometimes it drove me mad, but I loved her and I was very worried when the shells exploded closer and closer to her house. In early August, Ukraine went on the offensive in the Donbas, and the battle was fought on the outskirts of Donetsk.

"What have we done to deserve this?" my mother asked me. "We just wanted to be with Russia. Why won't these fascists just leave us alone? Why on earth did they bring the war to us?"

A military medal has two sides, like a coin. Each of us sees it differently and each of us believes that what we see is the truth. I chose the side that was right for me.

"Ukraine just wants to get their land back, Mom," I said. "Was it not you who asked Putin to bring in troops? He did it. Now you're reaping the fruits of your own recklessness. Look, we didn't start the war, the Russians did, so we have no reason to apologize or express regret for our treatment of the Russian zealots in our land. As soon as Russia gets out of here, the war will be over."

"Russia will protect the Russian people," my mother said.

"What the hell are Russian people doing in Ukraine?" I demanded.

"We *are* Russians," she replied. "We live here. Russia only provides us with humanitarian aid and political support."

She was referring to Putin's clever tactic in Ukraine. The official position of the Kremlin was to deny any involvement in the war. "We are not there," Russian diplomats and propagandists kept repeating. Meanwhile, humanitarian convoys from Moscow delivered weapons and ammunition to the rebellious republics. Half of their army consisted of Russian military men. Even though Moscow always stated that they were volunteers following "a call of the heart," they were actually regular forces. Only very naive or cynical people could regard this as "humanitarian aid."

"Stop it, Mom," I told her, wincing. "Please. We agreed not to discuss these things."

"It was you who started," she said accusingly.

Softening my voice, I said: "Mom, you just need to have a little patience, okay? This war won't be long. Our troops are advancing rapidly on Donbas, so I suppose I'll be back in a few weeks."

"Son, you probably read the wrong news stories because you are absolutely wrong," my mother said. "Ukrainian nationalists are never going to win. In less than a week, they will be surrounded and defeated."

The Ukrainian media gave out the opposite information, so I preferred to believe them. High spirits prevailed as the nation prepared to celebrate the twenty-third anniversary of its independence from the Soviet Union. On Sunday, August 24, 2014, residents of Kyiv flooded the city center, smartly dressed and cheerful, many in *vyshyvankas,* traditional Ukrainian embroidered shirts. In their hearts, they celebrated liberation—not from the Soviet Union, but from Russia.

I remember that sunny Sunday vividly. Luba and Svitlana were there with me. Khreshchatyk, Kyiv's main street that goes through Maidan, was filled to capacity. Patriotic songs blared from loudspeakers. A huge number of people waved yellow-blue flags, chanted "Glory to Ukraine," and applauded the passing soldiers and tanks. The minister of defense saluted the troops from an open-top limousine, his expression firm and determined. President Petro Poroshenko, an overweight man with puffy eyes and an unusually deep voice, stood on a high podium, proudly towering over the crowd, shouting that Ukraine was fighting a war for freedom. For some reason, he kept calling it an "antiterrorist operation in the east of the country."

My family and I shared the enthusiasm that overwhelmed the thousands of people gathered around. Tears of pride and inspiration shone in our eyes, and I also shed a tear when volunteers led a group of military invalids through the streets. Many of them had lost their arms and legs, and some were driving in wheelchairs.

My memory still retains the image of one veteran with a black patch over his eyes. His face was stern and distant. Not only was the war over for him—so was his life! He had traded his eyes for the cheers of a grateful crowd. It was an unequal exchange, monstrously unfair. Soldiers who had lost parts of their bodies at war were surrounded by healthy, happy, jubilant people who hadn't shed a single drop of blood for the sake of victory.

Young men without their limbs were unable to walk again; those without hands couldn't hug their children and wives; those with deformed faces had no hope of regaining their original looks. Their deaths and their wounds were real, while their momentary glory was a mirage. It was damned unfair, I felt, and I wondered if others felt it, too. My excitement was gone, replaced now by sadness. Suddenly, all of us—Luba, Svitlana, and I—were depressed by what we had just seen.

As we were leaving the crowd, I noticed two young men in military uniforms walking beside me. Their faces were tanned to leather by the sun. Without saying a single word, they looked over people's heads as if seeing something that others could not. They knew something about the war that we didn't, and it wasn't long before I discovered what it was.

In a grim twist of fate on Ukraine's Independence Day, our forces were trapped in Ilovaisk, a small town in the Donbas region. A separatist army, backed by Russian tanks and artillery, was far stronger than the government troops. After days of being under siege in Ilovaisk, commanders of the Ukrainian forces had begun to negotiate an agreement that would allow them to withdraw from the town.

In the early morning of August 29, Vladimir Putin claimed that a humanitarian corridor for besieged Ukrainian soldiers should be established, allowing them to leave Ilovaisk. At 8:00 a.m., soldiers and volunteers, many of them injured, retreated in two columns. Tired and unarmed, they passed the first ring of encirclement safely, but within a few miles, their columns came under the merciless fire of Russian artillery. The area was now a shooting range, with unarmed, defenseless people the targets in that "bloody corridor" prepared by Putin. Hundreds of bodies were thrown everywhere by the force of the blasts. The Russians posted selfies and videos on social media platforms, proudly posing over the corpses lying at their feet; others played football with severed heads.

As we watched, tears of outrage welled up in our eyes, and millions of fingers clenched into fists. The Ukrainians were unable to respond; there were not enough troops or weapons to oppose the occupiers. For years, we had lived in the neighborhood of an enemy who stabbed us in the back while telling us it was for our own good. Now, violated, Ukraine was paying the price of its nonchalance with the blood of its sons and daughters.

In September 2014, demoralized by the defeat near Ilovaisk and threatened by a full-scale Russian invasion, President Poroshenko was forced to sign a twelve-point ceasefire deal called the Minsk Agreement. On the surface, its provisions included prisoner exchanges, deliveries of humanitarian aid, and the withdrawal of heavy weapons. In truth, it was a disguised surrender pact stating that Donetsk and Luhansk would be granted "special status" while the Russian presence and Russian militants would be protected by law.

However, the agreement quickly broke down after violations by both sides. After the Ilovaisk massacre, this conflict hadn't the slightest chance of being resolved peacefully.

CHAPTER 4

The Noose Tightens

TALKS BETWEEN THE RUSSIAN AND UKRAINIAN PRESIDENTS IN MINSK ended without any signs of progress. Though Russia still denied its military presence in the east of Ukraine, insisting it was local guerrillas who were causing the problem, the Russian army still attacked Ukrainian troops with heavy artillery and air force. Vladimir Putin had boasted that he could take Kyiv in two weeks if he wanted to, and insisted on a large-scale Ukrainian military pullback. Fierce battles for Donbas continued.

For eight years, until the first Russian missiles landed in Kyiv, this war was observed as if it were a football match. We fans were rooting for our team, while the team members were dying by the hundreds. War is a despicable crime; it steals the lives of the combatants while also taking the humanity of those who passively stand by while the tragedies unfold.

Was I obsessed at the time with the war? Frankly, no. I was preoccupied with plans for my future career. My long-term cooperation with Moscow had sullied my reputation in the eyes of Ukrainian publishers. One by one, they refused my services or treated me with contemptuous silence.

In October 2014, when I celebrated my sixtieth birthday, I was insecure as a writer as well as financially challenged. With less than $3,000 in my bank account, I was edging close to panic. I saw no prospect of getting a steady job to support my family and our pensions were so meager they barely kept us fed. Luba was unable to help us since she'd lost her business and all the benefits that came with it.

Svitlana, with her Donetsk background, couldn't find a job in the capital where discrimination against natives of Donbas had always existed. It was as if we were the ones who had brought the war to our living space, wherever we were in Ukraine. And perhaps, in part, we had. This war had arrived in the country at large but was born in our hometown.

Writing was my only source of income, but since *American Thinker* did not pay for my pieces and the doors of publishing houses were closed to me, I was on the edge of a financial abyss. For the first time in our lives, my family was close to real poverty, and the reality of the term "financial assistance for internally displaced persons" in Ukraine was ludicrous.

Sergiy had his own family to take care of, so he wasn't able to help the three of us as much as he would have liked. Nor could I return to the Eksmo publishing house. Only a miracle could save us.

From the way that my wife and daughter often looked at me, I knew that they, too, were waiting for a miracle. I shrugged and told them that we were going to spend the autumn and the beginning of winter together somewhere warm and congenial, perhaps the Turkish Mediterranean. Didn't we deserve it, after everything we'd been through?

This unexpected adventure would probably drain all our financial reserves, and my common sense told me it was not the time for such indulgences. I don't know how to explain it, but I had always believed that money came and went, just like breathing. The more you spent, the more you received. I always felt that money loved movement and activity, so grasping and clinging to it would cause it to dry up.

When we arrived in sunny Antalya from rainy Kyiv, we found ourselves in paradise. It was resplendent with exotic blooms and green palm trees framing superb views of the bright blue sea. However, within a couple of days, our vacation mood had been darkened by the realization that there were many Russians in Antalya! When we had reserved our lodgings in a small apartment, we had no idea that it was located in the heart of the Konyaalti district known as "Russian Antalya." Its name was fully justified by a row of eight giant Matryoshka dolls in the central square, a majority of bilingual Turkish and Russian shop signs, and an instantly recognizable Moscow accent we heard wherever we went.

To make clear our statement of resistance, all three of us wore yellow and blue bracelets on our wrists and spoke to each other exclusively in Ukrainian, pretending we didn't understand Russian when someone spoke to us. We were quite aware that our behavior seemed childish, if not foolish, but we needed to show our contempt for the country that had stabbed in the back those whom they had once called their "brothers."

While in Antalya, in addition to the bracelet in the colors of the Ukrainian flag, I often wore a T-shirt with the inscription KYIV. One early morning I went to the sea alone. It was Sunday and the city was still asleep. The streets were empty, and the colorful shutters over nearly every window were closed. The pinkish-white blocks of three-story houses stood out clearly against the bright blue sky. I suddenly felt happy and strangely free. The war in Donbas was finally losing its hold on me.

Ahead, at the intersection of two streets, a noisy group of guys appeared. They were passing each other a bottle of alcohol, drinking from it in turn, and laughing merrily. One of them, slim and lanky, screamed and swallowed from the bottle more often.

At first, I mistook them for Turks, but soon I heard them speak Russian. The lanky one was yelling something like: "Hey, buddies, thanks for the great welcome! Next week I ought'a be back at the war, but until then, I'm gonna have some fun! Yahoo!"

As I came closer, I looked at him sharply and saw that he appeared to be a Georgian. He looked back at me with large, dark eyes, and then his gaze riveted on the word "Kyiv" on my chest. He froze, his hand wrapped around the bottle's neck. His friends went silent. The pavement was so narrow that we were unable to pass each other, but I had made my way through a cluster of his rough-looking pals blocking the street.

A chill ran down my back, but it was too late for me to turn back or escape. My pride wouldn't let me. All I could do was to keep moving forward.

The five continued to stare silently at me as I approached. At the last moment, two of them slowly moved to the side, making way for me, but the lanky guy with a Georgian appearance stepped forward and snapped, "Hey, Uke! Go home! Soon we will be in Kyiv, so get ready. I'll hang you from the nearest lamp post, Uke! It's a promise."

With that, he walked past, pushing me with his bony shoulder. The guys followed him, looking back at me.

I kept walking, my heart beating wildly under my Kyivan T-shirt. These youths radiated danger—I could clearly sense it—and the most dangerous of them was the Georgian-looking guy who had called me "Uke."

A couple of months earlier, gruesome news footage had emerged showing the same youth as a rebel chief, standing in front of kneeling Ukrainian prisoners of war. These men were battle-hardened soldiers who had defended the Donetsk airport from May 26, 2014, to January 22, 2015, with a ferocity that had earned them the moniker "Cyborgs."

In this video, the bastard called himself "Givi." He had asked for a knife, cut off the chevron of a Ukrainian officer, and then forced him to eat it. He then proceeded to repeat this with several other prisoners.

"Givi," it turned out, was a commander of the Somalia Battalion, notorious for his cruelty during the war in the Donbas. Once he admitted to the *Kyiv Post* newspaper that he had personally executed more than a dozen Ukrainian prisoners of war. He was killed in 2017—may the earth be hard and heavy upon him.

Back in the winter of 2014, Russia, Ukraine, France, and Germany made sluggish attempts to kickstart negotiations to end the violence in Donbas through the Minsk Accords. These were largely useless and unsuccessful efforts. Despite ranting about peace, Russia had been deploying increasing numbers of troops to the Ukrainian war-torn border region. Putin was not limiting himself to Donbas alone—his intended prize was our whole country, from one end to the other. Not yet ready for an outright military invasion, he chose to undermine our strength by digging under the political, ideological, social, and economic foundations of the Ukrainian state, like a mole burrowing down to escape the light.

The fully paid establishment stooges were preparing to build new political parties in Ukraine, each striving for the right to run for office, buy up industries, and control TV networks. Hordes of propagandists tried to convince Ukrainians that they were a dependent nation, tied to Russia by bonds of the Orthodox faith, the affinity of souls, and centuries of common history. Gas and oil valves were in the hands of Putin, who skillfully used them to destroy our economy. His expectation was that ultimately the devaluation and rising prices of gas and oil would persuade us to turn our backs on the West and once again become submissive vassals of the Kremlin.

But we refused to give up. This was a struggle not for life, but to defy death—and every year we became stronger.

Meanwhile, the professional tide finally began to turn in my favor, and after a series of rejections, I managed to get a contract with the Kharkiv publishing house. The publisher hired me to write several books for $500 each, but this was not enough to sustain us in the capital city of Ukraine. Therefore, we moved to the suburbs of Kyiv for the next four winters, where rent was far more affordable. My son's friends generously donated a home for us to use, free of charge. They used it only from spring to early autumn. It was actually a summer cottage heated by a fireplace. For four long winters, I was busy chopping wood and keeping the fire going. During breaks, I would write novels about travel and adventure in exotic countries.

The cottage stood at the edge of the village, facing the wasteland of peat bogs, covered with waist-high yellow grass. In dry months, the grass often caught fire, filling the air with suffocating smoke. Fires burned until rains put them out, as peat is a major fire hazard.

In winter, we were haunted by the smell of burning. Maintaining a fire day and night was no easy task. Pinewood, full of pitch and turpentine, burned brightly but gave off a lot of smoke. Dense wood tended to smolder, stinging our eyes while we sat by the fireplace.

Luba was constantly cold and spent a lot of time in front of the fire, which made her eyes red and watery. This did not save her from periodic uterine inflammations. Back then, we didn't know what this would lead to. I had often heard that Man is the creator of his own destiny. It's true. Looking back, I believe that most of our life tragedies are created by us.

On weekends, Svitlana and her future husband, Alexander, came from Kyiv to visit us. We barbecued, played board games, and drank wine in front of the fireplace. We enjoyed the company because when we were all together, the house didn't appear unwelcoming or stark. But on

Sunday evening, our dear guests would leave and Luba and I would be left alone.

Our loneliness was sometimes brightened by the presence of Sergiy's small daughter, Severine. Luba would bake pies and I would walk with our granddaughter through the snow-covered fields, pulling her on a sled. But those joyful moments were short-lived. Our only permanent companions were mice and a family of weasels who lived in our attic and woke us up at night making a huge fuss above us.

Although I kept in regular contact with my parents through telephone calls and Skype sessions, our conversations brought me nothing but heartache. Almost invariably, our talks turned into political debates and mutual accusations. My mother hated Ukraine. She and my father viewed themselves as "belonging" to Russia.

Looking back, I can't blame them. Their lives were coming to an end. The brief gap between sunset and darkness had left them wandering in limbo in the twilight of their lives. Both Mom and Dad refused to face the truth. Worse, they blamed my wife for being a "bad influence" on me, their only son.

They considered me a defector who had moved into the enemy's camp. Luba had come from an all-Ukrainian family, which hung over my parents like the Sword of Sorrow. They refused to let me speak of her or even mention her name. This crack in our family tree was about to widen and deepen in the most dramatic way.

It happened in April 2016. With the approach of spring, we felt especially cheery. We cleaned up the trash that was left in our backyard after another winter and prepared to move back to the city. It was like finally returning from exile!

One fine morning the phone rang. Luba's stepmother told her that her father had died during the night. In fact, it had been suicide. In his late eighties, Viktor Ivanovich had been rapidly losing his memory, his vision, and his ability to walk. He secretly took a bottle of vodka and locked himself in the garage. While sitting alone behind the wheel of his car, he drank the entire bottle and died on the spot. His heart, which had survived two strokes, could not bear the load. Apparently, he did it deliberately.

I was stunned. I had never seen this man drunk or drinking anything other than beer and house wine. A few days before, he had called Luba on her birthday, patiently waiting to speak with her so as not to overshadow the celebration. Then he was gone—forever.

The night before we received the news, I awoke to a touch on my shoulder. I shifted a bit and saw Luba sleeping with her back to me, breathing through her mouth, her arms relaxed. I put my head back on the pillow and was suddenly aware of a strong scent of alcohol in the bedroom. Luba and I had gone to bed absolutely sober. Where had this strong scent come from? I realized where the next morning, when I heard the sad news.

My parents knew about the tragedy, but neither of them expressed sympathy for Viktor's tragic death. Luba rightly took this as a deliberate insult. I saw it as even more significant: their silence was a confirmation of their rejection of *everything* Ukrainian, including my wife and her late father.

I tried to ease her pain when Luba and I were on our way to her father's funeral. I phoned my father to tell him that we were on our way east. All he said was a curt, "Good luck," which was an odd thing to say, given the circumstances. My mother remained silent.

Since then, a high barrier has separated Luba from my parents, and it appears that a relationship between them is no longer possible. Both Sergiy and Svitlana immediately supported their mother's boycott of my parents. It was left to me to be the only one who kept in touch with them. Our family tree has now been uprooted, which saddens me. Now, we are creating a new one without them—if one can actually do so.

The next year, when Luba made a short trip to Donetsk, she didn't even think to visit my parents. She had gone back to check out our apartment and pick up some things. I was surprised when she called me upon her arrival, her voice thick with tension.

"I really regret coming back here, Sergey," she said. "I'm afraid we will never be able to return to this place."

"Why? Is everything that bad?" I asked.

"It's worse than I expected! I'm afraid to leave the house. There's nothing but human scum on the streets—armed men, drunkards, junkies, felons, and tramps."

This was Moscow's policy in living color! Replace the one million refugees who had left Donbas with those from the poorest sections of Russia. Local authorities had provided empty apartments for the use of the Russian newcomers, and anyone with a weapon could take anything from those without one, be it a car, a property, or a life. Utter one harmless word in Ukrainian and you could be accused of espionage, get arrested, and be tried in a court-martial. The Russians were giving the world a living demonstration in Donetsk.

With growing concern, I asked Luba if she could hear gunfire.

"It's quiet now," she answered. "But the corner of our house was damaged by a shell. Many windows have been shattered. It looks like we'll have to sell the apartment. It's impossible to live here."

But now, we could never sell our apartment! At the beginning of the occupation, its value had fallen by more than 70 percent. Even if a solvent buyer could be found, it would be too risky for us to try to take money out of Donetsk. Along the roads were checkpoints and guard posts where people were searched. So now, we would have to abandon our apartment with all its contents. Our contents!

I would have given a lot to bring back photo albums, some books, and other trifles I valued, but now it was too late. Our home, sweet home would have to exist only in our memories. Gradually, we would forget the color of the wallpaper in the rooms we had spent years making our own . . . but in a way, it felt less painful. A vivid memory can hurt more than an older, duller one.

For a while, my loss of income did not allow me to buy a new apartment in Kyiv. However, in 2018, things began to improve. My new books were selling well in Ukraine, and the publisher offered me a contract to write one book every six weeks. The variety included crime thrillers, action-adventure themes, and historical romances. My advances had doubled and then tripled. Writing books at such a frantic pace was a difficult but ultimately valuable experience: I learned to work with concentration and perseverance, forgetting to rest even on holidays.

This allowed Luba and me to settle into the comfortable area of Kyiv. She was happier now; she no longer had to freeze during the long winter nights, covered with half a dozen blankets. However, I was concerned about her health. She had begun to complain of frequent pain in her lower abdomen.

Alas, these warnings were so subtle they failed to warn us of a gathering storm within her body. In truth, our heads were filled with other concerns. We had finally found a landlord who rented us two apartments in the same building. One was for Svitlana and her husband, Alexander, and one was for Luba and me.

I had just celebrated my sixty-third birthday when Svitlana gave birth to their first child, a girl, whom they named Erica. Now, Luba and I had *two* beautiful granddaughters who needed care and attention! Of course, it was the adults who would be forever blessed by the tender charms of our sweet granddaughters.

While our three families were (for now) living in peace and harmony, the Ukrainian nation was divided in half. The war was smothering the eastern borders and affecting the forthcoming presidential election.

And then, suddenly, a new personality entered the political scene! Volodymyr Zelensky was a comedian and actor, known for his irreverent jokes and clownish gig. For some reason, however, Ukrainians found him appealing. They were tired of war and pervasive corruption. When he actually ran for president of Ukraine in April 2019—and won—everyone was stunned!

At first, people were concerned about how he would assume his responsibilities as president. Like many politicians, he had a record of involvement with unsavory characters. He had also been a pawn in the experienced hands of the controversial oligarch Igor Kolomoisky.

After his landslide win—a powerful rebuke to his predecessor, Petro Poroshenko—Zelensky claimed that he intended to bring peace to Ukraine by getting a face-to-face meeting with Vladimir Putin. As it turned out, however, he came under mounting pressure from patriotic forces to be *tough* with the Russian president. Recognizing the importance of this first test as a president, Zelensky *did* stand his ground and denied the Russian dictator the concessions he had expected.

Putin was infuriated! He had expected compliance and obedience from his opponent. Since then, Zelensky has become such a despised enemy of Putin that the oligarch stopped referring to the Ukrainian president by name. For him, Zelensky would always be known as the leader of a "gang of neo-Nazis" or, at the very least, the head of the "Kyiv regime."

To be honest, I was not an early enthusiast about Zelensky. His hoarse voice, his temper, his posturing, and his way of communicating with the nation via short videos and tweets were, to me, highly annoying.

However, my perceptive son and his young, ambitious entourage saw it differently. They viewed Zelensky as a new player in a rotten political scene that needed to be demolished. They were not embarrassed by their hero's former extravagant escapades. Ukrainian youth were tired of seeing the same old politicians repeating the same boring mantras. They wanted radical change, and I must admit that over time, I have actually seen such changes take place—as dramatically as anyone could have imagined!

More surprises were in store, but this time it was the arrival of two threats to Ukraine's survival. In the spring of 2020, the COVID-19 pandemic hit Ukraine in full force. Inexplicably, it was accompanied by massive, out-of-control wildfires around Kyiv. Everyone was convinced that the arson was being committed by Russian saboteurs. Smoke covered the horizon and hung over the city like a whitish shroud. The streets were empty but for a few passersby wearing masks, now needed to filter the air from two threats: COVID-19 and smoke from raging fires.

"Social distancing," "mask mandates," and "lockdowns" were the new vocabulary, ruling our behavior and refocusing our lives. The military conflict in Ukraine was no longer a top news story and seemed more like a half-remembered nightmare. Everyone in my family suffered from the coronavirus and found that it was unpleasant, but thankfully not fatal.

Meanwhile, the SARS-CoV-2 virus was mutating, generating a variety of viral strains that would soon begin their world tour.

In May 2021, Luba, Svitlana, and six-month-old Erica went on a six-week vacation to Antalya. Alexander and I had a lot of work to do in Kyiv, and we got together in the evenings to play boardgames and drink beer. It was a time of temporary bachelor freedom.

One morning, I woke up feeling ill. My whole body ached, my head hurt, and I felt dizzy. When I sat down at the breakfast table, I realized that I could not possibly keep food down. However, the symptoms disappeared after a few hours. I took my temperature, and it was normal. I wasn't coughing or sneezing and didn't feel sick, so I decided to go downstairs to join Alexander. When we sat down to play a game of Brass, he looked at me closely and said, concerned, "Sergey, you're looking very pale."

"It's nothing," I said. "Let's play. I'll probably go to bed early tonight."

I refused the beer he offered and tried to focus on the game. But half an hour later, the chips became heavy in my hands and Alexander's voice sounded distant. It echoed as though my ears were underwater. I was in a daze.

I muttered that I had to go, got up with difficulty, and took a few steps from the kitchen to the front door. Then, a terrible weight fell on my shoulders and knocked me into . . . nowhere. When the darkness dissipated, I found myself flying over a deserted grassy field with occasional patches of shrubs and trees.

The daylight was gray and somber. I kept flying and circling over that field, thinking that now I saw the place of my death. I was going to die in this land of emptiness, stillness, and hopelessness. I felt deeply sad and lonely. I hated the idea of being dead, but somehow I was being pulled toward it as if by gravity. Was there no one who could stop this?

"Can you hear me? Hey, can you hear me?"

I opened my eyes. Alexander's face loomed over me, frightened and so huge that it obscured the ceiling with its intolerably bright lights shining down on me. I squinted and sat up. Alexander breathed a sigh of relief. He told me that I had been unconscious for about two minutes. My heart had stopped beating, and I had stopped breathing. I was essentially dead until Alexander gave me mouth-to-mouth resuscitation and chest compressions to bring me back to life. The ambulance hadn't arrived, and my son-in-law was close to panic. How could he tell Svitlana that her father had died in his arms?

We agreed not to tell our wives about the episode. It would have upset them and spoiled their holiday. I didn't want to go to the hospital, but I did agree to stay in bed for three days. When our wives returned home, I felt completely healthy except for a lingering feeling of weakness.

I believed that I had been attacked by the latest variant of the coronavirus. As the weeks passed, the memory of it all began to dim, then vanished. I would return to the grassy field of death again, but not until next year, in another country.

CHAPTER 5

A Life Smashed to Pieces

In March 2021, when American president Joe Biden was asked whether he thought Putin was a killer, he replied, "Mm-hmm, I do." He also told an ABC News reporter that Russia would "pay a price" for attempting to meddle in the 2020 US election and described Putin as having "no soul." Some three months later, the two leaders shook hands as they greeted each other at Villa La Grange in Switzerland. Politics is a dirty business, and everybody knows it. Politicians have to wash their hands often.

Putin's latest game was the dirtiest in modern history. In April 2021, while President Biden, German chancellor Angela Merkel, and a whole array of Western leaders delivered pro-peace speeches, Russia was amassing 120,000 troops along the Ukrainian border. Even more worrying was that every day Kremlin officials and propagandists covertly and directly threatened Ukraine with military punishment. There were not just troops on the border, but paratroopers, ballistic missiles, and electronic warfare systems jamming communications were now focused over the entire territory of Ukraine.

Western allies were rattled, fearing an invasion could be afoot. Now Putin was in his element, expecting that Western leaders would beg him not to start a war. This, after having believed that they were succeeding in bringing reason to the war-mongering dictator.

On April 23, 2021, Russian state media reported that troops were returning to their bases after taking part in exercises near the border with Ukraine and in Crimea. Ukrainians took a slow, deep breath and relaxed.

But despite Russia's announcement, we learned that in May, about a hundred thousand Russian troops were still on our border, along with their killing equipment.

As we were living a few steps from Svitlana, I saw her every day and noted the anxiety on her sweet face. I tried to comfort her, but at the same time I wondered if I was making a mistake. Was it true that the Russians would not carry out their threats? What if they were actually planning to attack us? Given their powerful army and huge resources, they had every chance to win. Could it be time for us all to pack up and sit out the troubled times under the protection of NATO?

My primary concern at this point was the safety of my daughter and grandchild. What kind of future awaited them if they lived in an occupied country, or worse—a country at war?

When I was much younger than today, I experienced a terrible dream. I stood at the window of our Donetsk apartment with baby Svitlana in my arms while the mushroom cloud of a nuclear explosion slowly, majestically rose over the city. This image remained engraved in my memory. It is impossible to describe the sense of despair I felt while clutching my priceless daughter to my chest. Were we *not* going to escape this nightmare? As the deadly wave approached us, its strength began to build faster and faster. I watched burning buildings collapse, swept up into the force rushing toward us. And there I stood, frozen, little Svitlana in my arms. I knew I would not be able to save her . . .

When I awoke, I couldn't tell if I was alive or dead. Later, I told my daughter about my dream. Even then, as I spoke, I felt despair building within me.

"It's been a long haul, Dad," she said. "The Cold War, an arms race . . . It's impossible not to have those thoughts."

I agreed with her. After all, we always choose to believe what we want to believe.

Today, the world is convinced that Putin wouldn't dare launch a nuclear strike against Ukraine. Perhaps now, as you read these lines, this has already happened. No prophet can predict the actions of a madman. In 2021, no one believed that Putin would actually attack Ukraine. His troop maneuvers were regarded as just another bluff in the geopolitical game. But with one miscalculation, the people and the planet supporting them—everyone alive—would be gone.

On my daily walks in Kyiv with my daughter, our conversations invariably revolved around war topics. We would start discussing anything from religion to our favorite desserts, and suddenly the topic of Russia's military preparations would come up. It was impossible to separate the country, Russia, from its growing threat to our family's survival.

Prior to this, Svitlana had not expressed any interest in politics. She wasn't apolitical, but her main areas of interest were spirituality, mysticism, and a passion for self-improvement. She'd kept herself in shape with gymnastics, yoga, and jogging as a young adult, and she continued these practices as a young mother. We often shared our worries and deepest secrets, and always wanted to be a good example for each other. Our sense of solidarity had made us close friends as well as father and daughter. Ours was the natural attraction of kindred minds.

Svitlana has always had amazing intuition. I was convinced more than once that she was able not only to read my thoughts but also to foresee the future. However, in the case of Russia, the future was impenetrable to us all. It's hardly a coincidence that politicians are particularly fond of the "suspense genre" when it comes to writing, reading, and viewing entertainment.

In June 2021, the Biden White House had temporarily frozen $100 million in military aid to Ukraine, a plan originally made in response to menacing movements by the Russian troops along Ukraine's border. It was put on pause as the Biden–Putin summit approached. The White House statement declared that further developments would depend upon Russia crossing territorial red lines: "We have also prepared contingency funds in the event of a further Russian incursion into Ukraine. As President Biden told President Putin directly, we will stand unwavering in support for Ukraine's sovereignty and territorial integrity."

Biden's actions were taken as a sign of weakness and hypocrisy by many Ukrainians, including me. In retrospect, however, we were basing our feelings on superficial evidence. We did not take into account the political interests of the United States and the friction that existed between the American president and Volodymyr Zelensky, who represented our country.

History is created by people, including individuals vested with power and influence over nations. The personalities of Joseph Biden and Volodymyr Zelensky were too contradictory to allow them to throw themselves into each other's arms. The relationship between the two leaders, fraught with friction and a lot of gripes, was far from convivial. Their tensions were inherent to their differing responsibilities and positions. The two men didn't seem capable of creating a positive collaboration.

In 2019, the impish forty-one-year-old actor, Zelensky, was swept to the summit of Ukrainian power. His previous experience as a president was ironic, to say the least. He had played the role of an "honest president" in a popular sitcom, *Servant of the People*. Biden, seventy-six, was a highly experienced politician with a long, distinguished record of accomplishment as a US senator and vice president. It was Biden who was a true leader, able to grapple with the coronavirus pandemic and a shattered US economy. Separated by thirty-five years, Biden and Zelensky had represented largely opposite generational poles and political systems.

After reviewing an intelligence dossier on the Ukrainian president, Biden must have experienced strong doubt that this man could pull this country out of the swamp of epic corruption. Leaders around the world used to throw up their hands in frustration when trying to assist Ukraine's emergence from its dark political past.

Joe Biden was no exception. Back in 2014 while serving as vice president, he had made his attitude toward corruption perfectly clear, calling it "a cancer that eats away at a citizen's faith in democracy."

How did Zelensky take those words, having had a long-standing association with the odious Ukrainian billionaire Igor Kolomoisky, the man who had been hit with US sanctions for "significant corruption" in Ukraine? In 2015, Zelensky's television shows were being broadcast on Kolomoisky's TV channels, and the oligarch was Zelensky's main backer in the 2019 presidential election.

President Biden had a personal grievance as well as his own political motives regarding Ukraine and the man who now represented this country. In July 2019, then-President Trump had pressed Zelensky for weeks to investigate Hunter Biden, Biden's youngest son. Hunter had joined the board of a scandal-plagued Ukrainian gas company named Burisma. Zelensky succumbed to Trump's pressure and made contact with members of a rogue team of Trump's stooges sent to disrupt the Ukrainian government and run surveillance on Hunter Biden.

When all this came to light months later, such mistakes were neither forgotten nor forgiven. And now all of Ukraine was paying a high price for the naive actions of its ruler.

I was filled with indignation at the thought of this situation, which put Ukrainians at risk because of the personal ambitions of driven, ambitious men ensconced in government buildings on continents separated by the ocean.

As a new grandfather, I found myself extremely aware of the fragility of my granddaughters: they were so vulnerable, so defenseless. As I hugged them, I couldn't even speculate on what awaited them should war break out. They had very different personalities, but both girls had something in common: they trusted us. We were gods to them—super-beings who always took care of them, protected them, and ultimately decided their fate. Alas, many other "gods" would prove to be unworthy of the designation. They have built a world where the killing of children is possible.

Three-year-old Erica and seven-year-old Severine had no time to think about such unpleasant things. They lived their happy childhood lives. Dark-haired Erica, Svitlana's daughter, was a lively, exuberant, energetic girl—a curious mixture of stubbornness and flexibility. In sharp contrast was tender, outwardly shy, blonde Severine, Sergiy's daughter, who kept her feelings to herself and rarely raised her voice. Each of them held a special place in my heart, which was contracted more and more tightly in anticipation of disaster events.

Meanwhile, my sense of impending catastrophe was closing in. Vladimir Putin was unwilling to abandon his aggressive plans. Convinced that NATO allies wouldn't defend Ukraine in case of an armed conflict, he once again started to drill his tin soldiers on the geopolitical board.

In early November 2021, intelligence officials, reporters, and bloggers flooded the media with information about a new threat of a Russian invasion of Ukraine. As it turned out, (suddenly, always suddenly), Putin left military units near the Ukrainian border after spring exercises, with the number of Russian troops in the area totaling ninety thousand. They seemed to emerge out of nowhere, and satellite pictures showed around a thousand Russian military vehicles only 160 miles north of the Ukrainian border.

Despite the video negotiations between Biden and Putin on December 7, the increasing concentration of Russian troops on the Ukrainian borders continued day after day, night after night, both overtly and covertly, quietly and loudly, slowly, methodically, and incessantly. I had an image of a giant python coiling its body around its prey, squeezing it to suffocation. Was Putin ready to attack, or was he trying to blackmail the West to achieve his goals? Could he actually be insane, or was he an evil genius with a secret plan?

Most important, where and when would he stop—if ever?

Everyone was a news addict, intoxicated with suppositions and rumors. As we ate our breakfasts, we kept one eye on the morning news, grumbling to ourselves and each other about how the world was clearly going to hell. At dinner we would count the number of Russian tanks and aircraft aimed at Ukraine. Suppers were infused with the lengthy reasoning of military experts. Every time I started falling asleep, I saw the glowing screen of a cell phone in Luba's hand—her lifeline to the world outside our own.

The information war inflicted severe psychological wounds and injuries upon us. I found that I didn't recognize myself. Suddenly, I had no strength to write, and everything seemed to fall out of my hands. At the time, I was writing a book about the Devil's Sea in the Philippines. To hell with the Devil's Sea! Who cares about vanishing ships and flying saucers in the Dragon's Triangle? All this was rubbish, compared to the reality we faced every single day and night.

The Christmas holidays of 2021 were dreary. Ukrainians celebrate Christmas a bit differently than does the Western world. My family used to celebrate Christmas on December 25, though most Ukrainians prefer orthodox Christmas day, January 7 (like the Russians). Our main religious holiday is Easter, and spring was too far away. We wondered how the winter would pass. I don't remember praying. My meditation and spiritual searches had been left behind. I could not bring myself to read or think of anything sublime. The mood caught us all, as a family. We had all become very down-to-earth and practical. One foot in front of the other, and then walk forward.

A trip to the supermarket in Kyiv was eye-opening; it was over-flowing with customers. We bought canned fish, cereal, flour, and milk. Few people truly believed in the coming war. We consoled ourselves, pretending that everything would be fine. Historically, people have a natural habit of comforting themselves—even as they're being led to the gas chamber or the firing range.

On New Year's Eve, we gathered at our festive table. Alexander treated us to roast beef and salmon steaks. Cooking has been his passion, as evidenced by his slightly protruding belly. Good-natured, generous, and easygoing, Alexander is a wonderful husband and father. He has always been—and remains—a man you can rely on.

Sergiy was unable to take part in our celebration, recovering in bed from COVID. As we sat in the kitchen, little Erica slept in the room where the decorated New Year's tree stood with presents beneath it. Luba and Sveta wore their best dresses and looked very pretty. Alexander and I helped ourselves to whiskey while the women drank champagne. We all tried our best to be cheerful and in high spirits, raising toasts to happiness and prosperity, but at the same time we were painfully aware of the Russian troops on our border.

Exactly at midnight, the four of us got up, holding glasses of foaming champagne in our hands. It was time to make our New Year wishes. I believe we all said the same word to ourselves: "Peace."

Alas, this was not to be. It was now 2022, and soon we would learn that Peace would not to be on the calendar this year.

In mid-February, American officials warned us of the "very distinct possibility" of a Russian invasion of Ukraine in the next few days. Putin's rhetoric had grown more belligerent, more arrogant. He was demanding legal guarantees that Ukraine would never join NATO or use their missile strike systems. It was clear that he would not receive concessions. After listening to yet another menacing speech, the United States, the

United Kingdom, and many other countries, including Italy, Israel, the Netherlands, Japan, and South Korea, sent out an alert to their citizens: "Leave Ukraine immediately!"

Caught once again in the bewildering speed of a whirlwind, we began packing our bags with only the necessities as we prepared to leave Ukraine. Initially, we planned to fly to Turkey, but international insurers refused to cover flights in Ukrainian airspace. All civil flights were closed. The skies over Kyiv were strangely empty. Whenever we heard the drone of a plane, we knew it was a transport aircraft delivering antitank missiles to Ukraine.

Unfortunately, these military supplies did not inspire optimism. The US-made Javelin missiles were mostly intended for *guerrilla* warfare. No one was sure that we could stand against the full might of the Russian war machine, much less that we would survive the invasion! How capable would Ukraine's troops be, matched against Russia's? Their fate seemed sealed. There were many reasons for that, but in the eyes of the Western world, it was primarily the fault of the Ukrainians themselves. We didn't prepare for war. We did not buy weapons for defense. We didn't fight corruption.

Even so, we felt betrayed by everyone. On the world map, Russia looked like a monstrous beast, grabbing a heart-shaped Ukraine in its mouth.

Luba called Sergiy several times a day, begging him to leave Kyiv until things settled down. He told her it was not yet time, that he wasn't ready to leave. Luba thought otherwise. She dispatched me to visit Sergiy and try to convince him to leave.

"Do you understand what awaits you if the Russians enter the city?" I told him.

"Dad, you know I'm lucky, I always was," he said. "As a kid, I always was able to get out of anything, remember? I promise you I will leave when the going gets too tough. Until then, I will stay to assist in the city's defense."

I knew Sergiy had no intention of fleeing. He was a proud young man who had become a role model for Ukrainian youth and patriots who were committed to resisting the enemy.

I looked away and said: "Okay, son, it's your decision. But I'll be damned worried about you."

"You need not worry, Dad," he said. "So far I've always been all right."

So far, I thought to myself and sighed. Sergiy put his hand on my shoulder, squeezing it gently, which made me feel a bit better. I asked how long Tanya and Severine were going to stay in Kyiv. He replied that if the war started, they would leave in Tanya's friend's car and added: "Let's hope nothing will happen."

We all waited and waited. Luba refused to abandon her son in the hour of danger, just as Svitlana couldn't abandon her parents. As a result, we sat in our apartments among packed bags and suitcases . . . and waited

. . . even after February 17, when the US president had warned our Ukrainian president that the threat of a Russian invasion of Ukraine was now "very high."

. . . even on February 23, when Washington gave Volodymyr Zelensky an intelligence assessment that Russia was preparing to conduct a full-scale invasion of his country within the next forty-eight hours.

That was shortly before Zelensky urged the nation to remain calm and claimed that the "hype" around the danger of a Russian invasion was much bigger than the actual threat. He was very persuasive when he delivered his speech—in fact, every political leader should have an acting career behind them—just like Volodymyr Zelensky!

On the night of February 23, I awoke, startled, as if someone had shaken me. I got up and stared out the window at the crimson-colored moon, incredibly large and round, beginning to wane. I'd never seen such a red moon in all my life. It was a strange, mesmerizing sight.

I sat in the kitchen for an hour or two in front of my laptop, trying to work. It was still dark outside when I heard loud explosions from the airport area. I counted five of them around 5 a.m.

Farewell to dreams of peace. The war had begun.

CHAPTER 6

On the Road to the Unknown

EARLY ON THE MORNING OF FEBRUARY 24, 2022, RUSSIAN PRESIDENT Vladimir Putin emerged on TV to announce the start of a so-called special military operation. He could barely contain his excitement. He had waited so long for this moment, and now his hour had come.

Addressing his accomplices, whom he called "citizens of Russia," speaking clearly and decisively, Putin equated the government of Ukraine with a "gang of drug addicts and neo-Nazis." He proudly announced that Russia's goal was the demilitarization and denazification of an unfriendly country: ours.

In concluding his thirty-minute speech, he exclaimed, "I am certain that devoted soldiers and officers of Russia's armed forces will perform their duty with professionalism and courage." At this point, Putin raised his voice. Every word he spoke was like a nail being driven into his audience's collective brain. "This means that the decisions that I made will be executed, that we will achieve the goals we have set, and reliably guarantee the security of our Motherland."

After that, the most notorious Kremlin propagandists jumped onto the stage, ready to take on anyone who would dare stand up and object to what they had just heard. In their front ranks were the most prominent talking heads:

Margarita Simonyan, the editor-in-chief of the Russian television news network;

RT, a small Armenian woman with big cravings for beaver meat;

Dmitry Kiselyov, a bald, round-headed TV presenter on Russia 1, famous for his trained, almost balletic hand gestures;

Olga Skabeyeva, another state television presenter whose powerful jaws and steely, permanently squinting gaze might be found in a women's prison; and

Vladimir Solovyov, a loudmouthed supporter of Putin and his war, always dressed in a caricature of a military jacket with a stand-up collar, fashioning himself into a chubby version of Stalin or Mao.

The walls of their TV studios reverberated as they acclaimed in one voice that Kyiv would be taken in three days! They and millions of their compatriots were already celebrating the swift victory in the Blitzkrieg.

We weren't listening to them, nor to the Ukrainian news reporters affirming their growing panic. We were packing up! Before that day, it had felt as if we were ready for a long journey—but it was only an illusion. Luba and I dashed about the apartment, closing windows, turning off the lights, pilling our belongings into suitcases, and checking all the drawers and shelves to make sure we hadn't forgotten anything in the process.

Svitlana called us every two minutes, urging us to move quickly, quickly, quickly. But everything was out of our hands. For the second time in our lives, the Russians had chased us out of our home.

Still, outwardly, I kept my composure. I had to. I didn't want Luba to notice my confusion. We needed to gather all the strength and courage we had, because we could rely only on ourselves and one another.

It was already daylight when we all gathered downstairs near our Mitsubishi Crossover. The parking lot looked like a large disturbed ant-hill. Many lots were empty and littered with trash and cigarette butts; the remaining cars were surrounded by people with suitcases, trunks, and cardboard boxes. We did not look at them, just as others did not look at us, lowering their eyes.

Those who run away are always ashamed, especially if they're men.

Alexander, unshaven and disheveled, shifted the bags in the car's open trunk. Svitlana nervously fastened Erica into the car seat in the back. Our little princess wasn't happy about the upcoming trip. Even at age three years and four months, she knew something was wrong. I smiled at her reassuringly and waved hello. Erica didn't smile back at me. She was very serious and silent.

At that moment, I again was reminded of how much I hated Putin. In 2022, the number of children under seventeen in Ukraine was approximately twelve million. Russia's "special military operation" was not just directed at adults; it included every child in Ukraine, as well.

Luba and I barely found room for our suitcases. Some things had to be stuffed haphazardly inside the car. As soon as we climbed in, it became hot inside from five passengers' body heat. We all began to take off our coats, tossing them anywhere. I was afraid that keys, bank cards, or money would fall out of my jacket pockets. But who could think clearly when we were "on the run"?

Alexander turned the car onto the road toward the bridge across the Dnipro River. It was the only path that would lead us west. Not surprisingly, the bridge was jammed with cars, trucks, and buses moving mostly in one direction, trying to cross as rapidly as possible. People with bags and backpacks walked along the footpath. Trapped between cars ahead and behind, we frantically read the news on our cell phones.

Russian troops had moved quickly to hobble Ukraine's defense capabilities. It was a fast-paced, three-pronged invasion from the north, east, and south—simultaneously. Many Ukrainian military targets, including airfields, had been destroyed in just a few hours. There was fighting at various points, including just outside Kyiv, where Russian paratroopers had landed. At some point, I thought I heard machine gun fire. I kept it to myself—no need to add to the terror we were all feeling. It took us at least forty-five minutes to drive over the 450-foot bridge, after which we entered the next traffic jam.

"Sashko, can't you drive faster?" Luba demanded. We always used the shortened version of his name, in the Ukrainian manner.

"Faster?" he asked. "I'm sorry, Lyubov Victorivna, but what in the world makes you think that I can fly?"

He was making an extra effort to be polite, but we were all overwrought. Erica was the only one whose face was blank, staring out the window at the traffic. She quietly asked if we could go back home so she could be with her toys. Svitlana had taken some of Erica's favorite toys with her, but they were buried somewhere among the contents of suitcases.

And there was no home. Not anymore.

I asked Luba to give me a carton of milk. The nervous tension gave me heartburn and stomach pain from an old stomach ulcer I'd developed many years back. Now I drowned it in milk—just another disorder in this disorderly life.

It was pure vehicular chaos, and then, right in the middle of that Mumbai-like traffic jam, Sergiy called me on my cell, his voice unusually tight. He asked me to take his daughter with us. Tanya's friend had let them down and all the train tickets were sold out. Sergiy was afraid to leave Severine in Kyiv when it was being threatened with encirclement by Russian forces. We agreed on a meeting place and Alexander finally cleared the traffic jam.

Sergiy was waiting for us near the metro station, now quiet and focused. For the first time, his face reflected the gravity of a forty-two-year-old man; whereas only a few days before he was still boyish-looking and confident that he could overcome any obstacle.

While we waited for Tanya and Severine to arrive, Luba began to sob, trying to persuade Sergiy to change his mind and join us.

"How do you imagine it, Mom?" he asked with a tight smile. "Are you going to tie me to the car roof?"

He again promised us that he could always leave Kyiv, but I knew it was wishful thinking. I didn't know what to say, so I kept quiet. We had gone through this dialogue before.

Finally, Tanya and Severine arrived from the subway. The farewell was brief and chaotic. Only a few minutes passed before I found myself sitting in our Mitsubishi escape vehicle with Severine on my lap. She was quiet and sad. Tanya looked inside the car to say that she would come as soon as she could. Severine nodded silently, tears streaming down her face.

"I will miss you," she whispered to her daughter . . . and to us all.

We said our final goodbyes to each other and then pulled the car away from the curb, heading west. Still holding a milk carton in my hand, I turned back to cast a last glance at Sergiy and Tanya. Their figures moved farther and farther away, getting smaller and smaller by distance. Sergiy gave us a final wave and then disappeared around the corner.

"Sivi, that's great!" Erica exclaimed in her tiny voice. "Together we will have fun! Do you want a cookie?"

Within three minutes, the two little cousins were chirping and laughing merrily, as if quite content with their lot. Now, the adults could focus on the task at hand: to move fast, yet carefully. Alexander was driving as if his life depended on it—and all of our lives did. Svitlana sat beside him plotting our route to the West, concerned that we stay as far away from Belarus and the Black Sea as possible. Belarus was already occupied by the Russian army and was ready to invade Ukraine at any moment. The sea was filled with Russian cruisers and destroyers carrying missiles—aimed at us. We were truly on the path between Scylla and Charybdis.

Luba, Severine, Erica, and I shared the back seat. Since the car's trunk was open to the cabin, packages and bags kept sliding onto us every time there was hard braking. The four of us could not sit four in a row because of the bulky child car seat on the left and a pile of things on the floor. Severine was to spend the entire trip on my lap.

The first hour flew by. After two hours, my legs began to feel numb. The journey from the city to the outskirts took six hours instead of the one hour it normally would have taken. The highway heading west out of Kyiv was choked with traffic across five lanes as millions of residents sought to escape alongside us, fearful of bombardments while stuck in their fully packed family cars.

On our way we saw the miles-long queues of cars outside the gas stations, their parking lots jammed with vehicles. When the time came to use the toilet, Alexander stopped at a roadside rest area in the woods. On the edge stood two tanks with Ukrainian soldiers sitting on the turrets, dozens of cars around them. Everyone had to take care of their needs in a grove across the ravine filled with plastic bottles, crumpled napkins, and cigarette packs. One could only guess how many people had been there before us.

After leaving the highway, men and women dispersed in different directions. There was no time for delicacy and timidity—the niceties of civilized life are often the first to go.

As I walked among the pine trees, I saw a line of soldiers passing green ammo boxes from hand to hand. They worked quickly and smoothly, preparing for battle on the outskirts of Kyiv. The war was for real. It was close.

As we got back together at the Mitsubishi, a camouflage-colored jet fighter thundered through the gray sky right over our heads. It flew so low that it almost touched the tops of the trees. We followed it with wide-eyed fascination and listened to its receding roar. Was it a Ukrainian jet or a Russian jet?

"Grandpa, what was that?" Erica asked in her chirping baby-talk language.

"A plane, dear," I answered. "Just some plane."

"Did it fly up to Kyiv?"

"It flew somewhere," I said honestly.

We drove on, downing snacks to keep us going. Sometimes we were overtaken by ambulance trains with shrill sirens, and sometimes they moved toward us. Now and then I asked Severine to stand up for a while to rest my numbed legs. She was a light, thin girl, nonconfrontational and quick-witted. Erica tended to rebel a bit and was used to getting her way.

At dusk, both girls were exhausted and fell asleep. Severine grew heavier and heavier on my lap, but I was wide awake. Myriad thoughts played hide-and-seek inside my head. I looked ahead and thought about myself and my loved ones, about Kyiv and Ukraine, about our past and our future. Now, we were surrounded by darkness, saturated with the menace of war in the night air. The road ahead looked like an endless river of red rear lights. Oncoming headlights did not blind us. Military trucks were driving toward Kyiv with their lights off to keep them from being spotted by enemy aircraft.

After a while, we took turns charging our phones. Luba, Svitlana, and I scrolled through the news, exchanging brief remarks in an undertone.

"Oh, my gosh! The Russians captured the Chernobyl nuclear site, just sixty miles from Kyiv!"

"They crossed the border from Belarus, damn them . . . !"

"Zelensky has ordered general mobilization . . ."

"Fuck this clown! He didn't think beyond his nose . . ."

"Missiles are raining down around Ukraine . . ."

"The Russians are attacking us from three sides . . ."

"Their tanks were seen on the outskirts of Kharkiv . . ."

"They landed by sea at our port cities of Odessa and Mariupol . . ."

"Putin said he has repeatedly accused the US and its allies . . ."

"President Biden said . . ."

"Britain's Boris Johnson said . . ."

"In France, Emmanuel Macron said . . ."

Between conversations, we slept in snatches or nodded off. Severine lay across Luba's and my knees. Sitting in the strapped-in baby seat, Erica squealed through her sleep. Alexander, fueled by his devotion to his passengers, drove nonstop. Our three-hundred-mile journey lasted almost twenty-four hours.

Early the next morning, in the gray February dawn, we arrived in Lviv, an ancient city in the western corner of Ukraine, three hundred miles from Kyiv, near the Polish border. The road into Lviv was lined with improvised checkpoints identified by sandbags and cement blocks—local volunteers had been preparing for an invasion. Behind these makeshift barriers were haphazardly dressed men with hunting rifles and submachine guns. I wondered whether they were thinking these were adequate for impeding a Russian assault.

Morning in Lviv had empty streets and long queues to the gas stations. ATMs didn't work because they had either been turned off or had no cash inside them. Shop assistants shook their heads at the sight of our bank cards—all they would accept was cash. Alexander and I had to exchange some dollars for Ukrainian *hryvnias*. When we hit the road again, Sergiy called me to ask about our future plans. I told him that we had decided to go to Poland.

"Lviv doesn't look like a safe place for our girls," I said.

However, Sergiy was strongly against our going to Poland. He insisted that his daughter be brought to his friends in the suburbs of Lviv. Severine was supposed to stay there until her mother arrived. They were planning to live there together. Sergiy gave me the address, which meant that we would have to make a forty-mile journey in the opposite direction. Instead of going on to the Polish border, we were returning to Lviv.

The friends of Sergiy and Tanya met us with warm hospitality. They were a very large family living in a very large house. There were at least a dozen relatives and their acquaintances gathered under one roof—whom you ran into at every turn on your way to the bathroom or kitchen. The head of the house and his sons were busy building a bomb shelter in the basement. His wife, daughter, and daughter-in-law fed us Ukrainian borscht and dumplings. They tried to persuade us to stay with them, saying that they had enough space and food for us, so we shouldn't worry about imposing on them.

But how could we accept? Too many people lived there, each one along with their habits, tastes, and requirements. We didn't want to create embarrassment for them or for us, so we said we'd better go.

Before leaving, I went out to say goodbye to Severine, who was playing in the yard with her new friends. She sat on a rope swing made from a large tire, kicking her legs in and out. Her smile spread wide across her face, and her cheeks flushed red.

I asked her if she was happy and she told me, carelessly, "Yes!" That made me feel better, but at the same time, sad. It wasn't until a few minutes later that I realized Severine had done her best to hide her true feelings. When the others joined me to give her farewell kisses and hugs, she looked down so that we wouldn't see the tears in her eyes. Little Erica couldn't contain herself—she was crying in the car, repeating between sobs, "Let Sivi go with us, let her go, please."

Reassuring Erica, I told her a tale about two little sisters who would fly to each other in their dreams. She closed her eyes and said that she was going to sleep. She wanted to be close to her Severine. The war would not allow it, not for now, but hopefully she would have other opportunities to reunite with her older cousin.

CHAPTER 7

No Exit

ONCE BACK IN LVIV, WE DECIDED TO STAY THERE FOR THE NIGHT. ALEX-ander, exhausted, was unable to drive any farther, and Svitlana was too inexperienced a driver to take turns with him at the wheel. Neither Luba nor I possessed a driver's license, and Erica was now fretting, refusing to return to her car seat. We all needed some rest and couldn't even imagine getting back into the car.

The name *Lviv* means "the City of Lions." On this evening, it seemed that there were more stone lions on their pedestals than living people walking in the streets! Most of the hotels, cafés, and restaurants were closed. The locals ate and lived at home, and there were no tourists in Lviv. Refugees did not linger here, passing through in a hurry to reach Poland, Slovakia, Hungary, or Romania.

We settled in at a hotel in an ancient monastery with its typical stone walls, a wide-open cobbled courtyard, a massive temple, and several buildings, one of which appeared to be the inn. It would have been a perfect location for a Gothic horror film, but we weren't afraid of the ghosts. We already knew that there were worse things in this world than phantoms. Our room looked like a monastery cell, cold and damp, with a crucifix in the corner and a Bible on the table. We had a late supper of sausage, bread, and cheese and chatted about various meaningless things when suddenly a loud bang made us jump in our seats. It was a huge yellow balloon that burst in Erica's hands. The sound was like a gunshot ringing off the walls of the dim room.

Once again, we were brought back to our fears about the war, which was destroying more and more areas in Ukraine. On the second day, the world saw tanks enter Kyiv. In response, the city's officials began handing out guns to thousands of volunteers, along with instructions on how to make petrol bombs. Many Ukrainian cities were under attack, a number of civilian areas had been targeted, and hundreds of people had been killed.

Luba punched in Sergiy's number to find out what was happening in his area. He quickly reassured her that everything was all right. "Nothing to worry about," he added. This would become his invariable formula when talking with me and Luba. "Take-it-easy-don't-worry-be-safe-bye." We listened to this throughout the siege of Kyiv.

Before falling asleep, Erica crawled into my bed for her obligatory bedtime story. Afterward, she went into her dream world and I went into mine. Everyone fell asleep and everyone had their dreams, but we all woke up to the same disturbing reality.

Suddenly, we bolted from our beds at the roar of an air raid siren. It was the very first siren we had ever heard. In Donetsk, they had not used them. In Kyiv, there was no time to activate the alert and notification system. But here in Lviv, we had a taste of the present—and the future—when the sirens did the job they were created to do.

I wonder whether the explosions themselves are able to affect the human psyche as destructively as does the sound of blaring air raid warning sirens. The women were in a panic, and we dressed in record time and rushed to the nearby bomb shelter. Fortunately, the monastery had a cellar beneath the hotel. The receptionist showed us the narrow staircase that led us down to safety.

The lights of the city were now turned off as the area plunged into total darkness. The dank basement quickly filled with hotel guests, glowing phones in their hands. We all took our places on wobbly chairs along the walls. Some of us could not sit still and walked back and forth, and then down between the shelves holding cardboard boxes filled with apples. We also saw canned vegetables (all dusty and cobwebbed), interspersed with whatever else had been tossed down there: yellowish newspapers and magazines, old clothes, ropes, broken fans, and air conditioners. It was all junk placed in high stacks against the walls.

We saw two or three monks in the basement, their robes pushed out by fat bellies. (It has always been a mystery to me why ascetic priests often appear chubbier than average.)

To amuse little Erica, I carried her around the cellar, looking into all the nooks and crannies, hoping that a rat would not jump out at us. She was frozen with terror.

"Grandpa, why are we here?" she asked.

I told her that there were bad people who wanted to steal our land and hurt us.

"Then why don't we push them out?" she asked.

I thought, groping for the right answer. "They're too strong," I offered after a moment.

"Then why are we not as strong as they are?"

Some children's questions confuse adults. That's because their questions are simple and only require clear answers. However, I didn't have any answers. Ukraine had lived in the same neighborhood as Russia for centuries. We were periodically conquered and exterminated, exiled, and starved to death. So why had we found ourselves unprepared for this war? Why hadn't we become strong, as we should have been, given our history?

"Erica, honey, let me help you blow your nose," I said. She had caught a cold in the monastery's basement and when we got upstairs, she was sneezing and coughing. Soon afterward, we went to bed, exhausted in every way possible.

The next morning at breakfast, we had a quick discussion about what to do next. As far as we understood from conversations with Lviv residents, the city was bracing itself to join the theater of war. There were rumors circulating that Russian paratroopers had parachuted from three helicopters in the Lviv region near the town of Brody. Our troops had reportedly repulsed the attack, but no one knew when and where it might happen again.

So we decided to go to Poland, as we had planned the day before. Deep inside, I hated the idea, feeling torn between caring for my family and wanting to stay in the homeland to defend it in whatever way I could.

On the way from Lviv to the border crossing at Shehyni, we got into a queue that stretched for miles. It was an unmoving line of multicolored cars, trucks, and buses, packed with passengers and belongings, all waiting their turn to squeeze through the overburdened border checkpoint to Poland. Tens of thousands of Ukrainians had rushed to the west in search of safety as Russia mercilessly pounded their cities with airstrikes. Many cars had to be abandoned due to lack of fuel. Now they stood abandoned along a road completely congested with vehicles coming from the east. Endless lines of refugees headed for the border on foot, trudging along the highway's trash-strewn side of the road with their children, pets, and all the bags they'd been strong enough to carry. It was a pitiful, unforgettable sight.

Shivering in the piercing wind, people sought solitude in the bushes and turned their backs on the involuntary spectators. Time after time, someone carried the children's potty out of the car to empty it on the brown winter grass, now scattered with piles of excrement and crumpled paper. Some babies suffered from nausea or diarrhea, and mothers had to carry them out of their cars in subzero temperatures.

I walked about half a mile ahead along the highway to get an idea of the size of the queue. The far end was lost in the distance. Then I stopped by a group of men smoking and asked them what chances we had of crossing into Poland before dark. They replied that they had been standing there since early morning, and had advanced a hundred feet at best.

"Get ready to spend the night here, mate," they said. "Whilst the border may be meters away, it is also still hours away."

"If not days," one of them added grimly.

Discouraged, I returned to my family. We had very little food—only biscuits, bread, and water. Milk was long gone and no stores were within reach. We had just waited in line for four hours and moved forward four hundred feet. How much longer could we hold out?

Erica demonstrated heroic patience for a three-year-old, but she was weak and coughed all the time. Puffed up in the back seat of the car, she watched cartoon after cartoon and waited silently for us to finally give her the kind of coziness she deserved. She looked blank and joyless. It was breaking our hearts to see her so unhappy.

After the late lunch (if it could be called a lunch) we perked up slightly when we noticed that more and more cars were leaving the queue, turning around on the road and heading back. This gave us hope. Finally, the main vehicle stream slowly flowed forward. An hour later we saw in the distance the roof of the checkpoint building. We were beginning to anticipate the end of our torment when I noticed a police patrol blocking the road. I immediately knew that there was something going on there, something totally unexpected.

Helmeted policemen armed with machine guns approached the cars and peeked inside. After that, some owners of the cars had to climb out, and some had to turn completely around and drive in the opposite direction. We also saw men arguing with the police, or giving farewell hugs to their women.

Svitlana and I went down there to check out the situation. The police officer looked at me, and then at Svitlana. "Lady, your husband cannot go through," he said. "Today, a presidential decree came into force prohibiting men of military age from leaving the country. This applies to all male citizens from eighteen to sixty years old, without exception."

"I'm sixty-six," I said. "And I'm not her husband, but her father."

"All right, then," the officer said wearily. "Get back in your car and wait."

"What about my husband?" asked Svitlana quickly.

The officer turned to her and repeated, "All men aged from eighteen to sixty years old, lady. No exceptions."

We returned to the car and told Luba and Alexander the news. He immediately told us that we should go on without him.

"Svitlana, you can drive a car," he told her. "If nothing goes wrong, by sundown you will be in Poland."

"And you, Sashko?" she asked.

"I'll return to Kyiv by train," Alexander said. "I belong there, sweetie. The city needs men."

"Wives need their husbands," Svitlana cut in sharply. "We're not going anywhere without you, Sashko. I hate leaving you alone."

The discussion soon ended. My sweet daughter is the kind of woman who knows how to insist on what she wants.

When Alexander finally agreed to continue with us, we turned on our phones and started to seek a place where we could settle together. This was not an easy task. Apartments were rented out at much higher rates than before the war, and there were no free rooms in the local hotels. We found this out on the way to the small town of Truskavets. We chose it because it was close to the border, and the trip down there would take under an hour. Erica needed to be put to bed as soon as possible; she needed a proper meal and rest—as did the rest of us!

On the way, I counted all the money I had in my pockets and on my bank card. This should have been enough for about a year of a modestly comfortable existence. Alexander and Svitlana's financial situation was no better. They had recently spent all their savings to purchase our trusty van.

After some hesitation, I called my editor in Kharkiv. The publisher owed me sixty thousand *hryvnia* (around $1,500). This money could make our lives much easier and steadier.

The editor told me that my last book would never be published or paid for. War is reason enough for a *force majeure*, isn't it? Our contract had been terminated. The publishing house was no more. Meanwhile, Kharkiv had burned and smoked for days now, and the number of dead began to pile up. My book, my money, and my problems looked microscopic against the backdrop of these daunting events. I told the editor I wished him well and switched to the news channel.

The first video footage showed me a Russian missile hitting a local theatre and exploding, causing a huge ball of fire and blowing out the windows of surrounding buildings. I saw cars driving by the wreckage and saw dead and injured people lying on the sidewalks.

The commentary said that it had happened in Kharkiv's Freedom Square. What could be more symbolic than this barbaric act? The goal of the Russians in this war was very clear: they had come to destroy *how we exercised* our freedom. Destroying our freedom would be the next and final step.

Chapter 8

The Handwriting on the War

On a cold March morning, I left the hotel for a breath of fresh air. Walking along the alley toward the biggest park in Truskavets, I looked at the sky blanketed with heavy, low clouds. My bare hands were red with cold after a minute, so I tucked them into my pockets.

The park had a square decorated with a thirty-foot pole flying the Ukrainian flag. It looked like a yellow and blue patch stretching to the iron-gray sky. Suddenly, the anthem of Ukraine burst from the loud-speakers, causing a huge flock of black crows to fly up out of the treetops and into the freezing air, through the first snowflakes, circling and cawing excitedly. *Ukraine has not yet perished*, the male choir sang sternly. But there were no other listeners: the area was completely deserted.

The anthem ended and it became quiet. I listened to the silence. There was no wind, just the whispering of snow pouring steadily from the sky down to the patches of bright green on lawns. Spring had been defeated in the battle with winter. But the war was not lost. The victory of spring over winter is imminent and inevitable.

While standing there alone and watching the snow coming down, thicker and thicker, something clicked and I realized what I must do. I had just discovered my purpose: I was to create order out of the mental chaos that continued to plague me. I would write a book about the war that would blaze from miles away. Even here, away from the flames, I could feel the burn of its red-hot breath. This book would have to be written immediately to let the outside world feel what we Ukrainians felt every day, every hour, and every minute—even as the Russians continue to bring death and destruction to our land.

As I left the square and walked on, the first line of the book popped into my mind. It read: *The small resort town of Truskavets on the Ukrainian western border* . . . Once I "saw" those words in my imaginary book, I immediately felt better. My trepidations and insecurities were now being replaced with clarity and a powerful sense of purpose.

An hour later, when I was walking back to the hotel, the snowfall turned into a blizzard.

God damn it, I thought. The last thing we needed now, in March, was a blizzard! None of us had winter clothes and shoes, three of us were suffering from the flu, and the other two were about to catch it from us. We were short of money and lived in cramped conditions. In addition, we were all depressed by the bad news and our anxiety about Sergiy. Despite these troubles, I continued to feel uplifted. Now, I had a goal!

I turned around to shield myself from the razor-sharp wind blowing into my face. The snow was thick, quickly covering my footprints. Cars were sliding down the street like children on sleds. The trees were covered in snow, its weight pulling down the branches. But I knew that soon these branches would straighten up and be covered with green buds. The snow would melt, the earth would dry up, and winter would fade away. Wars don't last forever. They, too, would come to an end, and one day, a new life would emerge for us all.

I do not pretend to possess ecclesiastical wisdom, but suddenly I felt clear. I decided that today I would wait for the end of winter, just as tomorrow I would wait for our victory in this war.

I shall not give up, I promised myself.

When God stops believing your promises, you must then make the oath to yourself. However, it only works if you keep your word.

I took the elevator up to the fifth floor and entered our hotel room. It consisted of two bedrooms and a tiny hallway with a wardrobe and a door to the bathroom. The five of us spent day after day together and had gradually gotten used to the tightness of living conditions and lack of privacy. Erica shuttled between the bedrooms as she pleased, so our doors were never closed. She could choose any of the beds she liked to sleep in, and usually, it was mine.

We didn't have the courage to refuse Erica anything. The child was very weak. She had recovered from her cold, but now was refusing food, saying that she was afraid of vomiting. It took us a lot of effort to feed her something other than plain mashed potatoes or a glass of milk. On examining her, doctors found that she had an increased amount of ammonia in her urine. These were the consequences of the transferred infections and weakened immunity due to illness.

Svitlana, anxious about her daughter's health, lost so much weight that she turned into a pale shadow of her former self. Alexander had a fever and a bad cough. Luba suffered from flu symptoms, too, and complained of sharp pains in her lower abdomen. She and Alexander tried to treat themselves with healing mineral waters that allegedly could help cure many illnesses. So far, they weren't working.

The "hotel" in which we lived was not actually a hotel but a sanatorium with a restaurant for two hundred people and a medical center in the basement. Our room cost about a hundred dollars a night and required repeated re-booking, so we were constantly on pins and needles. In fact, we were all nervous and irritated, ready to quarrel at the slightest provocation. The nightly air raid alerts contributed to frayed nerves all around.

One day, the fire alarm sounded in the hotel. As panic arose among the guests, everybody ran toward the fire-exit doors. We hurried down, too, and spent a full hour under the open sky, shivering in the chilly wind, suffering from cold and anxiety. I cradled Erica in my arms, holding her close to my chest to give her a bit of warmth. She told me that she wanted to go home to Kyiv. I told her that we would definitely go back there.

"When, Grandpa?" she demanded.

"Soon," I answered.

She believed me. The problem was, I didn't believe myself. Each day began with the hope of a rapid victory and ended with a dreary realization that the war could continue indefinitely. My anxiety about the family never left me. It was constant and debilitating, like a toothache. One day,

I looked in the mirror and saw an old man staring back at me. The God of War does not necessarily swallow the whole human life in a single meal. With the same appetite, he takes a bite, then another, leaving less of you piece by piece, nerve by nerve, year by year.

For me, writing books was always the best way to protect myself from the blows of fate. And that was exactly what I did while in Truskavets. I devoted every free minute to it when not babysitting, shopping, or doing other household chores. Waking up in the very early hours of the morning, I would go down to the lobby and get to work.

It was a long, difficult process because I decided to write my memoir in English. I didn't have the money to hire a competent translator-interpreter. And, frankly, I didn't trust those unknown translators who offered their services via the internet. In order for a translator to create an *adequate* translation, a competent knowledge of the language and grammar is not enough. The translator I sought should also have literary talent. I couldn't afford to have my manuscript vivisected and taxidermied by some apathetic English teacher. I intended to convey my thoughts and observations to the public in their original form, not in a close copy.

The more difficult a task you set for yourself, the greater the effort you must make to achieve it. And the more effort you apply to your work, the more rewards you will reap. This was the third reason that prompted me to write in English.

Before that, I had made several miserable attempts that achieved nothing. My articles in the *American Thinker* were simply a trial run for me. From now on, I would really give this project my "all." I have read hundreds of English-language books and had a dozen electronic dictionaries at my disposal, so in a week, I prepared a solid proposal, which was sent to a good number of literary agents.

One of them responded immediately and expressed his desire to look at the first chapters of my book. His name was Roy. He happened to be the owner of a British literary agency with impressive experience in editing and publishing. His interest in me felt like the gesture of a celestial being who had extended his hand to me from the literary heavens.

Roy and I exchanged emails, and he always showed himself to be a big supporter of both Ukraine and my family. His interest inspired me to work like a dog. I slept four hours a night and lost six pounds. In order to fill the chapters with historical facts, I followed the news in Ukraine and the world with redoubled attention.

Official newsreels on TV and footage on social media showed me the same pictures: blackened ruins, palls of coal smoke over our cities, tongues of blazing flames, streaks of blood, and dead bodies with limbs stretched out or twisted, just as death's agonies had left them. It was a terrible but now familiar sight. It scared me. Was my soul hardened? Had I gained the ability to watch the horrors of war calmly sitting in front of the television, with my eyes dry and my heart beating steadily? If so, why should I be outraged that the rest of the world was not similarly shocked by the tragedy of Ukraine? All of us witnessing the action from a distance saw only fragmentary episodes of this ongoing tragedy.

Nearly two weeks into the war, the invaders from the East had advanced deep along Ukraine's coastline in order to establish a "land corridor" to the Crimea Peninsula, which Russia had seized from us many years ago. Mariupol, which stood in the way of that projected corridor on the Azov Sea, was already half-shattered and surrounded by Russian forces. Rats and dogs were devouring corpses lying in the streets of the burning city. Those who remained alive huddled in basements, melting dirty snow for water and breaking into stores in search of food. All attempts to evacuate the survivors failed, as Russian troops had fired on the convoys before they reached the city.

It's hard to believe, but the entire Russian nation rejoiced at the suffering of Ukrainian citizens. Kremlin propagandists openly called for drowning our children and razing our cities to the ground. Our enemies were not shy when expressing their wish lists. Political talk show guests brandished their fists and stamped their feet, promising to turn Ukraine into one giant version of Hell.

Backed by heavy shelling, Russian troops captured city after city in the southern and eastern parts of Ukraine. The number of our refugees passed 1.5 million, triggering the greatest refugee crisis in Europe since World War II, and Vladimir Putin didn't hide his contented smirk. "I want to say that the special military operation is going strictly according to schedule," he affirmed, opening a meeting with his security council.

In full accordance with his bloody "schedule," Russia took control of Europe's largest nuclear power plant at Zaporizhzhia. A fire started there after it was attacked and shelled, which could have caused a worldwide nuclear disaster surpassing even the Chernobyl catastrophe in 1986.

Putin used the capture of the nuclear power plant as another trump card in his dangerous game of rising stakes. He used nuclear blackmail time and time again to force the world to refuse aid to Ukraine. His propagandists threatened to turn the West into nuclear ashes. And it has always affected the mass psyche of Western citizens and politicians.

I will never forget Bogdana, an adorable five-year-old girl with blue eyes and golden hair, whom I met in the children's room of the hotel. There were plenty of toys and games for kids to play with, and when Erica finally recovered, it became her favorite spot for fun. After breakfast, she would jump up and down shouting, "Let's go, Grandpa! Come on, let's go! We're going to be late."

The children's room was always louder than a zoo and full of excited, happy kids of different ages. Many of the youngest ones were accompanied by their parents, mostly mothers. Bogdana usually came with her grandmother, as her parents were missing somewhere in the Kyiv outskirts. While the kids were playing, running, and yelling, we adults occasionally talked about all sorts of things, especially what each of us had experienced in the recent past. There, I learned much more about the war than reporters and observers told us. I heard a lot of stories about blown-up houses, dead neighbors, and lost relatives. Each Ukrainian story was unique, and this united us as if we had known each other long before we met in Truskavets.

Meanwhile, I noticed that Bogdana was always silent and kept away from other children, not taking part in popular games. I asked her grandmother what was wrong with her.

"Bogdana is shy," the woman answered. "She's afraid that the kids will not want to play with her. She is mute, you know."

"I hope she'll be healed," I said.

"It's not a disease," the woman said. "Bogdana refused to talk after she saw the news about a possible nuclear attack. The men on TV showed viewers a clip from an old documentary about the explosion of the atomic bomb. Bogdana only glimpsed it, and then ran to hide under the bed and wouldn't come out. When I managed to get her out of there, she mumbled something about an ugly mushroom and then fell completely silent. Since then, she has not spoken to anyone, not even to me. She just looks and smiles. She always smiles a bit when she is about to cry."

I don't know how, but I was able to get Bogdana talking. Her grandmother seemed too confused, nervous, and tense to inspire the child to relax. I guessed Bogdana needed a more delicate approach.

I squatted next to her and whispered, "No one will hear us if we're quiet. So you can talk freely, little darling. We can whisper."

It seemed to me that she nodded slightly.

"Well, then, tell me what you're scared of," I said. "You don't need to speak aloud. I can hear you if you just whisper back to me."

I lifted my eyebrows, waiting. Bogdana stared at me, hesitating. I leaned forward and put my ear next to her lips.

"I'm afraid of the bad man," she whispered, her voice so soft that it was barely audible. "A bad, bad man has an ugly smoky mushroom and wants to hurt everybody with it. He is the one who took my Mommy and Daddy away from me."

Choosing my words carefully, I told Bogdana what the Ukrainian soldiers would do to a bad man and his mushroom. Someday he would simply disappear and never do anything to harm her or anyone else. I told her that her Mom and Dad would definitely be found. She asked when, and I replied that I didn't know but I knew that it would happen, and by this time we were no longer whispering, but talking in an undertone.

Ten minutes later, Bogdana was laughing and playing dollhouse with the girls, while her grandmother was looking at her with tears of relief. I wished someone could dispel my fears as easily and quickly!

Actually, my fears were not for myself. I was afraid for Sergiy, who remained in Kyiv. Nearby towns were now occupied by Russian troops, and terrible rumors described mass executions, torture, rape, and robberies. It was obvious that the same thing would happen in Kyiv if the invaders broke into the city. What might await Sergiy and the rest of those who had stayed there?

When entering Ukrainian cities, the first thing the Russians did was "clear" the area, which meant killing young men whom they regarded as potential enemies. Sergiy was at risk of becoming one of them. When I thought about him, my heart sank. I dreaded what the Russians might do to him.

But Kyiv held out, despite fierce battles in the suburbs and rocket explosions in the city center. The main highway leading from the capital to the west of Ukraine was not cut off, making it possible to supply the troops and population of the semi-besieged city with food, arms, and ammunition. Miraculously, the way out still remained open.

It was a great relief for me and Luba to learn that Sergiy was going to come to Lviv. However, it was only for one day—to say goodbye to Tanya and Severine, who were leaving for France and an indefinite stay there. The church community of a small town, Camaret-sur-Mer, Brittany, overlooking the North Atlantic Ocean, provided free housing and education for Ukrainian refugees, God bless them.

Lviv was no longer a safe place. On March 13, 2022, a barrage of Russian missiles slammed into a military training facility roughly thirty-five miles from the city and ten miles from Poland; 35 people were killed and 134 injured. It was an ominous expansion of Russia's targeting and the closest attack to NATO's border.

It was abundantly clear that the time had come for us to leave Ukraine while we still could.

The snow had melted, it was becoming warm, and spring was fast approaching. The war was also approaching us with speed and reverberations that suggested destruction was on its way.

PART TWO
WEST OF HELL

SVITLANA MAYDUKOVA

Captain, this is madness! High time you thought of your own home at last, if it really is your fate to make it back alive and reach your well-built house and native land.

—HOMER, *ODYSSEY,* CA. EIGHTH CENTURY BC

CHAPTER 9

Toot! Toot!

ON MARCH 18, 2022, WE HIT THE ROAD AGAIN: AN OLDER MARRIED couple with their daughter and granddaughter, each with different manners, habits, tastes, notions, and everything else. Therefore, there were three pretty self-willed women in my care—women of different ages and at different points in life, from sixty-seven to three and a half years old, who, in turn, were going to take care of me, each in her own way.

Alexander was to return to Kyiv by bus. Our farewell took place on a concrete pad, located by the border checkpoint terminals. There, he got out of the car with a suitcase and a bag, and we gathered around him to hug him and say our goodbyes.

Erica did not show the least emotion and seemed completely undisturbed when she parted with her dad. She seemed to have a mental block protecting her from any sense of loss. She was also used to my being with her all the time and treated me like a second father, so she had no reason to worry.

Luba was somewhat aloof, not really saddened. Over the past four weeks, her relationship with Alexander had deteriorated to the point that sometimes they didn't even speak. They were too different to have much to share. Forced to face each other every day, they had several conflicts and were secretly glad to break out of a stressful in-law routine.

For Svitlana, this was the most painful moment. She would now be separated from her husband, not knowing if they would ever see each other again. Every young Ukrainian man could be sent to war at any time. Every Ukrainian could die during the shelling. Alexander was no exception.

When Svitlana returned to the car, her eyes were wet, but getting behind the wheel, she promptly wiped away her tears and stepped on the gas. This was a real test for her—her first experience of driving a long distance. Because she couldn't simultaneously drive and follow the navigation instructions, I sat beside her as the co-driver.

Poland met us with green, sunny landscapes as if to say, "Welcome! Feel at Home!" For an indefinite time, this was supposed to replace our homeland. We knew that we could hardly leave Poland, since we couldn't afford to live in Western Europe with its high cost of living. Thus, we were going to settle in a suitable local city not far from the border so we could return to Ukraine at any moment. Without thinking twice, we headed for Rzeszow.

An anticipated two hours of travel time stretched into six full hours. We lost our way twice and had to make a lengthy detour to get back onto the highway. Local gas stations, car washes, and parking lots with meters were *terra incognita* for us. Fortunately, the Ukrainian language was a bit similar to Polish, which allowed us to communicate with the Poles.

The vast majority of them treated us hospitably (although not as hospitably as the newspapers wrote about them), while some were arrogant and turned away. It was a foreign country, and we were refugees here, not tourists. We had to get used to it.

I will never forget the Polish salesman from a small grocery store where we went to buy water and a little food. As we wandered around looking at the shelves, we talked in Ukrainian, and the young man behind the counter took notice of us. He was blond with light-colored eyes and unshaven reddish stubble on his round cheeks.

Erica was in my arms, and she was very tired, hungry, and thirsty. One of us handed the seller two hundred *zloty*, which was about fifty dollars. Our purchases cost no more than ten bucks. The seller turned the bill in his hand and looked at us with cold eyes. I smiled politely at him. He didn't smile back. For a while he continued to sit motionless, staring at us, and then began sorting through the money in his cash register. He did it defiantly, slowly.

"Grandpa, I'm thirsty," Erica squeaked, holding my neck.

I gave the seller another polite smile and told him we were in a hurry. I knew a little Polish, because in my youth I liked to listen to the records of the group Czerwone Gitary, which were then considered "the Polish Beatles." Perhaps my speech was far from perfect, but the young man behind the counter understood me very well. Then he finally smiled at us. But it wasn't the kind of smile that radiates affection or sympathy. His lips stretched into the malevolent smile of a man who rejoices when he plays dirty tricks on others. Enjoying every moment of his triumph, he scooped up a handful of change from the cash register drawer and began to lay out the coins on the counter, one after another, slowly and solemnly.

Those two or three minutes seemed very long to me. All the shoppers were looking at us, everybody with a "How damned long will this take?" expression on their faces. Erica, who hadn't had her bottle of water, burst into tears. Luba and Svitlana tried to shame the seller. Ignoring them, he carefully counted out the silvery coins. Having finished with this business, he laid out our purchases in front of us without offering a bag. I don't know if he hated only Ukrainians or other foreigners, too. But his mockery would never be forgotten—or forgiven.

Of course, we also met other Poles, sympathetic, amiable, ready to help. There were many more of these than the ill-wishers. About 80 percent of Poles were definitely on the side of Ukraine in this war. Their support was invaluable and sincere. I'm sorry that the behavior of one prejudiced minority spoiled our impression of that beautiful country. Everyone knows how nasty a bee sting can be. During these painful times, stings from human beings can hurt even more.

Poland was very nice, with its smooth green hills, pine forests, windmills, and well-kept farms. I could spend hours admiring the beautiful scenery we were passing through if it were not for the need to follow the navigation map. In this country, we felt safe. For the first time in six long, disturbing months, we were other than insecure, afraid, and depressed. Our visit here had a healing effect on us.

Ukrainian media tended to exude optimism, too. Political scientists and military observers unanimously predicted a quick victory over Russia. This was an obvious exaggeration, but it could not be otherwise. Someone had to comfort the millions of Ukrainians who had lost their homes, their businesses, and their loved ones. Those who sacrificed themselves in the trenches hardly followed the news. They knew their own truth about the war, which was fundamentally different from the reports of newspaper and television reporters.

Residents of Ukrainian cities that were now charred ruins also knew the truth. And Western politicians were gradually awakening from the stupor created by Russia's unexpected and illegal attack on a neighboring country. They were inspired by the courage shown by the Ukrainians during the first four weeks of the war.

Now they faced a difficult choice. On the one hand, they recognized the value of weakening Moscow and raising the costs of their aggression. On the other hand, they wanted to minimize the risks of the war to prevent us from spiraling into a heavily armed confrontation between themselves and Russia because of their fear that it could all too easily turn nuclear.

The president of the United States is now the undisputed leader of the West, demonstrating to the world his determination and directness. Asked in Warsaw on March 26 what he thought of Putin, President Biden branded him "a butcher" and exclaimed: "For God's sake, this man cannot remain in power."

His words could become a motto for all the Western allies, who increasingly supported Ukraine. And they really inspired me, a writer wandering around a foreign country with a laptop, inside of which more new pages of this book were being created. To express my thoughts and feelings clearly, I spent hours in front of the computer's glowing screen looking for the right words. It was hard work, but it was worth it. My English vocabulary had grown, and I was now constructing phrases more and more confidently, using conjugated verbs and navigating the confusing identities of tenses. Writing slowly has taught me to be thoughtful and focused. Creating nonfiction about the war was not at all like churning out crime thrillers. But I liked it. And, most important, my literary agent liked it, too.

Roy proved to be a very paternal, very caring person. His emails always contained questions about my family and ended with warm words of support. There was no British stiffness in his attitude toward me. I was glad to have this gentleman at my side. He spoke of the publication of my book as an anticipated event in the very near future.

I was not going to leave Roy for anyone else and rejected the offers of other literary agents without hesitation. I preferred to stick with the one I knew—at least, I thought I knew him.

Roy signed an agency agreement with me and praised every paragraph that I wrote. I was overjoyed when he texted me that I would soon be having a Zoom meeting with an editor of a powerful publishing house. It seemed that I had terrific prospects. But at the same time, I was a bit nervous about the big test ahead of me. I had no particular experience communicating with English-speaking people. I had learned the language with my eyes, while my tongue remained mute and indifferent.

Back in the 1960s, my language tutorials had been the Beatles lyrics, Tarzan comics, and disheveled paperbacks with the 007 logo on their covers. Over time, they were replaced by Stephen King's novels and increasingly serious literature. Because I never had the opportunity to exchange a word with those authors, it was a one-sided, silent training. So how was I going to talk to the publishing house's editor? Would my tongue-tied speech repulse her? Or maybe she would take me for a swindler selling her someone else's manuscript? I needed to practice and needed it immediately, so I paid for five online lessons with different tutors.

An elderly English teacher, a bulky Hindu, and a Portland student all burst into smiles when they heard that I was Ukrainian. Each of them contributed to my learning, and each provided me with a spark of hope.

My impromptu lessons were held in the lounge hall of a large, respectable hotel in Lublin, Poland. Its name, Luxor, did not seem exaggerated to us. The hotel had recently opened and was trying to lure visitors with low prices, so we paid about ninety dollars for our bright, spacious room.

Owing to the frequent spring rains, it was quite chilly in the room. Our windows were directly above the hotel laundry, so we used to fall asleep and wake to the low rumble of washing machines in the basement. It sounded like music to us after the howling air sirens. The hotel's long corridors with framed arty photographs on the walls provided ample space for Erica to play with her new friends. The Luxor was half populated by Ukrainian refugees. They were all women, old and young, and children. I even saw strollers with babies who were surprisingly quiet, as if afraid of drawing attention to themselves. When you are a refugee in a foreign country, you learn to live by new rules. Alien rules.

The hotel didn't have a playroom, so on rainy days, its hallways served as a place of fun for a dozen children, along with their moms, grandmothers, and older sisters. The women were a fascinating mix: There was a small, mousy woman with heavily painted eyes who, right in front of me, received news of the death of her brother at the front. There was a fifty-year-old Kyiv lady who was jealous of her husband and called him every thirty minutes, demanding to know where he was and what he was doing at the moment. There were two teenage sisters who were worried about their kitty, left alone at home with only a two-week supply of water and food. There was also little David, who had recently lost his father and acquired the habit of silently running along the corridor from end to end, not stopping for a minute, his face focused and purposeful.

And there was me, keeping an eye on Erica so that she wouldn't get lost or drink the antiseptic liquid from the spray bottles scattered around the hotel. Being a good grandfather is harder than being a refugee but far more pleasant.

On sunny days we walked a lot in the area, Erica on my shoulders. Behind the hotel were lovely paths up into the woods, where we heard the frequent tapping of woodpeckers. The squirrels watched us with curiosity from the branches. I tried my best to feel happy in this pastoral atmosphere, but I didn't succeed. The phantoms of war accompanied me wherever I went, whatever I did.

Erica often asked me why I was so sad, so I would say, "No, sweetie. I'm just thoughtful."

Then, one day she said, "You better think of something fun, Grandpa."

It was great advice. Unfortunately, it was difficult to implement, as other concerns were taking priority. I was consumed by anxiety for our son. He was alone in Kyiv without our support and attention. Our problems were minuscule in comparison to his. Preferring not to upset us, he asked us not to call him too often, and for several days we did not know what was happening to him.

One day I made a video call to him on Skype. For once, I had caught him looking unusually somber and haggard. I asked what was wrong. He sighed and told me he was tired of the shelling, the street patrols, and the endless queues at stores with empty shelves.

"And I really miss little Sivi," he confessed wistfully. It was one of the rare moments I saw beneath the calm surface he usually presented.

I wanted to tear myself apart so that half of me could appear in Kyiv next to my son, while my other half stayed in Poland near my wife and daughter.

It wasn't possible, so I said: "I heard the Russians have been pushed back from Kyiv."

The small figure of Sergiy on the screen of my phone shrugged his shoulders and said nothing. I guess I frowned. Noticing my anxiety, he smiled and told me a couple of funny stories from his recent life. But the poor quality of the video did not prevent me from seeing his look, which said more than any words. He was weary, and he wasn't very good at faking a smile. My son was now a lonely-looking man whose family was away while he worked frantically to earn money for his family and his country.

"Son, do you want me to come for a day or two?" I asked.

His face became hard. He knew that I had picked up on his depression, and clearly he regretted his moment of vulnerability.

"I'm sorry, Dad," he said quickly. "We've got an air raid warning. So long."

My phone's screen went blank and I suddenly remembered that tomorrow was Sergiy's birthday. This made my heart ache even more.

I crossed the lawn and sat down on a bench among the conifer shrubs with waxy green needles. As I was sitting there, I remembered my parents. I phoned them every day, but I hadn't called them on Skype for a long, long time. They must be missing me, their one and only son. They would probably be happy to see me and hear some kind words from me.

I had periodically suggested that they move to Kyiv so they could live out their last years near me, but they always answered that they hated

Ukraine and considered themselves Russians. In the spring of 2022, they, like most residents of Donetsk, received Russian passports, and now they were foreigners to me. The war had erected the ultimate, impenetrable wall between us. But they were still my parents, my dear Mom and Dad, doomed to die alone without seeing me, their son, their grandchildren, and their great-granddaughters.

They had sent me money several times, and I had spent it on my family, but Luba never forgave them for abandoning us. Svitlana agreed. Sergiy had kept in touch with them for some time until political differences brought their relationship to a dead end.

The pointless dead end, dark and cold. A place that needs light and heat, at least a little . . .

As I sat on a bench between two conifer bushes, I pulled out my phone from my pocket. The screen was black. To revive it, all I had to do was to press a button. Such a simple move. Such a difficult move. I sat still, gathering my thoughts.

My mother had recently turned eighty-seven. I remember her as young and beautiful. She had always been kind to me. She had once had long brown hair and a movie star smile. She knew many poems by heart and sang wonderfully. When I was young, I was very much like her.

Years passed and I became more like my father. He was six years older than my mom. His birthday was now only seven weeks away. He would be ninety-three—such a venerable age. Until his seventies, my father had played tennis and boasted a trim, athletic figure. He also had an amazing memory and a mathematical mindset.

Where does it all go? My parents had lost their youth and their health. They had long ceased to leave the house and hardly walked around the rooms. Housekeeping, shopping, and cleaning were done by their relatives and neighbors. My parents had enough money to pay for their care, but they didn't have love. They didn't have their son.

I pressed the call button. Toot, toot. When had we last seen each other? When was the last time we chatted casually and reminisced about our happy times, putting aside our disagreements? Two years ago? Three?

To-o-t! To-o-t!

"Hello? Son? How nice to see you! It's a real treat for us!"

First, I heard my mother's voice. It hadn't changed. Then her image appeared on the screen. She had cut her hair and it was now short and curly. She noticed me staring and ran her hand through her silver curls, asking if I liked her new look. I said I found it "perfect."

She complained to me that she never could get used to her short haircut and smiled shyly. I noticed that my father was missing a lower front tooth. I swallowed hard. Mom was sitting in the same room where I had last seen her in person, eight years ago. My childhood home had turned into a nursing home while I was absent. During this time, my father had lost a tooth, and my mother, her luxurious hair. There are things that cannot be restored.

I asked my mother how they were doing.

"Great," she replied, nodding slowly with her grey head, "Just great, sonny. Don't worry for us." She raised her voice. "George! Come here, George! Have a glance at our son!"

My father appeared, looking unchanged, although he was stooped and moved with difficulty. Bending over, he asked me how I was doing, and I replied that everything was fine. We chatted for a bit and then he was gone.

"Your father is hard of hearing," my mom said apologetically. "He hates you to know that. You remember how proud he is."

"Oh, yes, I do remember," I said.

"And he's as stubborn as ever," she said. "His memory keeps failing him. And his health, too. But we will overcome this, son. We must wait for you. The war will end and you will come back, won't you?"

"Certainly," I said.

After we said our goodbyes, I sat on the bench for a few more minutes, listening to my heart. It was beating evenly and calmly. Something very important had just happened. I felt reconnected.

I inhaled the scent of conifer needles. It brought back my childhood memory of our New Year's tree, with gifts stacked underneath. I tore off a needle and chewed. It was fragrant and bitter. I tried to imagine what the next New Year would be like but saw nothing. The picture was still out of focus.

CHAPTER 10

Unpolished Polish

Boys love to play at war. This gives them the opportunity to present themselves as fearless heroes, winning or dying with weapons in their hands. I don't think it's normal, but I'm aware that as long as men make war, their sons will love to play at it.

In the United States, this psychological focus for boys has always been directed to the safest channel, highly romanticized and fictional, if not fantastic. There has long existed a cult of the "lone hero" or more accurately, the "cult of superheroes" such as Superman, Captain America, and a whole cast of similar metaphorical characters fighting the forces of evil, which had no prototypes in real life. Scenarios of games like "Cowboys and Indians" or "Cops and Robbers" also lacked any evidence of concentrated hatred and fury against the enemy.

The ideology of the USSR, however, focused on developing completely different qualities in children. The Soviet Union used all its propaganda to train them as the future defenders of the Motherland, glamorizing the ideal of heroic death during the performance of military duty.

Russia, as the successor of the Soviet Union, has successfully continued this tradition and brought it to the point of absurdity, using old ideological clichés in hundreds of military TV series, movies, books, and songs. The victory of the USSR over Nazi Germany (the Allies' contribution to the common victory had been largely downplayed or hushed up) was elevated to the rank of a national cult.

All of this had a strong influence on the mass consciousness, and very soon in Russia they ceased to be surprised at the sight of a baby dressed in a semblance of a military uniform, or a camouflaged pram designed as a tank. For students, "hours of patriotic upbringing" became compulsory in school, forcing them to engage in exercises like military men, marching with flags and singing patriotic songs.

Just before the Russian invasion of Ukraine, military hysteria was raised to its climax. Kremlin mouthpieces portrayed Ukraine as anti-Russia and called for the destruction of us as a nation, along with our culture, history, language, and customs. When hordes of men, inflamed by propaganda, invaded Ukraine, they were eager to fight and kill. They saw this as their calling. And the guns in their hands were not toys.

Paradoxically, the advantage of the Ukrainian soldiers was that they did *not* want to fight. All they wanted was to stop the war as soon as possible, driving the invaders from their land or killing them all; it never mattered. Russian troops prevented them from returning to their families, homes, and jobs. Consequently, it was necessary to destroy the Russian troops. Everything was extremely simple; it was impossible to think of any simpler way of achieving the goal.

So at the end of March, in the sixth week of the war, almost miraculously Ukrainian forces began to retake some areas from the invaders who increasingly fled the battlefields, abandoning tanks and armored personnel carriers.

For Russia, those were the days of the greatest shame and humiliation. Putting a good face on a bad game, Putin's spokesman, Dmytro Peskov, dully muttered that the retreat of the troops from the Kyiv region was merely a "gesture of goodwill." The clockwork heralds on state TV channels were chanting the same mantra. The decision to scale back operations around Kyiv, according to them, was taken in order to "boost mutual trust" in peace talks.

The "peace talks" never started. They became impossible after Ukrainian forces liberated the small town of Bucha, in the north of Kyiv. It happened on April 2, and from that day forward the name of the quiet residential community became a household name, and Russian soldiers were branded with the indelible moniker "bloody butchers."

Bucha!

When Ukrainian troops entered there, they saw the hundreds of corpses of men, women, and children left strewn along the streets, sitting in bullet-ridden cars, or lying across their toppled bicycles. Some had their hands tied behind their backs, some with blindfolds on, many of them bearing signs of torture and sexual assault. Others were found in mass graves, decomposing under the warming sun, barely covered with soil, their darkened arms and legs protruding from the red clay and heaps of garbage.

Similar heartbreaking, nauseating scenes were found in the neighboring towns of Hostomel and Irpin and smaller villages around Kyiv.

The brigade that had committed the atrocities in Bucha had been awarded the honorary title of "Guards" by Putin, who congratulated the unit for their "great heroism and courage." By so doing, he had placed himself next to Hitler, who in 1940 told his soldiers that he was freeing them "from the dirty and humiliating self-torture of the chimera called conscience and morality."

People without morality are beasts—it is as simple as that. Bucha has become clear proof of this. What normal human being can justify this? Who can ignore or turn away indifferently?

Later, while in Poland, I happened to meet the mother of a four-year-old girl who had survived the Bucha massacre. She was an ordinary woman in her mid-thirties, red-haired, freckled, more plump than thin. I think her name was Irina. We met at the playground our girls enjoyed visiting when the weather allowed.

I don't remember what triggered the story about Bucha. Most likely, it was news from there. An international investigation was going on in Bucha, and reporters from all over the world came there. It was a very painful, bloody wound in the collective heart of Ukrainians, so we often talked of it. "Do you know . . . ?" "Did you hear . . . ?"

"You know, we were there," Irina said. "Me and my daughter. I remember it as a nightmare, and I still can't believe we escaped from that Hell."

She talked about her days in Bucha very calmly, almost without emotion. Her daughter and my granddaughter sat on the swings next to each other, swaying gently as they held onto the iron chains. The sun was shining brightly, and the girls laughed and chattered to each other as merrily as the birds in the trees surrounding us.

We adults stood in the shadows, looking at them. The day was very warm for the beginning of May. Irina told me that she had arrived in Bucha a week before the start of the war. Her older sister's family was about to move from Ukraine to Germany and had to leave their apartment unattended for a year. Irina saw this as an opportunity to save on rent. Shortly before that, she had divorced her husband and her finances were low.

There were two reasons why she was not afraid of the arrival of Russian troops. First, Irina considered the Russians her "brothers" and didn't expect any trouble from them. Second, the Ukrainian media insisted that the idea of war was "impossible." Be that as it may, she came to Bucha with her daughter, Valya, and settled on the sixth floor of a multistory building.

When the war began, Irina and her daughter were trapped there. They had no car of their own, and they didn't have time to leave the city by bus or train. Everything happened very quickly. Suddenly, it was too late to run.

The Russians turned out *not* to be brothers but cruel and merciless enemies. They were shelling around the clock, and it seemed to Irina that all the shells flew over her house. Valya was crying all the time, as children do when they are scared.

One day, standing by the window, Irina saw a column of tanks and armored vehicles surrounded by soldiers. There were the Russians. From time to time the tanks turned to crush the cars parked along the street. As the column slowly drove by, soldiers suddenly began spraying bullets in all directions, firing at any movement in a window or on a street.

Irina and Valya hid in the bathroom and stayed there until morning. They spent several hours in complete darkness, wrapped in blankets. Their gas, electricity, and running water were cut. Irina was not able to charge her mobile phone and call for help. And who could save them?

The single mother and her daughter had to survive on their own. They had a supply of water in the boiler tank, and some food in the refrigerator in addition to flour, potatoes, and eggs. Some neighbors were setting up wood fires outside their houses to cook on them, but Irina did not dare to follow their example after seeing dozens of corpses lying in the street. These were the people shot dead by Russian soldiers, and no one could risk their lives trying to collect them.

Irina forbade Valya to go to the window, trying to protect her from shock. The refrigerator was empty, the eggs were gone, and Irina had to feed her daughter raw dough with raisins and buckwheat porridge soaked in water. Twice, she left the house in search of food, and each time it was a gamble. The Russians would shoot anyone they wished. They also robbed apartments and raped women. After committing a crime, Russian soldiers usually killed their victims and eliminated all witnesses, methodically checking neighboring houses.

Irina said she still could not believe her luck, being in Poland and living in a free hostel founded by local volunteers. She was looking for a job and did not intend to return to Ukraine. Her decision seemed logical, and I asked myself, how many Ukrainian women and children will remain in Europe after the end of the war?

The answer was obvious: many, many of them. Ukraine was losing not only men on the battlefields. We were losing tens of thousands of our young women who now settled in Poland, Germany, France, or God knows where else. They were looking for places to live safely, and they had every right to do so.

Unlike us, the refugees didn't stay in Lublin for long. They tended to take a break there, and then travel farther to the west in search of housing and work. We were the only ones who remained in the Luxor hotel for weeks. As before, we did not want to move too far away from Ukraine, hoping to return home in the near future. Russians had retreated to the north. What if the same thing happened again in the east and south, all over the country?

It looked as if NATO had finally realized the seriousness of the situation. The sky over Poland was crossed with contrails left by the fighters, alerted to conduct permanent exercises along the border. Columns of military equipment were moving along the roads toward Ukraine with Black Hawk helicopters patrolling overhead.

You didn't have to be a military expert to spot the increasing number of Americans in the country. President Biden casually mentioned that they were "helping train Ukrainian forces in Poland." The Pentagon, as usual, found it necessary to clarify the words of the president, insisting that US officers were only "liaising" with Ukrainian troops as they handed over weapons to them, but were not—(not for the world!)—training "in the classic sense."

American military personnel appeared at the Luxor almost every day. As a rule, they were strong, fit men with straight backs carrying huge, heavy bags. They spent one night at our hotel and drove east. There were usually groups of five to ten men. Sometimes there were women among them, mild-mannered and dressed as tourists. Those small parties of the military traveled in minibuses with tinted windows.

One day I happened to glance inside the van and saw a wooden box with a sign that read: "US Paratroopers assigned to the such-and-such Airborne Division."

The paratroopers didn't stay at the hotel for more than one night. I was sitting with Erica in the hallway as the team left their rooms and headed for the exit. Among them was a middle-aged woman and a man with rimless glasses on his narrow, intelligent face. All of them greeted us as they passed by with their bags and backpacks. I think their smiles and waves of "hello-goodbye" were directed primarily to Erica, not to me. She cheerfully and naturally shouted in response: "*Pryvit! Pryvit!*"

Hearing her Ukrainian greetings, the man with rimless glasses stopped in front of us.

"Ukrainians?" he asked, a friendly smile on his lips.

"Yes, we are," I replied and hoped that my upcoming Zoom with Random House would go without complications. This could be a good sign . . .

"These are challenging times for Ukraine," the man said.

"Uk-aine, Uk-aine!" Erica yelled in her ringing childish voice.

The military man smiled wider. "I'm American," he said.

"I know," I said. "Hello, America."

"Hello, Ukraine," he said. "I suppose we should visit your homeland someday, sooner or later."

"Sooner sounds better than later," I said. "I bet you'll be welcomed."

"Then, why not?" he said.

"Why not?" I echoed.

We smiled at each other. At first glance, this was a short, polite conversation about nothing. Nevertheless, something important was recognized between us. We both knew the American was going to visit Ukraine, but not as an ordinary "guest."

The man from the van conveying the US Airborne Division leaned over to Erica and in English asked her what her name was. To my surprise, she understood the question.

"Ei-ca," she replied.

The American caught her name correctly.

"I'm Saul, Erica," he said. "Wait a minute, okay? I'll be back soon."

In less than two minutes, the military man appeared in front of us again. In his hand, he held a dark red rose. I couldn't imagine where he got it from. He was like a magician holding out a flower to an admiring young girl.

"Good luck, little lady," he said. "Everything will be fine. Just remember this. Bye!"

He saluted us with a wave of his hand and left, this time for good. But his simple words gave me some rare but welcome confidence. It was a time when the whole world cringed in anticipation of Russia's possible use of chemical, biological, or nuclear weapons. Everybody, from the average citizen to those in the top political elite, had good reason to fear.

Even before the Russian troops poured across the border into Ukraine on February 24, the potential threat of a nuclear conflict had been raised. There was considerable speculation that Putin might become so angry that he might press that notorious red button. He enjoyed his role as the mighty Sauron. In the days before the invasion, he ordered a large-scale military exercise involving nuclear weapons. Then, as Russia attacked Ukraine, Putin unleashed belligerent rhetoric against NATO and the West, threating them with "consequences greater than any of you have faced in history" if they interfered.

Just days later, on February 27, he declared that he had ordered his country's nuclear forces into a state of "special combat readiness." In case anyone missed Putin's menacing message, Dmitry Kiselyov, a bombastic Kremlin propagandist, appeared on national Russian television and grunted between his teeth: "Now Russia's entire nuclear triad has been placed on special alert. Putin has warned the world. Don't try to frighten Russia!"

With Russian forces occupying the site of the decommissioned Chernobyl facility, as well as the Zaporizhzhia Nuclear Power Plant, Putin's blackmail diatribe sounded credible. To plunge Ukraine into a radiation nightmare, he could simply give the order to blow up one of our nuclear plants, and then coolly watch the agony of thousands of people. Russian propagandists even hinted that any member of NATO could become the target of their ruler. For example, Poland. *Most likely* Poland. Wasn't it the territory from which Western weapons had been supplied to Ukraine?

Lublin, only a hundred miles from the Ukrainian border, was no longer a safe place for my family. I realized it once and for all on a sunny spring morning when I went to the supermarket for water and food. The hotel provided us with breakfast and four small bottles of water a day—too few for the everyday life of refugees. To save money, we made our own tea and coffee and poured boiling water over oatmeal, which served us as supper. Our dinners also were meager. When you're on the run, you're forced to say goodbye to a healthy lifestyle.

Now, I walked along the highway on the narrow sidewalk, immersed in my thoughts. My work on the book was stalled in the middle of the second chapter. I hadn't had enough free time or space to move the story forward consistently. In addition, I sensed a change in Roy, my literary agent. He was no longer as enthusiastic as he had been in the beginning. His emails were getting shorter and less congenial. For the past two days, he had not responded to my message. This behavior seemed strange to me, especially after we had entered into an agreement and prepared a thirty-page proposal for publishers. And where did that promised editor disappear to? Roy remained silent and I remained tense.

Absorbed in thought, I walked with my head bowed. Every now and then my eyes stumbled upon cigarette butts and empty half-pint bottles of vodka scattered over the grass. After living in Poland for two weeks,

I had discovered that the Poles smoked and drank almost as hard as the Russians. Every nation has its own barbarian relics. They're like our bad habits. Some people get rid of them quickly and decisively, while others cling to their worst qualities.

My old habit, smoking, kept haunting me in times of trouble. Another habit was to hide it from my wife and daughter. I was not a heavy smoker. It only took one cigarette a day for the nicotine god to leave me alone for the next twenty-four hours. But he demanded the sacrificial fire and smoke every morning and didn't accept delays.

I stopped on the sidewalk, ready to pull out a pack of Camels, when my gaze swept around and froze. The peaceful Lublin countryside view was obstructed by the vertical black column of smoke rising high into the blue sky. The column was about two miles high, widening gradually from its base, hidden from my sight by broad green hills, with distant woods bounding the horizon. The smoke was impenetrably black and thick, like from a burning oil storage. I saw such smoke displays a month ago when Russian missiles hit Kyiv.

Just the day before, I watched a fragment of a Russian talk show where the guests excitedly discussed the possibility of interrupting the supply of foreign weapons for Ukraine through Poland by launching a sudden nuclear strike.

According to them, the most suitable targets for Russian tactical nukes would be traffic hubs on the Polish side of the border so that it could be seen as a brutal challenge to NATO. The voice of the TV host kept echoing in my head: "I swear they will piss themselves with fear. You'll see, they'll piss and put their tails between their legs."

As far as I could tell, the plume of black smoke didn't look like a nuclear explosion mushroom, but Russia could have used a conventional long-range missile to strike. If so, then the Third World War has already begun. Could it be? Really?

I looked around. It was a Sunday morning and not a soul was in sight, except for the cars and trucks rolling to their destinations on the nearby highway. I turned on my iPhone and started browsing the news about Poland. Nothing. There was nothing about Lublin either. No reports of explosion or fire.

I looked up. A cyclist was riding toward me from the side of the store. It was a Pole in his thirties, carrying goods on his bike. Black smoke was behind him. I asked him to stop, said hello, and pointed to the sky.

"Do you know what it is?"

He looked over his shoulder and exclaimed, "*Kurwa! Kurrrrwa!*"

Kurwa is to Polish what "bitch" is to English, a word for all meanings. In this particular case, it had a very limited meaning. The cyclist was obviously shocked and frightened. Turning the bike, he rushed in the opposite direction. He never once looked back at me and tried to call someone while pedaling furiously away.

For a while, I stood still and then went on. As I approached the supermarket, the smoke cleared from the sky, leaving behind a gray, ghostly trail.

The sellers of the store did not know anything about what had happened; nor did the hotel staff. News about the incident in Lublin never appeared in the press or social media. But something else took place that day that added to our anxiety.

As I walked with Erica, I saw Poles in gas masks and chemical protective suits at the far end of the hotel park. The instructor was teaching a dozen people how to use radiation dosimeters. They were employees of a reputable company who devoted their weekend to learning the basics of survival in the nuclear zone.

The Poles were preparing for the worst and it looked more than convincing. We decided it was time for us to change location. Nothing was keeping us in Lublin.

We headed to Warsaw and ended up in Lodz, an extremely untidy and dilapidated city that was so depressing that we didn't dare to spend the night there and continued our journey up to Bydgoszcz where I finally heard from Roy. In his email, now dry and businesslike, he informed me that no publishing house was going to receive my book, since it had no logical end, since the protracted war between Russia and Ukraine seemed to be endless.

"Sergey, I am grateful to you for trusting me with your work," Roy wrote at the end of his note. "But I am afraid it is not quite right for my list at this point, so I should probably step aside and wish you the best of luck with your writing somewhere else."

Somewhere, somehow, sometime . . .

Chapter 11

Hearts in Flames

We arrived in Gdansk, in the north of Poland, at 2 p.m. and stopped across the street from our prebooked hotel. It was a small private hotel on the outskirts of the city, without its own parking, close to a busy and noisy highway. There were construction sites all around, with attending cranes and concrete mixer vehicles. The grass on the lawns was gray with cement dust; the buildings were shabby and squat.

We had been seduced there by the low prices but immediately regretted it. I was the first to declare that we had made an error in judgment. Fortunately, we hadn't paid for the room in advance, so we had a choice. I asked my exhausted family to picture themselves living in this hole for some time. We intended to make Gdansk our permanent residence, and the hotel looked like a poor candidate.

Svitlana, who had made the booking, protested. She said she was tired of driving and needed to rest. I was not surprised. She missed her husband and was uncomfortable, to say the least, in her role as principal driver. For a woman accustomed to creature comforts, being responsible for the care of her child and older parents in a remote area of Poland was challenging and exhausting. Forced to share a room with us, she had no personal space. Svitlana's efforts to sell her picture books or illustrations had been fruitless except for the €500 she received from the *Guardian*. She had sold them a stark image from our joint experience in Lviv while in the dark bomb shelter at the monastery.

To our disappointment, the war was no longer a hot topic in the world press. The Western information market was saturated with war images and stories, as my unfortunate experience with the British literary agency proved. And as for children's books, Svitlana did not have enough time for concentrated work. Because she was a *foreign* author and artist, agents thought twice before venturing into a collaboration with her. Each such episode deeply wounded her pride. The work she produced was exceptional, and it was hard for her to be told, "No, thanks" for her efforts.

Meanwhile, I was deeply disappointed about Roy's sudden departure. It was truly a crushing blow. Only one day ago, I had gripped fortune by the forelock, and now my hands were empty. On top of that, I—like my daughter—was tired of the nomadic lifestyle. I had also quit smoking recently, so it was difficult to control my desire to cheat during the first days of abstinence. My lungs demanded the usual dose of nicotine, while my stomach could not do without milk and soda. To put it mildly, I was barely keeping it together.

Luba's health also left much to be desired. Any draft, any hypothermia caused an intensification of her illness. Now, she was unable to lift heavy things and often experienced discomfort. And she was worried about Sergiy. Maternal feelings are always stronger than paternal or sisterly ones. There were days when Luba was overcome with anxiety for her son.

The youngest of us, Erica, was the most tolerant and persistent under bad conditions. She behaved like a little heroine, enduring the hardships of our nomadic life. She always tried to reconcile the adults when we let ourselves express negative emotions toward each other. One of those breakdowns occurred in Gdansk.

Everyone's mood was already dark when, exchanging snarky remarks, we exited the Mitsubishi to take our belongings out of the trunk. The urban landscape reminded us of the worst examples of Soviet industrial architecture—everything was colorless, unattractive, and dull. It didn't look like pictures of Gdansk on tourist web pages. Our luggage was huge, battered, and heavy. In addition to suitcases, we had to carry a lot of plastic bags, bundles, and boxes. It was impossible to carry this whole heap topped with the bright green potty at one time, so we usually made several short trips, trying to hide this from people around. The massive amount of baggage eloquently characterized us as refugees, and in truth, hurt our pride.

While we were preparing to cross the road with our belongings, several locals gathered around our car launching angry tirades at us and pointing their fingers at a handwritten advert on the brick wall. It pointed out that parking of permanent vehicles was prohibited. In vain, we assured the Poles that we would take the Mitsubishi to another place as soon as we settled in the hotel. They didn't want to listen to us. They shouted, waved their arms, and unleashed a little dog that ran around trying to bite us.

Although the Poles saw the Ukrainian symbol on the license plate of the car, this did not deter them from aggression. They did not want to see Ukrainians in their yard and threatened us with the police. Finally, we were forced to retreat, putting crying Erica back in the car. Svitlana was on the verge of tears, too. After driving away from the ill-fated yard, she slowed down at the edge of the road and announced that she was no longer going to look for a hotel.

"From now on, it's up to you, dear Daddy and Mommy," she said, wiping a tear. "You didn't like my choice, so choose for yourself."

An hour of internet searching turned up nothing. Gdansk was a tourist city with overcrowded hotels. Our phones went dead before we got anywhere. We returned to the hotel among the construction sites, but our reservation had already been canceled, so we drove to the city center, stopping at every hostel, inn, or hotel we came across along the way.

It was a losing tactic. Gdansk is a city of islands, bridges, and canals branching off from the Motława River that flows into the nearby Baltic Sea. The narrow streets among the old Gothic buildings are often cobblestone and not suitable for driving. Parking spaces are few and hard to find, and in some places Svitlana had to squeeze our car into an illegal spot on a sidewalk.

As soon as we spotted a hotel, we stopped and asked for a room. Again and again, Luba returned and threw her hands up in the air in absolute despair.

"Fine, just fine," Svitlana would say and drove on. Erica sat in the back seat and stared blankly, clearly wishing she was anywhere but here.

She must have asked herself why we adults were so helpless and clueless. And we were. We were looking everywhere for lodging. There was no longer a plan: desperation was setting in. At hotels, we admitted that we were refugees from Ukraine who had nowhere to live, and the receptionists shrugged with distaste. They didn't care about the refugees. They were used to dealing with tourists. No one was going to do us any favors.

We had burned half the fuel in the Mitsubishi's tank and spent several hours driving through the labyrinth of streets. With the onset of dusk, Svitlana was completely exhausted. She put her head on the steering wheel and said: "This is the end. I can't drive anymore."

It is often said that God never gives us more than we can handle (don't tell this to the victims of wars, crimes, and disasters throughout the world). Svitlana squinted through the side window of the car and by chance saw a glowing blue sign against the dark sky. It was the Novotel Hotel. She asked Luba to make one last attempt. Half an hour later we were arranging our things in the hotel's lockers.

Novotel became our permanent residence in Gdansk and later in other Polish cities. It was a midscale hotel brand with hundreds of hotels worldwide. For several months we received significant discounts and privileges as regular customers. While we would have preferred to live in an apartment, it was too expensive to rent one for a short period on a daily basis. A long-term lease would have required us to pay several months in advance, plus a realtor's fee. It was cheaper to live in a hotel, especially all together in one room about twenty by twelve feet.

Our hotel breakfasts partly provided us with lunches and dinners, as we always tried to discreetly take something edible with us when we left the restaurant. During the day we bought soups in plastic containers and warmed them up in a sink filled with hot water. In the evening we boiled potatoes or pasta in an electric kettle. The maids were always happy to supply us with an extra bottle of water or bags of tea. (As a rule, they happened to be Ukrainians.) They also provided us with useful information about registering and receiving social assistance in Poland.

When you saw lonely women with small children on the street, you knew that before you were refugees from Ukraine. The women stood in lines for free secondhand clothes, looked for work, and wandered from block to block in search of kindergartens and schools for their children. They had fled from the bleeding Bucha, burning Kharkiv, and captured Kherson—everywhere the Russians had breached, leaving behind scenes from a horror movie. Most of these Ukrainian women stubbornly spoke Russian, as if they still did not understand who was to blame for their suffering.

Russian speech sounded on the streets of Gdansk more often than German and English. Mostly they were young men from Russia and Belarus who were hiding in Poland to avoid being drafted into the army. Often, they looked drunk, but I rarely saw them act defiantly. They didn't want to be deported, so they had to maintain their decorum. Some people understand only one language—the language of power and authority. You cannot keep a thug in line by addressing him with kind words and exhortations; he bends only before force. Force, or at least the threat of it, often is the only bargaining tool states employ to convey their intent to prevent aggression.

The Russians learned this lesson well during their interaction with the European police. However, Russia has heard nothing of the kind from NATO and the United States.

What was the collective response of the West to the atrocities of the Russian troops in the occupied territories? By shining a merciless light on the merits of this matter, let's examine the statement released by the G7:

> We, the G7 Foreign Ministers of Canada, France, Germany, Italy, Japan, the United Kingdom, and the United States of America, and the High Representative of the European Union, condemn in the strongest terms the atrocities committed by the Russian armed forces in Bucha and a number of other Ukrainian towns. . . . We express today our heartfelt solidarity with the Ukrainian people and our deepest condolences to the victims of this war and their families. We underline our unwavering support for Ukraine within its internationally recognized borders and express our readiness to assist further, including with military equipment and financial means.

In confirmation of the seriousness of their intentions, the United States, the European Union, and the Group of Seven nations were enacting new sanctions on Russia, targeting top Russian officials and family members, including Putin's adult children.

It was like saying to Putin, "Look, man, we don't like what you're doing, but we're incapable of reining you in, so feel free to keep going while we watch you with disapproval." That was how the uncrowned Russian tsar received the statement by the G7.

Only "old chap Joe" had the courage to tell Putin what he thought to his face. "This guy is brutal!" Mr. Biden said of him, adding that he believed Putin "is a war criminal."

The example of the eighty-year-old US president actually inspired the unexpected action of British prime minister Boris Johnson. On April 9, 2022, Mr. Johnson made a surprise trip to Kyiv to meet the Ukrainian president, Volodymyr Zelensky. He promised him a major new infusion of British arms and financial aid, and was the first G7 leader to arrive in Ukraine since the beginning of the war.

Thanks to the efforts of the NATO members, the political pendulum swung in the other direction: slowly and heavily, but powerfully—toward an increasingly determined confrontation with Putin's Russia. And it was a decisive turning point in the war, which at that time was invisible to anyone. Outwardly, everything remained the same. Ukraine was torn apart by war, and millions of refugees sought salvation throughout Europe.

Some found refuge in France, like Sergiy's family. Some were attracted by the high social benefits in Germany. Others received free accommodation in Britain and Scandinavia. But most of us refugees settled in Poland, and this country became our temporary home. We will always be grateful to the Poles, who were the first to support us Ukrainians. In 1939, they experienced something similar when Hitler and Stalin simultaneously attacked their country, while the rest of the world remained indifferent. Their historical memory did not allow them to remain indifferent.

During World War II, the old city of Gdansk (then the city of Danzig) was razed to the ground by the Soviet army. At the tail end of March 1945, it presented an apocalyptic sight of a sea of ruins. I couldn't help thinking about it when I walked around Gdansk.

I asked myself, Will the destroyed cities of Ukraine ever be rebuilt? Why do barbarians always seek to destroy the achievements of civilization? Is it envy? Is it hatred for everything beautiful, elegant, and perfect? Or does the reason lie in the fact that blunt force is not achievable without leaving destruction in its wake?

Looking at mysterious buildings and towers, small yards and squares, bridges and sailing ships on the river, I tried to force myself to enjoy the views, but couldn't. My mind was poisoned by the war. I didn't feel part of the colorful tourist masquerade going on around me. I couldn't remember us smiling while walking around the city. We didn't go to the cafés to drink coffee or beer. We didn't buy fancy clothes. It wasn't about the money. It was about our mood.

This mood was clearly visible on our faces, I think. Luba and Svitlana were not the lively, cheerful women I remembered from Kyiv. I, too, had changed, and not for the better. We were very lucky that Erica didn't let us sink into depression. Erica and faith in the victory of Ukraine were strong forces for positive thinking, despite our moodiness.

Why was victory so important to me? My family tree had no Ukrainian roots, as my genetic code carried only a few of the mutations common among Ukrainians. I do not consider myself a patriot or an ardent admirer of folk traditions and culture. I'm not a nostalgic person and I don't have strong romantic ties to any place in Ukraine.

If I had enough money, I would rather live in Canada, Australia, or Scotland, or somewhere else with a pleasant climate and environment. I do not know Ukrainian history at all, just as I do not know the history of Poland or Japan. So, what's the basis of my attraction to Ukraine? Why do my eyes sometimes fill with tears? What makes me clench my teeth and fists? Why am I donating money to the Ukrainian army instead of spending it on my family? Why, why do I so passionately wish victory for Ukraine?

The answer is obvious. Because war and crime cannot leave me indifferent. Because cruelty, meanness, and violence disgust me. Modern Russia is the embodiment of these worst qualities. All dictatorial regimes and all terrorist organizations receive the support of Russia. Without it, our world would be a much safer and happier place. And that is what determined my choice to support Ukraine.

The Ukrainian people entered into a fight against an empire of evil that terrified all nations. That's what makes me proud to belong to Ukraine. Not the blood flowing in my veins—but the blood spilled by Ukrainians on the sacrificial altar of history.

Their resilience and readiness for self-sacrifice were fully manifested in the southern seaside city of Mariupol. The courage of its defenders was truly epic, becoming Ukraine's own version of the Battle of Thermopylae or the Alamo.

For Putin, Mariupol was a coveted prize. The city stood in the way of one of his key objectives: the creation of a land bridge linking Russia to the occupied Crimean Peninsula. Night and day, Russian jets, ships, and artillery pounded Mariupol with everything they had, while Russian correspondents and war bloggers milled around, covering the assault like some crazy kind of football match.

To the Ukrainian command, the besieged port city on the Azov Sea was the perfect place to stop the Russian troops for a few weeks more, thereby gaining the time to prepare for new battles elsewhere on the southern and eastern fronts.

As a result of this stand, Mariupol suffered a devastating, six-week siege and was bombed literally into charred ruins, the streets littered with bodies later devoured by starving dogs and cats. The city became a trap for citizens and soldiers alike. The encirclement was so dense that there was no possibility to reach its defenders either by land or by sea.

For weeks, a furious Russian assault met relentless Ukrainian resistance. But it was too unequal a warfare, as Russian forces outnumbered the Ukrainians dozens of times and prevailed in the air, in artillery, and in tanks. At the beginning of April 2022, after a month of an epic, agonizing struggle against overwhelming odds, Ukrainian marines and volunteers of the Azov battalion were forced back to the Azovstal steel plant, a massive industrial complex nearly three times as large as Central Park in New York City.

Surrounded on three sides by sea and ringed by thick, high walls, the plant appeared as impregnable as a medieval stone fortress. Surrounded by superior Russian forces, roughly three thousand Ukrainian heroes, short of food, weapons, ammunition, medicine, and largely without any communications, were barricaded inside, ready to fight to the end. Wounded soldiers, their injuries bloody and leaking, would be laid on the concrete floors in cold, dark bunkers, where gangrene ate them alive to the bones and the surgeons carried out amputations of their legs and arms without sufficient anesthesia.

Deep beneath the steel plant, more than twenty feet underground, there were dozens of bomb shelters, a legacy of the Soviet Union, preserved since the Cold War. Up to a thousand civilians, women and children among them, were holed up there for weeks, hiding from Russian shells and bullets and struggling for survival, deprived of food and clean water. The civilians and soldiers were starving, rationed to a single meal a day, mostly canned meat or oatmeal mixed with rainwater and fried like pancakes.

Attacks and the shelling of Azovstal did not stop for a minute. It was a meat grinder of a war. Every day, dozens of the Azov fighters were killed. But the survivors held on. They continued to fight as if they were made of steel instead of flesh.

I couldn't wrap my head around it. How was this possible? Where did these soldiers get the strength and courage to endure the endless series of terrifying trials? I wasn't able to imagine these apocalyptic scenes. Nobody was. Even after the world had a chance to peer inside Azovstal, thanks to the videos from there on Telegram channels, it was still unimaginable. There were bunkers filled with badly wounded men, and episodes of fighting when bullets were digging into concrete walls next to soldiers, and night battles with the flashes and thunder, and messages of deputy commanders, and babies in diapers made from plastic bags, and children pleaded to see the sun again, and their mothers, who were seemingly on the verge of despair, on the verge of collapse, on the verge of life.

And there was a Ukraine female soldier, twenty-one-year-old Kateryna, better known by the call sign "Ptashka" (bird in Ukrainian), who decided to do something for her nation and moved Ukrainians to tears with a patriotic song, performed somewhere in a dark basement among her comrades in arms:

Well, we were born at a great hour of Ukraine
From wartime fires, with our hearts in flame,
So we were nurtured by the shared pain
And we were fed by rage that still remains.

Even a year later, when I rewatched it to translate the lyrics into English, I experienced the same storm of emotions that had run through me in the spring of 2022: anger, sorrow, guilt, awe, and something deeper, something that had no name because it was an amalgamation of so many different emotions, from fury to love.

Equally, my heart flamed with love and suffering for another Azovstal defender, a young man called Orest, who was filmed singing the Eurovision winner, "Stephania," to the sounds of bombs falling:

Stephanie, Mother, can you hear me pray?
The fields are blooming while you're turning gray.
Stephanie, sing to me a lullaby,
I need to hear your voice as the years go by.

Orest looked so fearless. He looked so doomed.

I told myself I wasn't going to cry after I watched the video five or six times. It was like an internal dialogue. "Stop it, Sergey. Don't you fuckin' cry! Deal? Deal, Goddammit! I must be strong. Weakness doesn't help."

Long after midnight, I lay on my narrow hotel cot, looking out the window at the night sky. Not thinking. Not moving. Just lying and looking.

In the morning I woke up with the thought that I would never write this damn book about the war. It was too painful a process, too self-destructive. I was unable to keep my head cold while my heart was on fire.

I got up, turned on the laptop, and deleted all my drafts except for the first chapter. I can't say why I left the beginning—probably in memory of my first failed attempt.

CHAPTER 12

BANG! BANG! We're Alive!

THE NORTHERN CITY OF GDANSK RARELY FAVORED US WITH SUNNY days. It rained often and the cold Baltic winds blew. As we were close to the "Land of the Midnight Sun," we experienced long hours of May daylight and had to adapt to shortened nights in the northern latitudes.

I liked to walk around Gdansk in the early hours, when the streets were free from tourists and free from attractions. By this time, the nightly revelers had finished their beer and dispersed to their homes and hostels. The air was clean and humid. Wild ducks and swans sat on the glassy river surface. Approaching the edge of the embankment, you could see a fur seal emerging from the water to look at you with its black, shiny eyes. In the park of our hotel there lived a wild fox that would return from its hunt in the early morning. The fox liked Gdansk, and so did I.

Foreigners, consisting principally of Englishmen and Germans, often lived in the Novotel hotel. In the evenings they drank together in the lounge, and in the morning each table, awash with beer, was cluttered with empty bottles and glasses. I had found a place to work at the far end of the ballroom at a single high table for booklets, flyers, tourist guides, and the like. I found a bar stool and put it under the table. I would arrive at four a.m., when everyone was asleep. The hotel security at first watched me suspiciously, but soon they stopped paying attention to me. Maybe they became used to my presence as part of the interior. I didn't mind.

Lifting the lid of the laptop, the first thing I did was turn on music, mostly old Beatles tunes from the sixties or Tamla Motown stuff.

Headphones isolated me from the outside world and allowed me to concentrate. I leaned over the screen and got to work.

After the failure of my "wartime memoirs," I decided to write a completely different kind of book. This was also nonfiction since it was important for me to sell the first couple of chapters up front, and not the entire book. I needed an advance payment and I just couldn't write fiction anymore. It made me sick.

The military theme was too painful for me to continue pursuing. Instead, I plunged into the true-crime genre, describing my insider experience of working for the mafia in the 1990s. Maybe this topic would draw attention to me!

The start was unsuccessful. I prepared sample chapters and a query letter which included a book overview, and sent it all to Roy, who answered me with an icy email. Again, he wrote that no publisher would want to take my book—this time, because it would cast a shadow on the heroic image of Ukraine during its war with Russia. I asked him what topic he would suggest to me. He had no answer. He proved to be a true English gentleman and left without saying goodbye.

As for my true-crime book, he was wrong. About a dozen literary agents responded to my query letter. The first of these was Claire, an agent based in Tucson, Arizona. Oddly, the moment I got her email, I was listening to the Beatles's "Get Back." It was a sign of Fate, no doubt about it because young Paul McCartney was singing about Jo-Jo, a man who "left his home in Tucson, Arizona, for some California grass."

But that wasn't the only thing that made me choose Claire. It wasn't even her impressive bio on Publishers Marketplace or her impeccable courtesy and precision to detail. She really seemed to *care* about my book. And that was what I was looking for.

When I once thanked her for her time and patience, she replied, "You're worth it, Sergey." It inspired me, and I began to believe in myself again.

"No rush . . . take your time," Claire kept telling me. But I was in a rush; indeed, it was a feverish rush to get to work. I felt that this time I would succeed. Every day I wrote a thousand words, and my English got better and better.

Our first face-to-face meeting via Skype left me feeling dazed. While we exchanged introductory phrases, everything was fine, but Claire sometimes spoke more quickly than I could follow. I could only smile politely and nod my head. I began to feel insecure again and out of my depth. How was this going to work?

I tried to make our communication purely written, but my tactics failed. From time to time, Claire felt the need to ask me questions, face-to-face. Then she would call me on Skype. She wanted to make sure my extraordinary true-crime story was, indeed, true. She delved into the most minute details of my biography. I began to feel more secure again.

We have worked together for over a year now, and I speak English quite often. True, my tongue still doesn't quickly respond to my brain's impulses, but that is no longer a problem. I found in Claire a friend who understands me and has taught me so much about the world of publishing.

May 2022 was the month when Washington and Kyiv also reached a full mutual understanding. If Mr. Biden and Mr. Zelensky looked back, all they would see was the long and winding railroad disappearing on the political horizon, which they had just left behind them. America and Ukraine had become military allies. Nobody expected such a transformation.

Back in February 2022, a few days after growling convoys of Russian tanks rolled across the Ukrainian border, the US secretary of state, Antony Blinken, a man who was respected by Joe Biden, repeated his claim that America's goal was to stand behind the Ukrainian civilians.

The White House did not remain indifferent. The States sanctioned the Kremlin's Russia, targeting political élites, government-owned enterprises, and a few oligarchs to pressure Putin to put his troops back in the positions from which they started. But it was like closing the stable door after the horse had bolted.

Yet in just over nine weeks, US officials had framed America's role in more aggressive terms, and Ukraine rapidly transformed into a theater of a full-scale proxy war with Russia—a decision that has had global ramifications. The goal was to bleed Russia without a direct clash of arms, as the USSR once bled the States by supporting pro-Soviet proxies in Korea, Cuba, and Vietnam.

Despite war weariness after more than a decade in Afghanistan and Iraq, it was time to remind the world of the power and military superiority of the United States. Americans' sense of moral responsibility and their determination to curb the aggressor was reinforced by tens of billions of dollars in aid to Ukraine.

Putin's ill-conceived assault has left Russia in an extremely exposed position—potentially, that of a cornered rat. Ironically, as a teenager, he once chased a huge rat down the hallway of his apartment building. He was armed with a ski pole and felt like a fearless hero. But soon the chaser turned into the prey. Cornered, the rat turned on the boy, trying to bite him. Terrified, Putin fled into his parents' apartment and slammed the door in the rat's muzzle, its teeth bared.

He himself described this incident to his biographer and added that the lesson for him was clear: never put an enemy's back against the wall. You never know what they'll do when they're desperate.

Feeling trapped, Putin resorted to rat tactics. His rhetoric became bolder than ever. On April 27, he warned that any country interfering in Ukraine would be met with a "lightning-fast" response from Russia. "We have all the instruments for this, such that no one can boast of," he said, in an apparent reference to the Russian nuclear and missile arsenal.

Instead of scaring off Western leaders and causing them to leave Putin alone, his threats had the opposite effect. The world was no longer afraid of him; people were tired of feeling like victims.

When a maniac with a chainsaw has settled in your area—one who kills your neighbors and promises to visit your home next—it's time to act. You're not going to wait until the chainsaw breaks or the psychotic killer grows old and dies. You will look for the most effective way to get rid of him. This was exactly what happened in May 2022.

One day we made a short voyage on the coast of the Baltic Sea, and we were impressed by the columns of military equipment moving toward us from the seaport. The only thing that poisoned our joy was knowing that this Western aid was coming late. The delay of our allies was paid for with the blood of thousands and thousands of Ukrainians. Money, iron, and gunpowder are replaceable. Human lives are not.

People from all over the world supported Ukraine with whatever they could: with letters, songs, articles in newspapers, words of sympathy, free housing, clothes, food, protests near Russian embassies, Ukrainian flags flying in the most remote corners of the planet. And of course, there were monetary donations, donations, donations. Ordinary people did not wait for UN sessions and meetings of parliaments and congresses. They gave their money to Ukraine generously and sincerely.

I will never forget the sight that met my eyes at the St. Mary's Church in Gdansk, the largest brick church in the world, a majestic construction 350 feet high with thirty chapels, capable of holding twenty-five thousand worshippers at once. When I entered, I saw exactly how big it was, and I lifted my head, admiring the incredible high vaults supported by marble pillars in white and suddenly realized how small I was, and I passionately wanted to believe that God was invisibly present among all these crucifixes, frescoes, arches, candles, tabernacles, and tombs from the dark medieval times.

It was impressive. Sometimes I wished I was a Catholic, dipping my fingers in holy water, kneeling and praying to the stone ceiling above my head. Architecture can influence us no less than music and cinema.

In search of the sublime feeling, I often came to the church in the morning, before the service began and the tourists appeared with their cameras and chatter. The building had many entrances, so each time I came I entered from another side. One day I entered an unfamiliar hallway, dimly lit, with a single arched window in the ceiling. There was a three-foot-tall glass box filled to the brim with euros, zlotys, pounds sterling, and God knows what other bills. The announcement on the wall invited visitors to leave money there for Ukraine.

The box was not guarded by anyone, except for the surveillance camera on the wall. You could put money into the slot of a giant piggy bank, or you could take it out of the temple without hindrance. But no one coveted this money. It was like an inviolable shrine.

I left my pocket money in the glass box and went outside. There was the typical drizzling Baltic rain. It was chilly, but I felt warm inside. I had faith. Faith in people.

Once I took Erica to the temple and she liked it. After that, she often asked me about God and Christ and invented her own religion, mixed with fantasies and fairy tales, as bizarre as those of adults.

After the rains, Erica and I used to walk around outside the hotel, picking up snails from the footpaths. The rescued ones stubbornly crawled back out of the grass and fell under the feet of pedestrians. The paths were stained with crushed snails. Frowning, Erica asked me if this was like God trying to keep people out of danger. At three and a half years old, she was a very bright and perceptive girl. When I replied that yes, stupid people behave like snails who don't want to be saved, Erica said, "I saw one girl step on a snail on purpose. Let's not let evil people onto the paths."

I thought this might be the right way to rid the world of Russian aggression. They should have been isolated from the rest of the world, like North Korea or Iran. Instead, they had been placated by a world afraid of angering them because of their nuclear power.

Leaders of all advanced countries gradually came to the solution proposed by my granddaughter. Russia was losing supporters, remaining in the minority. Russians ceased to be welcome guests in the civilized world. They were the black sheep of humankind. It was a natural selection process. The world sought to shield itself from the malignant cells of this political cancer.

One of my memories illustrates this.

One morning, Erica and I had breakfast at the hotel restaurant. For us, this was a real luxury, since the buffet at the Novotel cost about $25. Sveta and Luba insisted that I accompany Erica to the restaurant. They said that our little sweetheart should eat properly at least once. Probably, they were also worried about me, who suffered more than the rest from the dry food.

Erica and I were sitting at the table eating our soup and scrambled eggs when a Russian boy ran up to us. Pointing his plastic pistol at us, he began to "shoot" us. Erica stared at him, holding the spoon in front of her open mouth.

The boy was five years old. He was very sweet, with big blue eyes and golden angelic curls. But his face did not arouse our sympathy. He was very annoying, continuing to spin around us and saying "Bang, bang, you're dead."

"Grandpa, I don't like him," Erica said. "Let him go."

"Can't you hear her, buddy?" I said to the little boy. "You are disturbing us."

"Bang, bang!" he shouted. "You're dead!"

His parents, a married couple in their thirties, were sitting not far from us. I looked at the boy's father and said, "This is a bad game for your son. Do you want to explain it to him?"

"Aw, hell, no," the man said. "It's just a damn game. My kid is having fun."

He grinned. He was pleased with himself and his son.

Erica bent down, hiding behind the table from the annoying boy.

Hotel guests were watching us for our reaction. Actually, I wanted to take the toy gun from the boy and throw it away. Even more, I wanted to smack his father's grinning face.

But if I did, how would I be any different from the Russians? And what would foreigners think of us? *Aha*, they would think, Ukrainians are fighting the Russians.

However, I completely misjudged the public reaction. People raised indignant voices, warning the Russian family to behave decently and properly. Someone called the administrator. Finally, the father was forced to take away the toy from his son. The boy yelled in protest and struggled as his parents turned red.

A minute later they got up from the table, leaving dessert uneaten. I smiled gratefully at the customers and received a dozen smiles in return. Then everyone returned to their breakfast. The incident was forgotten. But not by me. Some small things can grow much larger if they mean a lot.

At the beginning of June in Gdansk it was only slightly warmer than it was in April. The nights became very short. The sun woke us up at five o'clock in the morning. At 9 p.m., when Erica and I used to go to bed, it was still quite light outside. We decided we were tired of Gdansk and needed a change of scenery. When people's thoughts and hearts are out of place, they may think they'll find peace of mind somewhere else. This race can never be won, of course. Because what we are really trying to do is to run away from ourselves.

During the month of June we changed cities several times, of which I vaguely remember only Wroclaw, Krakow, and Katowice. In each of them, we stayed for about a week. All of them were very different. Each one had its own atmosphere, its own spirit.

The Wroclaw hotel was surrounded by tall pine trees and the whole ground beneath them was littered with cones. Erica picked them up and her hands and dresses were constantly stained with pine resin that didn't wash off.

The hotel in Krakow had windows that didn't open, which made our life uncomfortable. On the other hand, there was a magnificent, free, swimming pool equipped with an artificial current. In the pool, we met three young Albanians. When they found out that we were from Ukraine, they got up from their sun loungers and gave us a small standing ovation.

In Katowice, there were many abandoned mines which reminded me of Donetsk. There I met a Briton who was married to a Ukrainian girl. He told me that he would never return to Britain and was looking forward to going to Ukraine after the end of the war. I didn't tell him that it might not happen very soon.

By that time, Russia controlled a fifth of our territory, and the front line extended for more than six hundred miles. Russian forces in eastern Ukraine were intensifying attacks on key cities and seeking to occupy the Donbas region. In June, Putin called the seizure of Donbas the final goal of the war. He didn't mention "denazification and demilitarization" anymore and assured everybody that "everything is going according to plan."

His plans were constantly changing. His goal remained unchanged. This can be summed up in five words: genocide of the Ukrainian people. Putin did not have any other goal and still does not.

The price of his manic obsession was very high. The land of Donbas was saturated with blood and littered with corpses. Since February 24,

Russia had lost over ninety thousand soldiers, including both the dead and the wounded.

We were also taking fearful losses as fifty to a hundred Ukrainian troops were being killed every day. All these were mostly young, intelligent, healthy men—businessmen, restaurateurs, artists, and musicians among them. Behind every soldier killed were widowed wives, orphaned children, and heartbroken parents. Russia sadistically celebrated every bombed-out Ukrainian mall, every station, every school. They couldn't get enough. They drank blood like vodka. While Russia was getting rid of its alcoholics, unemployed, and prisoners, Ukraine was losing the flower of the nation.

Hundreds of our brave men holed up in tunnels beneath the Azovstal steel plant in Mariupol were forced to surrender. Russian commanders guaranteed them compliance with military conventions, but of course, this was a lie. As always.

The first to leave Azovstal were civilians. The evacuation was humiliating and harrowing. The people were strip searched and interrogated with demonstrative brutality. Those who seemed suspicious to the Russians were pulled off the buses and taken away in an unknown direction. Children were pulled out of their mothers' hands. The poor women remained surrounded by Russian soldiers, who earned themselves the notoriety of rapists and marauders. Some of the civilians were forced to record videos in which they falsely testified that the Ukrainian troops had forcibly kept them at the plant as hostages. Their faces were frightened, and their voices trembled. They were morally destroyed, having lost hope for the future.

Their hometown no longer existed. Mariupol's streets were blasted, and its apartment complexes bombed to the ground. Experts estimated that around twenty thousand of the city's residents had been killed during the siege. A further ninety-five thousand were deported to filtration camps across Russia. Their fate is still unknown, just as the names and the exact number of people killed in Mariupol are unknown.

In order to cover up the traces of its monstrous crime, the Kremlin ordered soldiers not to dismantle the rubble of the destroyed city. Instead, the military trucks took out whole concrete fragments mixed with human remains to the outskirts of the city. Some bloggers wrote that this terrifying mixture of crushed stone and bones served as the bottom layer for a road being constructed. The path of all conquerors is always paved with corpses.

Could the last defenders of Mariupol rely on the mercy of such a savage winner? Definitely not. After helping civilians to leave, the defenders continued their desperate resistance for some time, until the General Staff of the Armed Forces of Ukraine stated that they had completed their combat mission. At that point, President Volodymyr Zelensky personally gave the fighters approval to surrender because their situation became hopeless.

On May 16, they began to capitulate to surrounding Russian units. Many of them were seriously injured or in a state of severe exhaustion. They supported each other and walked on handmade crutches to the buses. Everything around was cordoned off by Russian soldiers. They checked the prisoners for weapons and shook out the contents of their backpacks on the ground. The event was filmed by TV reporters. Russian television presented it as a great victory, emphasizing that Ukrainian troops had surrendered on Russia's terms and that their former courage had been broken.

Kremlin's newsmen claimed that the prisoners were transported to hospitals or taken to a prison camp in the Donetsk region. No one could either confirm or deny this. Nor could they verify the claims that allegedly more than twenty-five hundred defenders from Azovstal were captured by the Russians. Almost no information about the conditions of their captivity was publicly available. However, from what we knew about our enemies, the Mariupol defenders had to go through all the circles of hell.

The fantasy of Dante Alighieri was not enough to describe the horrors that awaited the Ukrainians in Russian captivity.

CHAPTER 13

Bitter Medicine

ESCAPING FROM THE CITY HEAT AND HUSTLE, WE ENDED UP IN NOWY Targ, a small town in southern Poland, with about thirty-three thousand inhabitants and wonderful views of the green foothills. Perched at an altitude of two thousand feet, the town delighted us with cool July nights and provincial picturesqueness. It was the most comfortable place to live in Poland, which very few refugees reached. Although the maids at the hotel were, as always, Ukrainians.

For a long time, Ukraine was a servant of Europe. Now it served as Europe's protector and squire.

One of the maids advised us to settle in a house rented by several Ukrainian families at the same time. We visited there and decided that we would rather stay at the hotel. The house was a hybrid of a kindergarten and a hostel. It was filled with thick smells of fried fish, onions, burnt milk, and deodorants. Children's voices sounded everywhere. Their moms and grandmothers were constantly scurrying around the floors, crowding into the kitchen, or sitting in the common living room in front of the TV turned on at full volume. There was no place for me to work. Meanwhile, recently, I had been working hard.

We needed money. We needed it badly.

Half of our savings were gone. In the summer we started receiving financial assistance from the United Nations, but this covered only half of our expenses. It was obvious that the war would not end this year or next.

What would we do when the money ran out? My only hope was Claire and her connections in the US literary world. However, she urged me not to push her. Claire felt we weren't quite ready to go on stage. She said we'd only get one chance, and we couldn't afford to fail. In the summer and fall of 2022, we redesigned the proposal and sample chapters several times, searching for the right focus.

It was tiring and discouraging at times, although I enjoyed working with Claire. I learned a lot from her and I was impressed with her professionalism. And yet I was nervous. Luba and Svitlana constantly asked me if I should find another literary agent who would not be so meticulous but . . . I didn't dare. I was like a gambler who had put all my money on one card. I couldn't get up from the table and quit the game.

Besides, I trusted Claire's opinion. She knew what she was doing. I was far from her first author, so she knew how to create a book. My haste was due to financial difficulties, but if an artist sets money as his goal, he usually achieves little.

Intense work, nervousness, lack of adequate sleep, and irregular meals were undermining my health. Sometimes I felt so bad that I wanted to just lie there without moving. But each time I forced myself to get up and do what I had to do. The disease did not recede. The pain in my stomach got worse, now gripping my chest and head. But I was afraid to show my weakness, complaining of fatigue or malaise, so I just hid it from my family. I came up with more fun adventures for Erica and kept up a happy façade. I drank milk and believed that one day I would wake up healthy. Belief in miracles is not limited to children.

If not for my illness and not for the war, I would be happy in Nowy Targ. It was the perfect place to relax. The hotel was away from busy highways. It overlooked a large stadium where football and tennis players sometimes trained. To the left was the small old-fashioned railway station, which almost never had passengers. To the right and behind the hotel were vast wastelands with wild apple trees and raspberry bushes. In the waist-high grass, grasshoppers chirped and butterflies fluttered over white, yellow, and purple flowers. Separate brick houses under tiled roofs, hiding among the trees, did not obscure nature.

As I walked through the fields, I saw rabbits and amazing birds whose names I didn't know. Humankind has become very distant from nature in recent decades. We vaguely recognize oaks or poplars, but most of the trees we see remain a mystery to us. Where is the alder, and where is the aspen? What is the name of the grass we trample on? What are the names of the flowers we admire? I remained in complete ignorance and it did not change anything for me. Shrubs were shrubs, grass was grass, and that was enough for me.

Somehow, I felt anxious in the wastelands. I didn't understand what caused it. Something was bothering me. Perhaps this was because in the vicinity of the hotel, I often encountered death, in one form or another. It could be a cat smashed on the road, or dead moles, shapeless as little fur gloves, or swallows that were slamming into the window panes and dying from a broken neck. For some unknown reason, all these tiny dead bodies constantly appeared in my field of vision, as if my eyes were searching for them. We see what we think—and we think about what we see.

One day Erica and I saw an unusually motley mouse splashing in a large rain puddle. The little animal had an unusual coloring. Orange with black stripes and white stains, it looked like a miniature tiger. We stopped near the puddle. The mouse paid no attention to us, continuing to wallow in the muddy water.

"Look, she's taking a bath," I said.

"She's so cute," Erica said.

The cute mouse suddenly stopped floundering, rolled over on its back, and froze. It appeared that all this time the mouse hadn't been swimming; it had been drowning.

The sight paralyzed me. I couldn't bring myself to pull the mouse out of the water. I had an instinctive aversion to anything dead. Under normal circumstances, all living beings dislike death. No one loves to touch dead bodies, even if they are just mice.

For a few moments, concentric ripples spread slowly across the water, and then the surface became smooth and calm, like glass. The mouse was motionless. Death took her suddenly and swiftly. Irrevocably, that's the exact word. Death, whatever it was, wherever it came, was final, unlike life. But how could it be? If life is temporary, then why isn't death also temporary? Once death is eternal, it means that it cannot start, as it can never end. It would look completely illogical. But there is nothing illogical in nature. One follows from the other, and they are interconnected. Either everything is eternal, or everything is temporary, and no other way.

It seemed to me that I was about to comprehend something incredibly important when Erica brought me out of my reverie.

"Grandpa, why didn't you save the mousy?" Erica asked.

Tears welled up in her eyes, ready to come down. She was shocked by what she had seen. Until now, she had not seen how the life of a living being could be cut short. The "foreign" appearance of insects and snails made it difficult to generate much empathy or kindness from Erica. The little mouse's dramatic agony aroused her sympathy.

We talked about it. I did my best to explain to Erica the meaning of death. She listened attentively to my explanations and ran to pick flowers. I thought she had forgotten the incident, but the next day she asked me to take her to the same place. The puddle had dried up, and the body of the mouse was almost indistinguishable among the brown lumps of mud.

"She's ugly," Erica said. "Eww!"

Death is always ugly, no matter how it is dressed up—there's nothing beautiful or romantic in it. Writers and filmmakers are like funeral directors who are fixing hair, putting on make-up, and restoring a hideous corpse to transform it into something poetic, or heroic, or mystical, or romantic, or even symbolic. But death is primarily pain, suffering, grief, and horror.

All this time, the defenders of Mariupol were a symbol of Ukrainian resistance, as people of steel will and great spirit. However, in reality, they were people of flesh, blood, and nerve endings, who were hurt and scared. Yes, they overcame pain and fear, but this did not mean that they didn't experience it. They were not made of steel or granite. They were not cyborgs or monuments—they were living people. Dying people.

In the summer of 2022, hundreds of them still remained in Russian captivity. On July 29, their guarantee of safety was brutally violated: an explosion destroyed the building on the territory of the former penal colony in Olenivka where Ukrainian prisoners of war were held. More than fifty of them were killed. Most likely, this was done to hide the signs of torture on the prisoners, although this could have been an act of revenge or another manifestation of innate cruelty. Sadism has long been the norm of behavior in the Russian army.

On the same day, July 29, 2022, a horrific video was posted on Russian channels that showed Russian soldiers torturing and castrating a Ukrainian prisoner of war with a green-handled knife. Their victim was bound and gagged with black tape. One of them wore a distinctive black wide-brimmed hat and blue surgical gloves. He approached the Ukrainian who was lying face down with the back of his trousers cut away, reached down, and mutilated the helpless man. Then Russian soldiers showed the prisoner his cut genitals and shot him in the head. Simple as that.

Modern science believes that several tribes of cannibals still exist in some of the remotest corners of the world and can be seen living as they have done for thousands of years, enjoying torture and murder, and using human flesh in their bloody rituals. Why don't scientists turn their attention to the country that occupies one-sixth of the world's surface?

The general reaction of the Russians to the nightmarish video was not only approving but jubilant. They were happy to see the cruel execution of the Ukrainian. Their comments on the video abounded with calls to castrate and kill all Ukrainians. It was a real national madness. I have never seen anything like this on Ukrainian social platforms. And I have never read news about the torture of Russian prisoners of war. They could be beaten during captivity, but then they were fed and kept in acceptable conditions. War can kill and harden hearts. But war cannot turn all men into beasts.

This thought was of little consolation to me. The horrible footage broke me mentally. I tried to imagine the feelings of helplessness, horror, and impotence that the unfortunate prisoner must have experienced in the last minutes of his life. Just thinking about it was enough to make my skin break out in a cold sweat.

Rage.

Shock.

Panic.

Dread.

I was flooded with these emotions from the tips of my toes to the top of my head. I was sick. I felt ill. And I felt guilty.

A few days earlier, the former editor-in-chief of the Kharkiv publishing house had called me. My heart leaped. I had no doubt that Vitaly was going to offer me some kind of job, like in the good old days. And so, it happened.

Behind Vitaly stood a mildly successful Ukrainian film director and producer who was about to start a new project called *Azovstal: Hearts of Steel* for Western audiences. It was to be a comic book series of twelve 36-page volumes. The first one had the working title, *Mariupol, City of Mary.*

The producer had an editor, an art director, and artists, but he didn't have a writer. He was willing to pay me $600 for a short synopsis in English. Each episode was supposed to bring me at least $1,500. It looked like a financial lifeline had been thrown to me from heaven. I had received an opportunity to quickly provide money for my family.

When I had agreed, the project seemed serious and worthy. But as we worked out the details, the storyline took a turn in the wrong direction. The producer and Vitaly saw the main characters of the comic as superheroes. They demanded elements of mysticism and action from me. I objected, but they insisted. They said that we were doing a great thing for Ukraine by glorifying its heroes. I tried to convince myself that it was so, but I had realized the false underpinnings of the project. We were going to sell lies in beautiful packaging. By describing the defenders of Azovstal as superheroes, we belittled their real feats. It was a dirty business.

Not listening to the voice of conscience, I continued to write. On July 29, I did not work, demoralized by the news from Olenivka and the castration video. But the next day, on Saturday, I had the completed synopsis in front of me. All I had to do was reread it and email it to Vitaly. But I couldn't bring myself to do it. My own syrupy text made me want to vomit. I put off the work for tomorrow.

Tomorrow is never what it seems while it's still today—July 30, 2022, turned out to be the best confirmation of this truth for me.

Saturdays were always special at Nowy Targ's hotel. It was the day the children's animator arrived, a young Polish girl with her boxes full of surprises. She usually gathered the kids in the courtyard of the hotel, arranging rides, outdoor games, and competitions for them. But on July 30, it rained all day, and the girl found that the yard was empty, except for me and Erica.

My granddaughter never missed the Saturday holidays. She adored those days, and she didn't consider the rain a hindrance to her favorite pastime. The girl saw Erica's pleading look and said that the celebration would take place no matter what. The three of us went down to the basement playroom. It was hot and stuffy there. I felt myself sweating under my sweater. Erica was also dressed too warmly for indoor play. I told the animator that I would go upstairs and fetch a light dress for Erica. "Five minutes," I said, showing her my spread fingers to be correctly understood. She smiled knowingly and said that Erica would be fine.

In spite of this, I worried. I had never left Erica in the care of other people. Svitlana would never let me do that. I wouldn't have done it myself if I hadn't been in a bad state that day. After being in the basement for several minutes, I felt that I was about to lose consciousness. I hoped that if I changed my clothes and got some fresh air at the window, my malaise would go away.

I took the elevator to the third floor and trudged toward our room. Luba and Svitlana had gone shopping in the city and were supposed to be back in about half an hour. I had to hold out until they returned. It was only thirty minutes . . .

As I pulled the sweater over my head, I almost fell over. My vision darkened and my ears were ringing. I felt myself running out of air. My reflection in the mirror was pale as death. I wanted to lie down on the bed and not get up until the dizziness went away. But what about Erica? The thought of her haunted me. She was alone with an unfamiliar person, and she was not even four years old.

I took her dress and left the room. The corridor seemed incredibly long to me. How many steps will I have to take to reach the end? I took the first step, then the second. It was hard work. My feet felt like lead.

I didn't try to call Svitlana because that would require extra strength, which I didn't have. All my energy went into keeping myself upright. Erica! I should have been next to her, keeping her safe.

I finally made my way to the elevator and squatted down, gathering my strength. The corridor was empty. That was good. I didn't want anyone to see me in this state. What would they think of me? I was ashamed of my weakness.

I began to feel as if my dizziness was easing up, and I slowly rose, holding on to the wall. My legs were trembling. I had the awful feeling that I was going to fall down any minute. I was on the edge of collapse. For a few moments, I was unable to move and gulped in a lungful of air. I decided that I needed to go back to the room to lie down on the bed. I'd rest a bit, get up, and go back to Erica. She had best not see me like this. This would scare her.

I managed to take only two small steps. The floor, covered with blue carpet, rushed at me, its geometrical pattern darkening to black. It hit me right in the face with all its might.

The flash of pain was so intense that for a moment I was blind. When my vision returned, I saw a grassy field below me. The tall grass was dark from the rain, though I felt no wetness, no cold. Dusk was close and the bushes scattered across the field were almost black. I was all alone, not just in the area but in the whole world, in the whole universe.

Time stood still while I flew straight ahead through the gray air. The field had no edges. It was monotonous, unchanging, and constant. Its sight made me feel sad and lonely. The way I was feeling reminded me of how I had felt long ago when I had first seen the same wasteland with the same small islands, shrubs, and trees. Then, a long time ago, Alexander had dragged me out of there, but now I had returned to the place where I was to die. Only this time I knew precisely where it would be! I was now in the Polish city of Nowy Targ. I didn't immediately recognize the area, because until then I had never seen it from above. Nevertheless, that was it—the grassy plain around the hotel where I had passed out.

I flew on and on at a height of about twenty feet but still stayed in place. The same landscape scrolled before my eyes: wet grass . . . a tree . . . another tree . . . raspberry bushes . . . a deserted road . . . a grove . . . wet grass . . . a tree . . . another tree . . . The field below me wasn't endless; I just couldn't leave, since I belonged here. I was destined to stay here forever, flying like a feather driven by the wind. It was much worse than complete oblivion. I thought it would be better if I didn't exist at all. Nonexistence was the only way out of such an intolerable existence. I was about to plunge into darkness when I remembered Erica. Where is she, and what has become of her?

My love, my sweet darling, what happened to you?

It wasn't my silent scream. These lamenting voices were heard from somewhere far away, outside my head. I opened my eyes. Luba and Svitlana were kneeling in front of me, stretched on the floor. They were crying.

"Daddy, Daddy, what happened?"

"Darling, are you alive?"

"Erica," I muttered. "At the basement. In the playroom. Her dress. Run!"

I handed Svitlana Erica's little dress. But she didn't leave until she and Luba had helped me up. My face was numb. The carpet under my feet was soaked with blood. Blood trickled down my chin to my neck and chest.

"Your nose, Dad," Svitlana said. "Oh, my God."

"Go find Erica," I said weakly.

They took me to a room and laid me on a cot. Svitlana ran away. Luba held my hand and asked how this happened to me. I replied that it was payback.

"I shouldn't have written that stupid comic script," I said. "Tomorrow I'm going to send Vitaly to hell."

"You did your job, Sergey," Luba said. "And you made money for it."

"I only made my nose bleed," I said. "Nothing beyond that."

I can remember only vaguely what happened next. While Luba wiped my face with a damp towel, I screamed every time she touched my nose. When Erica saw me, there was horror in her eyes. I think I managed to smile at her, and that scared her even more. The ambulance arrived an hour and a half later, so the first aid I received was given by the sports doctor of the children's football team, who, fortunately, lived next door. He put a band-aid on my nose and said that I had a very bad fracture.

"It's nothing," I said and fell asleep.

The Polish doctor spoke pure Russian. He was a big man with hairy arms and a large, curly head. He wrote something in his journal for a long time, sitting with his back to me and asking me many stupid questions before he wanted to know the reason for my collapse.

A comic book about Azovstal, I thought and said aloud, I think.

The doctor also didn't know what was wrong with me. He looked at me suspiciously, as if he suspected me of cheating. He asked me what I drank and how much. I replied that I don't drink alcohol.

"Everybody says so," the doctor said.

He took my blood pressure and gave me an injection. Two orderlies put me on a stretcher and took me out of the room, refusing to allow Luba or Svitlana to come along to the hospital. I went alone. On the way, I recalled my flight over the Polish wasteland and asked myself how it was possible that I had seen this place back in Kyiv, two years earlier. There was no answer. There was no suggestion. I only knew that death is a very unpleasant thing and that it would be wise to live as long as possible.

In the hospital, orderlies put me on a gurney and rolled me to the ICU. The waiting room was beyond packed. It was a large municipal hospital, the only one in the whole city. I had the impression that half the inhabitants of Nowy Targ were there on this Saturday evening. The injured entered in an endless succession with their burns, fractures, dislocations, and bruises. I continued to lie on the gurney, a cannula in my left arm attached to an IV with several bags of what looked like saline. I don't think it was painkillers. My face, from the bridge of my nose to my chin, burned with pain.

Patients passed me as they were taken into the various rooms, while I was lying on a gurney in the middle of the waiting room. It was cold there. A draft blew in through the open doors. I saw a nurse passing by and asked when it would be my turn. She replied that it was up to the doctor. He was a young man in his thirties wearing an unbuttoned white medical coat over a red turtleneck sweater. I could see him sitting at the table whenever someone opened the door to his room. Waiting for the right moment, I called the doctor and asked how long I would be lying there with a broken nose.

I spoke Ukrainian. Usually, the Poles had no problem understanding me. But this doctor heard me, all right. I saw it in his expression.

The next time I addressed him in English. He again left me unanswered. I knew that he was doing this deliberately, and it made me nervous. When the nurse disconnected my cannula from the drip, I got off the gurney and looked into the doctor's room.

Finally, he turned to me. Sour-faced. Pouting. I told him that I came to remind him that I needed someone to take care of me. He abruptly told me to leave his office. I said that I had been waiting for two hours. The doctor looked at me maliciously.

"You will wait as long as it takes," he said. "Even until tomorrow morning. So get back to your place and don't interfere with my job."

"Isn't my nose part of your job?" I asked.

From that moment on, the doctor spoke to me in Russian, and it was clear that this was his native language. Later I learned that a third of the staff of Nowy Targ's municipal hospital consisted of Belarusian doctors, and this predetermined their attitude toward me, a Ukrainian. Belarusian president Lukashenko was a close ally of Putin during the 2022 invasion of Ukraine, allowing Russian missile launchers stationed on its territory to shoot at Ukrainian troops and cities. For decades, Belarus has been a submissive vassal of the Kremlin. Its inhabitants have long lost their national language, speaking Russian from birth. The doctor sitting in front of me was a typical representative of the *Bela*-Russian people.

"I'm not here to help Ukrainian alcoholics," he said, grinning maliciously. "So, you get out, now, and wait till I serve the rest of the patients."

Patients and staff who overheard our conversation stared at me. Probably, with my face swollen and bloodied, I looked just terrible. A real night brawler from the bar. The doctor looked at me triumphantly.

"You're damned unreasonable," I said—"and you've no right to talk to me like this."

"I have every right here," he snapped. "Unlike any Ukrainian trash."

It was too much. I slammed the door and went out. In the hallway, I remembered that I still had the cannula in my arm. I approached the first nurse I met and asked her to relieve me of the needle. She looked at me with fright and spoke quickly in Polish, shaking her head. I pulled the needle out of my vein and walked out into the pouring rain.

CHAPTER 14

Crippled Inside

THE NEXT MORNING, I CALLED VITALY AND TOLD HIM TO COUNT ME out of the *Azovstal* comic project. Seeing my disfigured face on his screen, he hurried to agree and hastily hung up. It seemed that he suffered from hemophobia and could not stand the sight of blood. Or maybe he, too, mistook me for a brawler from a bar. I didn't care. Despite my painful injury, I began to feel like a man who had dropped a heavy weight from his shoulders and at last was free to do as he pleased.

In order not to frighten the hotel guests, for several days I wore medical masks that I had kept in my suitcase since the COVID-19 pandemic. This created an inconvenience for me at breakfast in the hotel restaurant, but I had a more serious problem, which I did not tell the others. There was something wrong with me. It wasn't the old familiar pain in my stomach. Amazingly, I had no pain or heartburn. What worried me was the blood that oozed out of me in the toilet. I suspected that I had hemorrhoids and was ashamed to admit it to my family. Sometimes men are so stupid.

The best confirmation of this stupidity was my reluctance to have nose surgery. However, it was not only my carelessness but also considerations of the economy. I hated to go back to the Polish municipal hospital, and at the same time treatment in a private clinic might hit our pockets heavily.

We were again forced to save. My whole calculation was based on the success of my book for the American market. In August, Claire and I discussed crime fiction. I wasn't keen on the possibility of turning my memories of the mafia into a fictional narrative, but later, I realized that she was checking to see how flexible I could be. In the summer of 2022, I was just a beginner who was not very skilled in writing English-language prose and, more specific, *Americanized* texts, and who thought too much about immediate success. People always want fast results. Instant coffee, instant money, instant victory.

In fact, the faster you create something, the less attention there is to quality and endurance . . .

I reminded myself of these words every day as I rewrote page after page according to Claire's comments. At least I had my trusty agent and editor behind me. My daughter didn't even have that. As Svitlana's first reader and regular translator, I saw that her picture books were very touching and imaginative, but the literary agents preferred to stay away, not willing to risk a headache with this Ukrainian newcomer. Svitlana couldn't find anyone who *cared* the way Claire did. While the others were "professionals" too, they lacked one vital attribute: compassion—the willingness to "lend a hand."

When I got up before dawn and went to work, I passed the blood stain near the elevator. The maids had failed to wash it clean. The pink spot on the blue carpet was a reminder that my body was not in order. I stepped over it.

My nose treatment turned out to be free. This was courtesy of an amazing private surgeon, a Polish woman in her seventies, who refused the fee. She did it with her bare hands, strong and experienced. I sat in a chair in front of her while her fingers set the broken bones of my nose. There was no anesthesia, so I had held back my pain as this woman did her job, speaking sweet, soothing words, "Be patient, dear . . . a little more . . . it will all be over soon." She was a doctor from God, and her name was Bozena, which meant *Godly*—the most appropriate name for her.

At a critical moment, she said, "You can scream, dear, there is nothing to be ashamed of."

I didn't scream. My pain was nothing compared to what Ukrainian prisoners experienced in Russian captivity.

After the surgery, my nose was left slightly crooked, but I didn't think about it. I was worried about my internals. Every time I had a bowel movement, I noticed that my stool was pitch-black and the water had a pinkish tint. Bloody tint.

Google stated unabashedly that this was the result of life-threatening internal bleeding, the symptom of acute perforation of a stomach ulcer. My recent fainting was caused by profuse blood loss, and it continued.

The best thing I came up with was to remain silent, hoping for a miracle. People are strange: Jim Morrison was right. We bide our time when immediate action is needed, and we act spontaneously when it is better to wait. Isn't it strange that our rational world is conquered by such irrational beings?

One of the reasons for my silence was my unwillingness to cause more trouble for my daughter. She was very upset by her separation from Alexander and deeply felt the difficulties of our living together. Several times I saw Svitlana crying, secluded in her Mitsubishi. In addition, she was hurt by the indifference of literary agents. The last thing she needed was a sick father.

And yet the day came when I was forced to seek medical help. Svitlana took me to a private clinic where I was told that I had to swallow a tube with a camera on the end so my stomach could be evaluated. It was excruciating, but I survived. I didn't want to return to the place of my death.

The medical examination confirmed the presence of a perforated ulcer in my gut, and the doctor wrote me a referral . . . to the same municipal hospital that I had escaped from a week ago. He didn't want to take responsibility. My case was too serious. The private doctor clicked his tongue and said I had better hurry.

So I ended up back at the ICU, where there were two different IVs attached to me. Svitlana was sitting next to me, holding my hand. When the Belarusian doctor saw me there, lying on the gurney, his eyes widened. After our memorable meeting, I had complained about him to the head physician of the hospital, and apparently, this had some consequences. If the look of a Belarusian could kill, I would have died on the spot. He took the orderly aside and spoke softly to him in Polish. As they talked, they cast sidelong glances at me. Then they both left. The fluids from the IVs continued to drip into my veins.

"I don't like it," I said to Svitlana. "There's no way in hell I'll stay here."

"You have to and you will, Dad," she said. "Be brave."

After about ten minutes, an orderly moved me in a wheelchair to an adjacent room. There a doctor was waiting for me, a nervous individual with a pointed foxlike face. The bright light reflected off the lenses of his thick-rimmed glasses, making it impossible to see his eyes. Printouts of my analyses lay in front of him on the desk. He spoke quickly and vividly in Polish. Svitlana and I shrugged our shoulders, not understanding a word of his tirade. He switched to poor English and announced that either I would agree to an operation or I would die. Very soon. Maybe today or tomorrow.

Svitlana turned pale as a sheet and said that we agreed. I said nothing. I noticed two disturbing details. First, the fox-faced doctor was in too much of a hurry, though he hadn't even examined me. Second, I was almost sure that I had seen him on that ill-fated night when the Belarusian doctor had refused me medical help. Probably, he was present somewhere nearby, among the medical staff. And he could well be on friendly terms with his rude colleague.

I looked at the orderly who had pushed me down the long hallway: squeak, squeak, squeak. His face was closed like a man plotting some kind of joke. Svitlana silently walked beside us. It was night outside; the windows were black. Why did this small town need such a big hospital, housed in two or three high-rise buildings?

The chair wheels turned. The hallway around the corner was empty.

"Where are you taking me?" I asked.

"Into the ward," the orderly answered cheerfully. "The doctor will visit you tomorrow. Now you need a good rest, so you're going to go to bed."

I understood him perfectly, although he spoke Polish. A cold shaft of suspicion pierced through me.

"The doctor told me it is urgent," I said.

"This could wait till tomorrow," the orderly said. "Don't worry. Everything will be fine, just fine."

I looked up at Svitlana. She looked down at me. The orderly rolled my chair up to the elevator. Squeak, squeak, squeak. We took the elevator to the fourth floor, where an inscription read, "Surgical Department."

We stopped outside a wardroom, the door of which was open. There was a terrible stench of feces and urine. A dirty diaper lay on the floor. The only window was closed. Three of the four beds were taken by decrepit old men hooked up to IVs. I was struck by someone's pale foot with long yellow nails stretched out from under the covers. Then I saw a bald head on a pillow, its toothless mouth sunken, its eyes closed. The room was so small that all the patients lay very close to each other. Too close. The fourth bed was against the wall, waiting for me. But I flatly refused to cross the threshold of this stinking closet.

"Don't you have another room for my father?" Svitlana asked indignantly.

"All the rooms are occupied, *pani*," the orderly replied, smiling radiantly.

He lied. It was the revenge of the Belarusian in the red turtleneck sweater, I had no doubt. The surgical department was quiet and empty. I didn't see a single nurse or patient in the hallway. All other doors were closed. The doctors at the municipal hospital found a way to get even with me by giving me a place among the dying elders. My mind raced. I was not going to stay there or put my stomach under the scalpel of some mad surgeon.

I tried to get up, but the orderly's hand pinned me to the chair.

"Don't be nervous, *pan*. We're only trying to help you."

I threw his hand away, got up, and walked to the exit. Svitlana accompanied me silently. She had seen everything that I saw and did not dissuade me.

We went down in the elevator with the nurse. When the doors parted, she whispered quickly in Ukrainian: "Well done. They're all crazy there."

Since then, I never returned to the Nowy Targ municipal hospital. We found another private clinic belonging to 80-year-old Miroslav, a doctor with snow-white hair and the sensitive fingers of a piano player.

He didn't use a computer but an ancient typewriter while preparing my medical record.

Miroslav had neither an assistant nor a nurse, but he had experience. He was understanding. He put me on a strict diet and gave me medicine—0 small yellow pills that I had to take for forty-five days. He had put me back on my feet. Within a week my ulcer healed. Two weeks later, I was able to carry Erica on my shoulders again, doing it stealthily so as to keep Luba and Svitlana from knowing.

For his miraculous treatment, Miroslav did not take money from me, saying that this would be his contribution to helping Ukraine. *Dear Miroslav, dear Bozena, will you ever read these lines? When I remember Poland, I always think of you two. You were the ones who made me love and respect your beautiful land.*

Despite some friction, Poland was the country that gave shelter to millions of Ukrainian refugees when we flooded across its border in the wake of Russia's invasion. Almost overnight its citizens formed a grassroots volunteer army to help the displaced and suffering Ukrainians. Many Poles were donating money and welcoming refugees into their homes.

Over 1.5 million Ukrainians were estimated to be staying in Poland in the summer of 2022. That was more than double any other country in the EU. Some 185,000 Ukrainian refugees had found jobs in Poland, and Polish schools were prepared to accept up to 300,000 more Ukrainian children in September.

Meanwhile, the war was raging in the east and south of Ukraine. Virtually every city in the country had suffered rocket attacks from Russia, from Murmansk and Kursk, to the Caspian and Black Seas, and everywhere. However, the Ukrainian troops were beginning to hit military targets in Russia more decisively. For a long time, Ukraine did not have long-range missiles and drones for this. But thanks to the increasing assistance of our Western allies, the situation began to change.

In mid-August, the first known major attack on a Russian military site on the Crimea took place. Nine Russian warplanes were destroyed in a deadly string of explosions at an air base in the annexed peninsula.

Military experts vied with each other to acclaim that this would lead to a significant escalation in the war.

The threat of a nuclear catastrophe had risen sharply again. It was not necessary for Putin to launch ballistic missiles or planes with atomic bombs in order to act out an apocalyptic scenario.

Europe's biggest nuclear facility, Zaporizhzhia Nuclear Power Plant occupied by Russia in the beginning of its invasion of Ukraine, could become an infernal explosive device. The efforts of scientists around the world, UN representatives, and experts of the International Atomic Energy Agency were in vain: Russia stubbornly continued to use the plant with a total capacity of about 6,000 megawatts, enough for about four million homes, as its military base and a trigger to global disaster.

Kyiv was separated from Zaporizhzhia by only 320 miles. Svitlana did not dare to go back home with Erica. Luba and I could not leave our daughter alone. We were tied together by family bonds as if we were in some sort of chain gang.

Love can make people happy. Love never makes people free.

I think I already mentioned that the name "Luba," means "love" in Ukrainian, didn't I?

We met way back in 1977. We got married in 1978 when we were both twenty-three years old. In 1980, our son was born. Three years later, Luba gave birth to our daughter. Luba and I have lived together for forty-five years and during that time we were never apart for more than a month. We became an extension of each other, fused together tightly, like two halves of one whole. In moments of crisis, we sometimes tried to live apart, but each time it turned out to be impossible, just as it is impossible to tear ourselves in two.

Can this be called happiness? I can remember many happy moments of our life together. But I also remembered times when we couldn't stand each other. Our relationship was much more than love. It was destiny. This is the correct definition. Love is only *love* in the beginning. Then, if you live together long enough, it becomes your fate. Your life. Your way of existence.

I realized how much Luba needed me when I opened my eyes on the floor of the hotel and saw her sobbing above me. It was not long before I would be shaking with fear for *her* life. It was a lingering fear that lasted a very long time and has not gone away to this day.

For some unknown reason, billboards in Nowy Targ announced that this was the City of Owls, accompanying the slogan with huge photographs of these ominous birds. Their round, yellow eyes were watching our every move.

I didn't like it. In horror films, I had seen that owls were often used to set the atmosphere for mystery—and terror.

CHAPTER 15

Troubles Arrive in Pairs

MY RAPID RECOVERY MADE A STRONG IMPRESSION ON MY WIFE. WHILE I linked this to my refusal to write the script for the *Azovstal* comic, Luba viewed Dr. Miroslav as a magician who could work miracles. She turned to him with complaints of pains in the lower abdomen. Miroslav's diagnosis ended her hope for a miracle. Luba had a tumor in her pelvis. Possibly malignant. *Highly likely* to be malignant.

Only a thorough medical examination, including an MRI, a CT scan, and ultrasonography could refute or confirm the diagnosis. Dr. Miroslav, with his typewriter on his desk, didn't have the appropriate equipment. It was possible to make an appointment at the municipal hospital, but not until December. We couldn't wait that long, so we hit the road again, heading to Warsaw, the capital of Poland.

I thought that Luba would be horrified to find out about the presence of a malignant tumor in her body, but seemingly she wasn't, or perhaps she never believed that it was possible for her to get sick and die. None of us could believe it.

We thought, well, we'll go to Warsaw, find a suitable clinic, and there our fears will vanish in the haze. The doctors who examine her will say that she was misdiagnosed. She will be given a prescription, she'll heal, and we'll exhale with relief. That was our plan. We were going to be as optimistic as possible.

The Warsaw hotel greeted us with free drinks and bad news. Three adults were not allowed to occupy one room. We were supposed to pay for *two* rooms, which would double our expenses. Instead, we found a way to get around their objections. Officially, Luba was not listed as a hotel guest. She had to live with us illegally. She was better suited for this role than either Svitlana or me because we often took Erica for a walk. It would be difficult for us to sneak past the reception unnoticed.

So, Luba became the one who went underground. We came up with various scenarios to get a third towel and an extra room key for her. And we tried to keep our secret from the maids, although they always seemed to notice everything. Yet they didn't give us away. Fortunately, they were mostly Ukrainians and had a strong sense of solidarity with their compatriots. Their Ukrainian speech sounded like music to our ears.

The first few days in Warsaw were peaceful. Instinctively, Luba delayed her visit to the doctor. She and Svitlana spent their free time looking for a suitable hospital. I continued to write.

In September, Claire and I went full circle back to the true-crime genre. I had to shorten the dialogues and supplement the text with many realistic details. The book took on a new format and shape. Claire and I often Skyped, coordinating our efforts. She was not only my literary agent and not only my editor but also my reliable friend to whom I might open my heart. In confirmation of this, we still had not entered into an agency agreement. There was no need to seal our relationship with signatures. She trusted me as I trusted her.

Normally, professional relationships don't involve complete disclosure, but this was a special case. I could tell Claire about my afterlife experience, and she could share her thoughts and feelings with me. She convinced me that we should take the time to "do it right." In my naivety, I had believed that publishing this book would solve my family's financial difficulties. I also thought my advance would be at least about $10,000. These thoughts inspired me and lifted my spirits.

My only regret was that I could not share my joy with my loved ones. Luba was completely absorbed in her illness. Svitlana spent all her time near her mother, encouraging and reassuring her. Erica was too young to know what this really meant. Sergiy was too far away for a heart-to-heart talk. Skype is able to connect people who are thousands of miles apart, but it's just not the same.

I was convinced of this again and again during video calls with my son in Kyiv, Severine in France, and my parents in Donetsk. In the beginning, the pain of being separated from them was sharp and it was breaking my heart. Later, the pain dulled, becoming constant and habitual. But it still hurt me. Every day, every hour.

My attitude about the war was exactly the same. It was a constant source of pain for me. The war had not become a routine, which was strange. It was so far away. And it had been going on so long. I wasn't in the fight. My family and I had not seen the war with our own eyes. So why did it bother us so much? Maybe we should think about emigrating somewhere far away, to Britain, Canada, Australia? Should we cling desperately to the unfortunate, torn, defeated Ukraine?

These thoughts came and went. My attitude toward Ukraine and the war remained the same. We had a country. The enemies wanted to take it away from us. We wished death on our enemies. There was no malice or vehemence in this attitude. When rats or cockroaches invade your home, you want to get rid of them. This is not rat phobia or cockroach phobia. Similarly, we did not experience Russophobia. We looked at the problem from a practical point of view.

In August, I watched the progress of the Ukrainian army with bated breath. Russia backed farther and farther away, snarling like a wounded animal. Our troops mounted a long-awaited counteroffensive in the southern region of Kherson.

The attack was swift and victorious. I felt a mixture of triumph and anxiety. How would Putin react to another defeat? Retaking Kherson might mark a devastating blow to his bloodthirsty ambitions in Ukraine. Then what would he do?

After the failure of his special military operation, the Russian president became increasingly unhinged. Watching fragments of his speeches, I realized that I saw a real madman in front of me. His actions and speeches were inconsistent and irrational. Losing control over the situation, he lost control over himself. While speaking on television, he fidgeted in his chair and held on to the edges of the table with both hands to keep them from shaking nervously. But his legs betrayed his true state. They were incapable of staying still, constantly moving and stomping, as if their owner was tapdancing to music heard by him alone. The world no longer feared him, despite all his antics and threats. My abstract fear of the nuclear threat had also disappeared. This was replaced by another fear, much more specific.

It happened early in the August morning. I was sitting in a deserted spacious lobby on the second floor of the hotel. It was a great place to work, apart from the lack of tables. I had to sit on the couch, putting my laptop on the chair in front of me. But no one bothered me there, so I felt rather comfortable. It was 5 a.m. A half-hour later, I would have an important conversation on Skype with Claire.

Looking up from the laptop, I saw Svitlana walking toward me. Her expression was unusual. She usually smiled in the morning. That day, her face was stern and slightly pale.

"Dad," she said, sitting down next to me. "I just read Mom's test results."

My heart leaped into my throat. Luba had been examined the day before and she was still sleeping, so Svitlana was the first to see the results. A tiny wrinkle crept between her straight, beautiful brows. I knew what the results were before I even heard. Things were bad and could hardly have been worse.

"When will we tell her?" I asked, my throat dry, my voice cracked.

"Not today," Svitlana replied. "The next test will show this more clearly."

"So we have hope?"

"Nothing but hope," Svitlana said. "Sorry, Dad. I need to be alone for a while."

She got up. I didn't stop her. A ringing void formed in my head. I stared at the screen, which had some lines in font size 12, Times New Roman. They meant absolutely nothing to me. The words didn't make any sense. Not everything in the world can be expressed in words. Sometimes they are redundant and even just useless.

Ten minutes later I had my call with Claire. We talked for quite some time, but my attention was momentarily elsewhere, and at the end, I wasn't sure what decision we had made. Claire looked at me, sensing something was amiss. I forced myself to smile at her across the Atlantic, got her to smile in return, and felt a little better.

Then I went to wander around Warsaw to put my thoughts back in order. These were fragmentary thoughts, mixed with short flashbacks. My first meeting with Luba. Our first night. Our honeymoon trip, quarrels and reconciliations. Past hurts and wrongdoings. Gifts and flowers. Broken plates and sleepless nights. Everything—all together and inseparable. The marriage life as it is. As it *was*.

I knew that our lives would never be the same. A gloomy diagnosis put an end to our former life. We had to cross the line and step into the unknown, as we had done many times before. So far we'd been lucky. Is it possible to always be lucky?

I returned to the hotel with a stony face and a crumpled heart. At breakfast, Luba gave me several glances.

"Are you okay?" she asked.

"I have some plot challenges," I answered. "Nothing serious."

"You look tired, dear," she said. "You should have slept more."

"I'll do it today," I lied.

I have never loved my wife so tenderly and reverently as at that moment. I wanted to hug her and kiss her, but then she might suspect something. I limited myself to touching her shoulder as I passed. She had such fragile shoulders, not adapted for a heavy burden. Would she bear the weight of the truth?

In the afternoon I took Erica for a walk. We built a house for grasshoppers and launched a paper ship through a puddle. I tried to look nonchalant, but Erica looked down at me and asked: "Grandpa, do you have a stomach ache again?"

"No, sweetheart," I answered.

"Then maybe you lost something?"

I thought that I had lost myself. For almost half a century, I got used to thinking that Luba and I would always be strong and healthy. But the truth revealed to me in Poland was different. We unwittingly crossed the Rubicon, beyond which old age awaited us with its illnesses and sad realities.

But that was not what my little granddaughter wanted to hear from me, so I said:

"When we lose something, we are bound to find something else."

"Something that's good?"

"Surely."

"Then smile, Grandpa," Erica demanded. "I want you to smile. You look right when you're smiling."

I obeyed. She was my little princess.

My other princess, the adult one, did not demand smiles from me. She was unsmiling herself.

I distinctly remember the day Svitlana received the results of Luba's last test. It was not encouraging. Our worst fears came true.

"What are we going to do, Dad?" Svitlana asked in despair.

"Live on," I said. "That's all we can do. Live on as long as possible."

It was time to tell Luba the truth. We didn't dare to do it right away. It was hard for us to bring the terrible news down on Luba, who was especially cheerful and happy those days. She felt great and seemingly forgot about her illness. But Svitlana and I remembered every hour, every minute. We felt like traitors acting behind Luba's back.

It was a rainy evening. I turned on the light so the room wouldn't be so gloomy. Erica was happily jumping around her grandmother. Svitlana and I looked at each other. She nodded; her lips drawn into a straight line. It was impossible to waste any more time.

Svitlana poked herself in the chest with a finger and cast an expressive glance at the door. I took Erica out of the room so my daughter and my wife could talk without interruption.

We walked under an umbrella until the night lights reflected in the rain puddles. Erica crunched the chips we brought along with delight. I dreamed of a cigarette. When we returned, Luba looked at me with teary eyes and asked how I could hide the truth from her. Her question was like a knife plunged into my heart. All I could do was throw my hands up—guilty!

Then we hugged and sat in silence for a while, hugging each other. Svitlana was reading to Erica aloud. It was a fairytale with a happy ending.

"Everything will be fine, my love," I told Luba.

That was all I could say.

"I don't know," she whispered. "I'm so scared."

Me, too, I thought.

I suspected that Luba's despair would be much longer and deeper, but she quickly recovered from the shock. She agreed to the operation, though she refused to do it in Poland. She wanted to see Sergiy before lying down on the surgical table.

On September 4, 2022, we left Warsaw in the direction of the Ukrainian border. Our "foreign tour" was over. We were going back to Ukraine after a long absence, and we were not the same as we'd been six months ago. There was no option: we had to change.

PART THREE
LIGHTS OUT, LIGHTS UP

SVITLANA MAYDUKOVA

I will fight
For the right
To live in freedom.

       —PAUL MCCARTNEY, "FREEDOM," 2001

CHAPTER 16

Home, Bitter Home

WE WERE DRIVING STRAIGHT EAST. THE MORNING'S BLAZING SUNRAYS bounced off the windscreen obscuring the road ahead and making us squint. Putting one hand on the steering wheel, Svitlana pulled down the car's sun visor.

I looked at my daughter and marveled at her profile. My heart warmed when I saw that she was smiling slightly. She might not have realized it, but she was smiling nevertheless, feeling rather happy. She was returning home to her husband, back to her everyday life, with its daily routines, needs, and rituals. She was returning to the normalcy of preparing food and eating, going out for walks and errands, practicing yoga, jogging and getting regular exercise, walking to the shop nearby or to the city center, and still having plenty of time for herself and her art.

I turned to Luba and asked her for water, using it as an excuse to look at her closely. Despite the upcoming surgery, my wife looked cheerful and well-rested. Her expression was almost happy. I smiled. It was strange, wasn't it? We were heading to a country where there was a war and people were dying, but this did not stop us from rejoicing at our return. Svitlana drove the car very fast. We were all eager to cross the border.

Toward noon we arrived at the customs and immigration security checkpoints, entered the line, and got through it smoothly. We didn't even have time to blink an eye when we were transported from Poland to Ukraine.

"Are we home now?" Erica asked from her child's seat.

"Almost," Svitlana confirmed and added: "I don't believe it."

But it was Ukraine, no doubt about it. Neat, well-groomed European views were left behind. They were replaced by landscapes more familiar to us with their cute huts, wooden fences, and two-lane roads, twice as narrow as Polish highways. In Ukraine, even bushes and trees looked different. Unshorn and unkempt, they grew up disorderly and freely. Indeed, it was symbolic of the very nature of Ukraine—freedom-seeking, desiring, defiant, willful, hard to grind or polish.

This land has never had its own tsar except for the Russian tsars, who for many centuries sought to invade and conquer Ukraine. All of them, from Catherine II to Vladimir Putin, did everything possible to suppress the Cossack spirit of resistance. Ukraine was drowned in rivers of blood, starved, and burned to the ground. But each time it was reborn, like a phoenix from the ashes, and claimed its well-earned freedom.

Russia failed to destroy the Ukrainian language and erase the national identity. We have not dissolved into Russian culture but instead have retained our distinctive character. Ukraine has always been *different*, and Ukrainians were ready to defend their independence at the cost of their lives. The war that began in 2022 made this truth plain for all to see. If Russia was a giant ferocious bear, then Ukraine was a wolverine, biting into the snout of the enemy and leaving him no chance to escape unharmed.

Russia was losing strength, confidence, and the presence of mind. Its commander-in-chief, President Putin, turned out to be not only a bad rat hunter but also a useless strategist. His initial military plan had projected a rapid advance into the strategic depths of Ukraine and a subsequent capitulation of government force. It failed because of poor preparation, even worse execution, and the heroic resistance of the Ukrainian people.

It became obvious that in this modern war, the Ukrainians held a notable edge despite the overwhelming size and awesome appearance of the Russian military machine as compared to that of Ukraine.

Over the few last months, with the help of the United States and NATO, Ukraine had built a well-trained and well-led army capable of executing complicated combat maneuvers. In contrast, Russia's military leaders learned that they lacked a fighting force capable of winning a war of occupation. This predetermined the outcome of the war, no matter how long it would last.

The first days of September 2022 had seen a stunning transformation of the battlefields of eastern Ukraine. A sudden and swift offensive by Ukrainian armored troops rolled through weak lines of the enemy defenses and recaptured around fifteen hundred square miles of territory. Multiple videos and local accounts depicted this as a chaotic withdrawal of Russian units, with mountains of ammunition, hardware, dead, and wounded left behind.

The Kremlin tried to portray the abandonment of Kharkiv as a planned redirection of efforts to the Donetsk region—but that claim was ridiculed even in Russia, where social media users described the pullout as disgraceful.

Commenting on the defeat of the enemy, Ukrainian President Zelensky said sarcastically: "The Russian army in these days is demonstrating the best that it can do—showing its back. And, of course, it's a good decision for them to run."

In the meantime, the White House warned that it was too early to predict the outcome. "The Russians maintain very significant forces in Ukraine as well as equipment and arms and munitions. They continue to use it indiscriminately against not just the Ukrainian armed forces but civilians and civilian infrastructure as we've seen," US Secretary of State Antony Blinken said.

Approaching Kyiv at a speed of 50 miles per hour, we had not yet seen the terrible traces of war with our own eyes. All our ideas about the war were mainly influenced by the reports we read, saw online, or were told. For us, witnessing the spectacle from afar, it was all rather abstract and remote. The sudden plunge into reality shocked us all.

About an hour from Kyiv, our eyes caught the first building destroyed by rockets. I guessed this was a factory or workplace of some kind, but it was difficult to identify because it was such a mess of broken bricks, concrete blocks, and twisted iron bars, everything blackened and distorted almost beyond recognition. There were many ruins, now to the left, now to the right: mansions and schools, shops and warehouse terminals crumpled like tin cans. I was running my eyes over ruined buildings, trying to imagine the force it would take to create this destruction.

Svitlana slowed down. Turning our heads from side to side, we looked at houses without roofs and windows, scorched trees, and overturned fences. In some places, the road surface had been pockmarked by tank tracks. Through the windows, we could see large bullet holes in the walls of some houses, and mutilated poplars, the tops of which were cut off by shells. It was not the war itself, but its ugly traces, that in themselves were frightening.

"Oh, my God," Luba muttered behind me, and it was the most eloquent of all possible comments.

Oh, my God, did you see it? How was this possible? Maybe you made up the wrong people? Or have we made up the wrong God for ourselves?

I hardly thought about those things then. I thought about the war. The suburb of Kyiv showed us how close the Russian troops had come to the capital, and what was going on here in the first days of the invasion. Would we be safe here? Or, will we find ourselves inside a closed trap during the next siege of Kyiv? How long do we have a peaceful life ahead of us? A week? Two weeks? A month?

I turned around to look at Erica, our cute four-year-old girl, busy eating dried sliced apples while watching a cartoon on my cell phone propped up in front of her. We bought those apples, along with tomatoes and some potatoes in a small village we passed through. Ukrainian grannies used to sell their crops sitting on small wobbly stools along the highway. If our world were run by grannies, it might be a bit old-fashioned, rustic, and a little sheepish, but not as cruel as smart men in suits and ties have made it. In any case, in such a world, no one would have to explain to little girls what war is and what it is for.

"Erica," I said sternly, "that's enough. Give me back my phone."

"Another five minutes, Grandpa," she answered without taking her eyes off the screen.

"Five minutes have already passed," I said.

"Those were the wrong minutes," Erica said. "Too short."

It would also be interesting to know what our world would have been like if children ruled it instead of adults. I sighed and turned away. Erica would rather watch cartoons than see burnt ruins. I couldn't blame her.

To our relief, the war zone was soon behind us. We entered Kyiv. Except for tank obstacles, concrete blocks, and sandbag barricades in the streets, everything looked the same, serene and peaceful: flashing traffic lights; shops with bright storefronts; fruit and vegetable stalls with big trays piled high with oranges, bananas, cabbages, and carrots; outdoor cafes under colorful umbrellas; lines of passersby on the sidewalks, covered with crowns of the green chestnut trees.

People took their children home from school or walked the dogs, or sat on benches in squares, or hurried home with their purchases.

It appeared that Kyiv had settled down to its normal life again. But this surface appearance was somewhat illusory. I felt that a hidden anxiety had settled here. Kyiv was not the same. Its inhabitants were not the same. They survived a severe crisis and this left an indelible imprint on their appearance and behavior. Mortal danger changes people. Severe trials leave scars.

Putin, who started the war to keep Ukraine in the orbit of his influence, received a nation that rejects the entire Russian world, along with its culture and history. Overwhelmed with petty jealousy and megalomania, he launched an unstoppable process of transformation. A chain reaction.

Kyiv urgently renamed its streets and dismantled monuments to Russian national heroes. The inhabitants of the city no longer wanted to walk along Moskov Street and look at the bronze figures of Russian generals and poets. Pushkin and Dostoyevsky became for Ukrainians what Wagner and Goethe were for Jews during World War II. Russian soldiers learned the works of Pushkin and Tolstoy at school. It didn't make them any more humane. Knowledge of *War and Peace* or *Swan Lake* couldn't stop them from cutting off the heads and genitals of Ukrainian prisoners.

Everything Russian has become taboo in our family. It was a conscious, rational decision. We had cut off the tentacles with which Moscow seized its prey, Ukraine, for too long a time. These tentacles were provided with suckers of old connections, habits, hobbies. Pulling them away from us was difficult and sometimes painful, but Putin's Russia left us no other choice. You cannot encourage a predator that is about to swallow you.

When Alexander occasionally turned on some Russian rock music in the car, Svitlana and Luba immediately lashed out at him, demanding that he switch to another channel. Under pressure from his wife and little daughter, he was forced to learn the Ukrainian language, which took a great deal of effort. Our return marked the end of his bachelor's freedom to do what he wanted, when he wanted, and how he wanted to do it.

We drove up to our house on the evening of September 5. Alexander was waiting for us in the parking lot, unshaven, uncut, and visibly plumper. Five months of loneliness hadn't done him any good. Erica had gradually weaned herself of him and did not look happy being embraced by her father. We had been away from home for so long. Everything seemed unfamiliar and a little surreal.

Upon entering our apartment, we rushed to open the windows. It turned out that when we had left, Luba forgot to take food out of the refrigerator. We could smell it as soon as we entered. When Luba carefully opened the door of the refrigerator an overpowering odor of rotten meat and cabbage filled the kitchen, and then the entire apartment. The stench was unbearable. We struggled unsuccessfully with it for days, using many deodorizers and disinfectants, until Luba found on the internet a way to eliminate unpleasant odors in the refrigerator. One fresh lemon was enough for this. Try it yourself, if one day you have to flee from the advance of enemy armies. However, I hope you don't need the recipe.

At night Luba and I slept like logs, tired from the long road and cleaning. Before going to the hospital, we had to set up our household again. We spent a few days doing laundry, shopping for groceries, and putting things in their places. During breaks, I worked and walked around. Walking around the familiar pathways gave me great pleasure. At the beginning of the year, it seemed to me that I became bored of living in one place and I was thinking of moving somewhere else. Since our return from our travels, my mind had changed. Upon arriving home, I didn't want to go anywhere. I was ready to stay in one place for the rest of my life.

It was impossible. The apartment did not belong to us. We had rented it from a nice couple, Ilya and Anna.

The two of them were both tall and handsome. He was fond of sports and politics, and able to talk for hours on his favorite subjects. She was a ruddy blonde, fifteen years younger than her husband, prone to mysticism and Eastern religions. For several years, we had wonderful relations with them.

The war had scattered us in different directions. Now we were to meet again and discuss an unpleasant problem. I hadn't paid rent from February to September and I couldn't do it right now. All our money was needed for Luba's treatment.

I met Ilya in a café where I explained my difficulties. He took a sip of his Americano and said: "You can pay later, Sergey, no problem. Don't rush. I understand. It's the damn war."

Anna readily supported him.

It is not often in the world that you meet such generous and magnanimous people. For a year and a half, they charged us only half the rent and never once showed me impatience or dissatisfaction.

I promised Ilya that I would pay him off when I sold my book to an American publishing house. In September 2022 it was akin to saying, "when the cows come home." Even so, Ilya just nodded. This simple movement of the head was worth a lot to me.

Moreover, Luba and I were not the only debtors of Ilya. Svitlana and Alexander lived in his second rental apartment and they also experienced financial difficulties. Instead of having a stable source of income, Ilya and Anna had two families who needed their support. I will always remember them with gratitude and respect. A friend in need is a friend indeed.

Indeed!

Sometimes I allowed myself to ask Claire when she was going to present my book to publishers. She was shaking her head and saying that it was still early. She wanted to see a flawless proposal and carefully polished chapter samples to boost our chances of success. This required time, which, alas, was not money.

In spite of all these difficulties and days of feverish work, I was always ready to drop everything to spend some time with my son. I missed Sergiy very much and our meetings were a feast to me. Over the summer, he got very tan and grew thinner, and his hair was faded and streaked from the sun. He looked strong, healthy, and handsome. During the war, he became a well-known artist and patriot in Ukraine. He was recognized on the street and any father would be proud of such a son. I was his father. And I was proud.

It was the right thing for Sergiy to stay in Kyiv, despite living under the constant threat of danger. In return, he received self-respect and the respect of others. The world's leading publications including the *New York Times*, the *Washington Post*, *Newsweek*, and the *Guardian* were pleased to put his illustrations on their covers and front pages. He had designed euro coins, gave interviews, and wrote his weekly column for the German magazine *Zeit*. This was a meteoric rise for the forty-two-year-old Ukrainian artist. Increased interest in Sergiy's artwork was strengthened by the fact that he saw the war with his own eyes and depicted it from up close, rather than from a distance.

We had spent six months apart and were in a hurry to fill the gap. Sergiy was taking me along the tangled streets of old Kyiv, treating me to fragrant herbal tea and feeding me homemade omelets and salads. We talked and talked and talked. We talked about everything, about the war and art, life and death, our hopes and plans for the future. Our long conversations stopped only at the chessboard, and then we started talking again. Mostly, it was Sergiy who told stories while I listened.

These were impressive stories that he would no doubt want to put in his own book, so I won't retell them in detail. Sergiy had learned to make Molotov cocktails, was arrested for violating curfew, carried humanitarian aid around the city, escorted foreign journalists to the front lines, and had been under shelling. He sketched wrecked Russian tanks and Ukrainian soldiers in trenches; he lived through food shortages and endless air raids. He told me that if he was drafted into the army, he wouldn't run and hide, and this was a deliberate decision of an adult man who knew the value of his own life and was ready to risk it for the victory of Ukraine.

All this time he had missed Severine very much, filling the emptiness of his living space with her things, toys, and drawings.

And he was worried about his mother.

Sergiy took on the mission of negotiating with doctors, organizing consultations, and financing treatment. Svitlana contributed the other half of the needed help. She and Sergiy accompanied Luba during visits to hospitals and supported her morally. These were very exhausting days, merged into one, a never-ending drudge of routine and one big blur in my mind.

One of the best specialists in Kyiv performed a successful operation on Luba. This was followed by twenty-four sessions of radiation therapy. Each time, Luba became weaker. Watching her suffer was unbearable, but I did my best to look calm and confident. I unquestioningly indulged Luba's whims and endured her bouts of irritation. This made me much more tolerant and accommodating than I had ever been before.

Our whole family rallied around Luba, supporting her and surrounding her with care. She received all our love, and it was healing. Together we fought her illness.

And the war continued . . . always present in, or behind, our thoughts.

CHAPTER 17

The Wailing Darkness

By the last weeks of September, after suffering setbacks on the battlefield, Russia announced a so-called partial mobilization (draft). In his televised address, Vladimir Putin explained it was necessary to ensure Russian territorial integrity. In reality, he urgently needed an additional three hundred thousand soldiers to drown Ukraine in blood, even if it was mostly the blood of his own people.

Mass murderers are usually sentenced to life imprisonment or the death penalty. However, Vladimir Putin continued to freely occupy the presidential throne of Russia, sitting on it quite comfortably and enjoying all the privileges of his position.

Addressing the West, he once again issued a thinly veiled threat that he could use nuclear weapons any time at all. "When the territorial integrity of our country is threatened," he said, "we will certainly use all the means at our disposal to protect Russia and our people. It's not a bluff."

Four hasty and bogus referendums were held in Russian-held regions of Ukraine—votes Putin was going to use as grounds to annex new territories and declare them Russian. He hoped that the fear of nuclear missiles would keep Ukraine from advancing in the zone of occupation. This didn't happen.

It couldn't happen under any circumstances. Putin left Ukraine no choice. Russia offered us nothing but death. It could be instant destruction by a nuclear strike, or the gradual extermination of all Ukrainians by any other type of weapon. In every liberated city where the Ukrainian troops entered, they found mass graves with hundreds of corpses bearing signs of torture and violence. The dead were buried in the surrounding forests and fields, and our army was accompanied by emergency service workers wearing blue plastic coverings. Digging into the ground, they opened more and more makeshift graves, bearing witness to Russia's war crimes.

It was not just a war. It was a genocide of the Ukrainian people. And it certainly was not a bluff, as Vladimir Putin said. He committed all possible crimes against humanity and could only be stopped by force.

The elimination of Putin would mean the end of the war.

He understood this very well. He constantly hid in underground bunkers, where rooms were equipped to imitate his Kremlin offices. He had multiple doubles and a whole group of actors from the Federal Security Service, who were used to shoot footage about the dictator's communication with the "people." When hosting visitors, Putin would seat them at the far end of a twenty-foot conference table, fearing an attack from them. He was afraid. And he couldn't stop, because the end of the war meant his removal from power and his death, one way or another.

On October 7, 2022, the Russian president celebrated his seventieth birthday. The Kremlin mass media trumpeted his twenty-two-year "reign," drawing parallels to Peter the Great and Joseph Stalin. We Ukrainians wished the birthday would be his last. We were not alone. It is impossible to imagine how many people in the world wished him dead.

On the other hand, all the planet's dictators, from lowly African chieftains to the powerful Chinese president Xi Jinping, have watched Putin with hope and expectation. His victory in Ukraine would open the way for them to increase their power. They were eager to redraw the political map of the world, so in some way the Russian president waged war on behalf of all dictatorial regimes.

Putin was imbued with a sense of greatness. But at the same time, he turned into persona non grata in world politics. At his birthday party, a bunch of secondary characters gathered around him. A few years ago, world leaders considered it their duty to congratulate the president of Russia and personally shake his hand. Now he was in almost complete isolation, receiving calls only from a noticeably short list of world leaders—including those from Kazakhstan, Cuba, and South Africa.

Could Putin's ambitious nature be satisfied with a tractor presented him by the Belarusian president or a pile of watermelons from Tajikistan's leader? Without a doubt, a burning resentment settled in his cold heart. He hated the West, but at the same time sought recognition and an honorary position among Western leaders. They ignored him. And two days after his seventieth birthday, Putin decided to show them what he was worth. As his whipping boy, he once again chose Ukraine. He still hadn't realized that he can make Ukrainians cry, but he can't intimidate them and bring them to their knees.

On the tenth of October, deadly missile strikes hit Kyiv and over a dozen other cities across Ukraine, many of which had not been fired upon since the early days of Russia's invasion in February. At least eighty-four cruise missiles plus twenty-four attack drones were used in the salvo targeting power plants, bridges, and civilian infrastructure. Museums, concert halls, passenger terminals, and children's playgrounds were also among the sites hit by Russian rockets. About a hundred people were killed or wounded.

This was only the beginning. Winter was approaching, and Putin was in a hurry to destroy Ukrainian infrastructure in order to break us with cold and horror. His trained propagandists promised to plunge Ukraine into the cave age, leaving the country without heat and light. Without hope.

These were the days when Luba was in the middle of radiation therapy.

I remember well my thoughts one day when outside the window, somewhere close, three powerful explosions sounded, one after another—BOOOMM . . . BOOOMM . . . BOOOMM. The earth trembled three times. Disturbed birds took to the sky.

This is it, I thought. The break is over. What awaits us? Luba will not endure the long journey back to Poland. And her treatment cannot be interrupted. So we will stay. What about my daughter and my granddaughter? They need to leave Kyiv. Immediately.

After the attack began, Luba and I sat in the hallway, the most protected place in our apartment. Every Ukrainian knew the "two-wall rule" during an air raid. When a rocket or bomb explodes nearby, you should be protected by two walls, not one. If the first collapsed, the second would cover you from debris and fragments. Unless, of course, the explosion is so powerful that it will destroy you along with all your walls and property.

Sitting on the cold hallway floor, I called Svitlana and told her to drive with Erica to the western border.

"No way, Dad," she replied. "Here we stay. Come what may."

And we all stayed. It was a damn easy decision with damn big consequences.

Throughout the fall of 2022, Russian missiles hit Ukrainian cities almost daily, killing people in residential buildings, crowded markets, bus stops, and malls.

In October, top US general Mark Milley condemned Russia's continuous missile attacks suggesting they met the definition of war crimes. How is this new? All of Putin's "special military operation" was a bloody crime. And there was no end in sight.

Ukrainian cemeteries were growing with fresh graves every day: hospitals were full of crippled citizens. At the same time, Russia occupied an honorable place in the UN Security Council, from where it lectured the West about good manners. It looked crazy and hypocritical. While the Russian foreign minister was ranting on the podium about peace and humanism, his country was shelling the peaceful cities of a European country. While he enjoyed his diplomatic immunity, the Ukrainians had no defense against Russian missiles.

In mid-autumn, more than fifty Western countries met in Brussels to pledge more weapons for Ukraine, especially air defense systems, but all this seemed far away. While the decisions of our allies went through long and complicated bureaucratic procedures, Putin only had to lift a finger to bring down tons of steel and explosives on our heads.

I met my sixty-seventh birthday under the howl of air sirens. Early in the morning of October 17, at around 6:30 a.m., Russia congratulated me with a wave of attacks, targeting Kyiv with twenty-eight Iranian-made "kamikaze" drones packed with explosives that detonate upon impact. They were called the *Shahed* because of their lethal and suicidal effect. Those damned things were relatively slow, although their small size and low altitude made them difficult to spot on radar. When I heard one of them approach for the first time, I assumed that a motorcycle was passing by somewhere nearby. The next moment the area reverberated with the rattle of gunfire as antiaircraft batteries tried to shoot down the approaching drones.

Later, the Kyiv authorities reported that only five of them had achieved their goals, but this was enough to ruin some critical infrastructure, with electricity cut in several areas of the city. And it was only an overture to a deafening symphony of demolition and chaos, performed by the Russian military orchestra under the baton of Vladimir Putin.

I would not be surprised if, during the eventual tribunal, we will learn that he watched the shelling of Ukraine on the television screen with absolute glee. The war had become an indicator of his self-affirmation and the only meaning of his life. Perhaps, while watching video reports, he would stop the image or zoom in on it. Here is someone's severed leg, there is a dead baby in the arms of a sobbing mother . . . Killing people by the thousands, tens of thousands, Putin could well imagine himself a god, omnipotent and inaccessible. I imagine his pulse quickened and his pupils dilated when he saw death scenes.

Beginning in October 2022, air raids on Ukraine and Kyiv became so regular and frequent that it never occurred to anyone to keep a record of them. Despite appeals from the officials for people to seek shelter, the city's streets were far from deserted. The sirens' piercing wailing and the low buzzing of the drones were now familiar sounds across the country.

None of our family has ever hidden in a bomb shelter. True, once I had been caught by an air raid when I was downstairs in the subway. Trains stopped moving, and gradually the station filled with passengers. We had to stand so close together that it was impossible to read the news on our phones. This went on for about two hours. Then the all-clear alarm sounded, and people dispersed in different directions to go about their business. No one looked nervous or irritated. It was an everyday episode for Ukrainians.

Another time, I got stuck in the elevator. I was coming down from the twenty-second floor when the power died. The lights went out and I found myself in total darkness, suspended a hundred feet up. I spent about forty minutes in captivity until I was freed by an emergency rescue team. They pulled many 24-hour shifts doing their work, but they were met by smiles and words of thanks and encouragement from me.

Climbing up to the twenty-second floor on foot was a tedious task, especially after shopping or in the darkness, lighting my way with a flashlight. The flights of stairs seemed endless. I memorized every chip on the steps and every mark on the walls as I made my daily ascents and descents.

The stairs were cold and busy. During the autumn shelling of Kyiv, I recognized by sight all the inhabitants of our building. Old people, and mothers with babies, and sick people were forced to do this urban mountaineering. My weakened wife did the ascent in twenty minutes. She accomplished this feat many times.

Another serious discomfort was caused by the fact that shops, hairdressers, cafés, and other establishments would close for the duration of air raids, so people were asked to leave the premises. This might happen several times a day. The alarm would start when Russian aircraft took off somewhere, and this could be a real threat or it could be false. Then a new alarm sounded, and we learned that the explosions had damaged the power plant, or the heat pipeline, or the communication line. Every day it got worse. Every day it got darker and colder.

In Kyiv, a schedule for power outages was introduced. At first, it was three-hour blackouts every four hours, then they became longer and more frequent. Sometimes we spent days and nights without electricity, water, and heat. The internet and telephone connections did not work. Our mobile cells would often run low, and we were left alone in the dark with each other and our gloomy thoughts.

We humans have forgotten how to spend time without reverting to beloved electronic toys. People no longer gather around pianos in living rooms, read books aloud, or write long, detailed letters to numerous relatives. Our eyes are unaccustomed to candlelight. Left with free time on our hands, we do not quite understand what it can be spent on besides movies and viewing pictures on Instagram. We have forgotten how to have unhurried conversations about this and that, patiently listening to each other. The light turns off, and you find yourself in a dark void. If, in addition to this, you are cold and waiting for an enemy air raid, then the night becomes especially dark.

Siren after siren sounds out from the darkness. It may be raining or snowing outside the windows. The beds are cold as ice and you have no opportunity to warm yourself with tea and hot food. You wrap yourself in a blanket and think, worry, think. Is our civilization really so stable? What will happen to all of us if one day some magnetic waves reach Earth and turn off the power plants? Who will survive under such circumstances? Surely these will be the most primitive and wild tribes, merged with nature. Our modern society is too fragile and totally dependent on electronics and electricity. A thin layer of living organisms on a stone ball flying across the universe.

In the fall of 2022, the apocalyptic scenario didn't seem suitable only for movies and books. It seemed as if it may very well come to pass. I have never discussed this with my loved ones, but I am sure that the world has never been so close to disaster as in the days when Putin believed in his omnipotence and the Western countries were not yet properly consolidated.

Joe Biden had to maneuver and be cunning, making concessions and pushing allies in the right direction. Among them were the eccentric Emmanuel Macron winking at Moscow, the cautious Olaf Scholz with his doubts and fears, and Viktor Orban straddling the Russian gas pipeline. All of them and many others required a special, individual approach. The US president persistently united them under the banner of the North Atlantic Treaty Alliance. It was not an easy job, given the fact that Biden had to deal with domestic political issues at the same time. Donald Trump's Russia-leaning ideas continued to have a strong hold on the ranks of the Republicans. But Biden managed a delicate balancing act, both politically at home and with allies overseas, and the allies held together. His sense of tact and balance seemed virtuoso.

Putin had three main trump cards in this game. Naked violence, hidden money, and blackmail. So far, he's played these cards quite successfully. As a former KGB officer, he skillfully used dirt and bribes, alternating between them as needed. And he never held back using brutal force.

On October 26, Putin staged demonstration exercises of Russian strategic nuclear assets at the height of tensions with the West over his war in Ukraine. Ballistic and cruise missiles were launched from Russia's far east to the Arctic. In response, NATO staged its own nuclear exercises over Britain, Belgium, and the North Sea. It was dubbed the "Steadfast Noon."

Putin's reaction was nervous and angry. Not daring to openly challenge NATO, he hit Ukraine again. Early on October 27, Russian forces launched a wave of cruise missiles at hydroelectric dams and other critical infrastructure across the country, inflicting very serious damage to energy facilities in Kyiv. About half of the capital's residents were left without water and power.

That night I was at home alone. After more medical procedures, Luba stayed overnight with Sergiy because she was too weak to climb to the twenty-second floor.

It got dark early. I tried to work or read, but nothing came of it. The computer battery had run out. My electronic reader did not have a backlight screen. I ate a cold supper and went to the window. The sky was pitch black, unlit from below. Apart from a few dimly lit windows across the street, the world was plunged into darkness.

My loneliness was complete and depressing. The silence made my ears ring. I tried calling somebody. Unsuccessfully. I was alone with myself. I got into a cold bed, surrounded by the cosmic void.

I made an attempt to think of something good. About summer and the sea, about the end of the war and a happy peaceful life. Those things seemed otherworldly. Unattainable.

I closed my eyes and saw nothing but that damn darkness. It was everywhere. It seemed endless.

CHAPTER 18

Boiled Frog Syndrome

IT IS GENERALLY ACCEPTED THAT THE ABSENCE OF POSITIVE EMOTIONS leads to an oppressed condition, dullness, irritation, or even aggression. Nothing like this happened to our family. On the contrary, we became more self-possessed and attentive to one another. Of course, from time to time we were overcome by melancholy and hopelessness, but the support of loved ones helped us to cope with this. Luba, who had completed her treatment, was the recipient of much care and love.

Doctors insisted that she undergo an additional course of chemo-therapy and some other procedures, but she flatly refused. "I don't want to live the rest of my life decrepit and infirm," she said. "I can barely move my legs after this goddamn radiation. I shouldn't have agreed to this. I've had enough."

Nobody could convince her. She firmly stood her ground. She believed that the worst was behind her, and we relied upon her inner strength. After all, it was her life, so we had to respect her decision.

In November, Luba felt so well that she did the cleaning and cooking on her own. Housework helped her feel healed. It was clear that she was recovering quickly.

By this time, we had acquired all the necessary items to survive the winter without heat, electricity, and water. We bought powerful charging batteries, various lanterns, torches, candles, and a camp stove with gas cylinders. We stocked up on water and food, which we kept cold on the balcony. We memorized the blackout schedules and didn't let ourselves be taken by surprise in the elevator.

Russia did not stop its efforts to destroy the Ukrainian infrastructure, damaging or demolishing some 40 percent of the country's energy system. During this time, Kyiv was in a privileged position compared to other cities. The capital was fairly well protected by Western air defenses. As a rule, no more than 20 percent of Russian missiles hit the target. But even this was enough to keep Kyiv in the dark and cold. Contrary to popular opinion, Vladimir Putin was not going to conquer us Ukrainians. He needed our territory; he needed Ukraine without *us*. His task was for us to die, to freeze, or to flee so that he can have our land.

On November 18, as Luba and I marked our forty-fourth wedding anniversary, Russia launched its mightiest wave of missile attacks on Ukraine in more than a month, leaving more than seven million people without power and the supply of electricity in a critical condition. As a result, our festive dinner was held by candlelight, in the best romantic tradition. Luba sipped her red wine, while I drank tea. Due to stomach problems, I had given up alcohol and practiced a completely sober life. I no longer felt the need to drug myself to get rid of stress. I made the decision to break this restraint on the day of victory over Russia. We talked a little about it.

Admiring the reflection of the flickering candle's flame in the ruby glass in her hand, Luba asked me when I thought this would happen. And I suddenly realized that I could not answer her question. Will the liberation of the territory of Ukraine be enough to call it a victory? Let's say the Russian troops retreat or even turn into a stampede. What will happen next? Russia is not going anywhere, even if it is defeated in *this* war. Sooner or later a new war will begin. Russia will never accept its shameful defeat. It will seek revenge. Always. Russians would only care about one thing—their vengeance. Revenge on Ukraine will become their national purpose.

"It might take a long time," I said. "Putin has enough missiles to bombard us for the rest of his life."

"He'll die someday," Luba said.

We too will die someday, I thought.

We sat for a while longer and were getting ready to go to bed when the lights came on. It always seemed like a small miracle after dark. "Let there be light," God said, and there was light. It was a vital invention. What more could you want in the dark than light?

"When the war is over, I'll take you to the sea, dear," I said. "We will lie in the sun and enjoy life."

"You know you don't like the heat," Luba smiled.

"Now I love it, darling," I said. "I want our eyes to squint in the sunlight and for the sand to burn our feet. Where are we going in the summer? To Italy? To Spain?

"We don't have money," Luba said, shaking her head.

"What do you think I work for?" I exclaimed. "We will have money. A lot of it."

She smiled. It's so great when the lights are on and someone smiles at you.

I worked tirelessly to make our dream come true. Luba needed rest and a change of scenery. It was my job to provide it for her.

Usually, writers are not included in the category of "wealthy people," with the exception of famous authors of world bestsellers. But the situation looks different if you write books in a ruined country and sell them to the wealthy West. I was not affected by the decline of the economy and weakened business in Ukraine. I depended only on the availability of electricity and the internet.

When the lights went out at home, I would take my trusty laptop and go to the Epicenter Mall. It was a fifteen-minute walk from our apartment, and I descended the cold flights of stairs and walked the familiar path between high-rise apartment buildings. I had to hurry to have time to write something before the next possible announcement of an air raid. When that happened, I would make my way back home without writing a single line.

There was a café in the Epicenter shopping and entertainment center that became my workplace. From the end of autumn 2022 to the middle of winter 2023, I went there almost daily. The mall had a generator for electricity and the all-important wi-fi. Crowds of people lined up at electrical outlets to charge their mobile phones. Shoppers gazed at the tempting shelves bearing stoves, blankets, heaters, and batteries. I usually retired to the L-shaped café where most of the tables were occupied.

There, I'd order an Americano coffee and take an empty seat in the far corner. Thus, tucked away from the crowd, I could shield myself from the noise around me by listening to the music in my headphones.

In December, my book was about half written and was now titled *Deadly Bonds: My Life Inside the Ukrainian Mafia.* Sometimes I asked myself whether this kind of memoir was timely during a war. Was "true crime" appropriate while readers were undergoing days and nights of the biggest and bloodiest "crime" in modern history? Doubts haunted me, but I drove them away. My literary agent was undeterred. She thought we could sell this book in the States, and I relied on her professional instincts. However, Claire pointed out that certain months were not good for sending submissions to editors, especially those before the Christmas/New Year season. We agreed to wait for a more propitious time after the New Year and once again, I struggled to contain the fires of my impatience by dousing it with cold calculation.

"Go slowly if you want to get on the fast track," I kept telling myself. I had heard this saying by an American general, and it stuck with me. Going slowly to achieve my goal was smarter than going fast to get nowhere.

Here at the café, I took a quick break from my writing and put away my headphones, listening instead to the conversations of my neighbors. They rarely discussed the war and shellings. Instead, they, too, drank coffee, ate snacks, and talked about ordinary activities. Putin's plan to plunge Ukrainians into despair had thus far failed. In fact, his missiles united us even more strongly in our determination to resist him to the end. The main mistake of the Kremlin strategists was that in their calculations they had not taken into account the peculiarities of the Ukrainian national character. Russian air raids filled us not with terror but with tough-minded persistence and resistance.

I discovered that when I was going through a particularly tough time, it helped to visualize our brave soldiers and tell myself they were a hundred times worse off than I was! Even when cold, tired, and hungry, they protected me as I confronted my problems and minor complications. How could I complain about the pain in my knees while climbing stairs when a freedom fighter at the same moment has lost his legs in an explosion of artillery?

Shame. Guilt. Those were the feelings that haunted—and still haunt—me since the beginning of the war. They arose in my mind as far back as 2014, when I was still living in Donetsk. I was not even sixty years old then, and I could still hold a weapon in my hands to defend myself and my country. Knowing that I wasn't a born fighter, I allowed thousands of Ukrainians to do the fighting for me. Ten thousand of those heroes had already died for my right, and that of my family, to live in the country we loved.

Nor did I go to war eight years later; I left it to others. I would do everything possible to stop my son from going to war, too. Was this pacifism? Practicality? Cunning? Or cowardice?

I kept telling myself that it was "not my job" to fight. Let the professional military do it! My job was to protect my family. But many thousands of Ukrainian men had chosen to go to war as volunteers, leaving their wives and children behind. I, on the other hand, had fled the country and spent half a year abroad, watching the tragedy from afar. I had donated no more than $200 to the Ukrainian army and written a couple of anti-Russian articles. This was my meager contribution to the common Victory Pot.

All these thoughts swirled in my head when two soldiers in pale-spotted uniforms sat down at my table. They put their bags on an empty chair and began to drink coffee from paper cups. One held in his hand the Ukrainian version of a hot dog: a boiled sausage tucked inside a little bun. The second man stared at his phone, periodically making scrolling movements with his thumb.

They were in their thirties, from which I concluded that they may have been officers or sergeants. There were no insignias on their jackets, except for the emblems of the Armed Forces of Ukraine—a black trident under a blue and yellow flag. They seemed tired or sad to me. I thought I should thank them by saying something like, "Hi, guys. Thank you for taking on this dangerous work. We're proud of you."

My tongue stuck in my throat and I couldn't get a word out. What was the point of my gratitude to them? They were either going to the war or coming back from it, while I sat in Kyiv on my ass and waited for them to drive the Russians out. I kept my eyes downcast and pretended to be absorbed in my work. It was my way of hiding my head in the sand. I hated myself. Finally, I looked up and muttered:

"My respect, lads. Glory to Ukraine."

One of them glanced at me, smiled, and winked. The second soldier finished his sausage and wiped his lips with a napkin. According to tradition, my greeting was supposed to be answered with "Glory to the heroes," but he uttered other words.

"How did you get here?" he asked. "I heard Kyiv got beaten up real bad yesterday."

"That's nothing," I said.

"It was hot, I suppose."

"Not so hot as out there in the war."

"Hold on," the soldier said. "Those sons of bitches will get theirs yet."

The soldiers finished their coffee, hung the bags on their shoulders, and proceeded out the door to a waiting military vehicle. I followed them with my eyes through the café window. I knew that we would never meet again. I don't know if they survived or died. I was sure they forgot about my existence as soon as they turned their backs on me. I was nobody to them. However, these men were ready to fight for millions of total strangers. We "nobodies" were their compatriots and their cheering section. That was reason enough for them to risk their lives.

My second meeting with the defenders of Ukraine took place somewhat later, during another blackout in Kyiv. At night, when the lights were turned off, it usually became so quiet in the house that Luba and I heard every step, every cough from our neighbors' apartment. Tonight, there was a small party going on above us. The men were talking and laughing loudly, which prevented Luba from falling asleep. Our upstairs neighbor often disturbed our peace at night, so Luba had wisely taken his phone number.

Now, she called him and reminded him that it was forbidden to make noise during the curfew. He apologized and promised not to bother us again. But half an hour later, the men had amped up the volume of conversation and then began singing! This activity was repeated several times. Finally, at midnight, I told Luba I was going to the twenty-third floor to calm down our neighbors. She resisted, fearing that it would come to a fight. Instead, she called the police, but they refused to come, considering the case too minor. An hour later, the men above silenced themselves, and Luba and I finally fell asleep.

The next day when I was going down the stairs, I met our neighbor from the twenty-third floor. He was walking upstairs toward me—a tall, thin man with a sparse beard, narrow shoulders, and the manner of a schoolmaster. When he saw me, he put his hand to his heart and asked for forgiveness for yesterday's noise.

"Please don't be angry with me," he said. "My friends were visiting me yesterday and we had a few drinks. They came from the front for a few days. Today we are going out of town together, so our silence is guaranteed!"

While the neighbor was apologizing to me, he was overtaken by two of his friends who were climbing the stairs behind him with cans of Pepsi-Cola in their hands. They were large men in uniforms, ruddy-faced and out of breath. Hearing our conversation, they squeezed past me and hurried upstairs like a couple of naughty schoolboys.

I didn't notice any signs of PTSD in their behavior. But I realized that one day these two men might not be so peaceful, along with two hundred thousand other soldiers who would return home with pistols, grenades, and paratrooper knives stashed away. Hard times awaited Ukraine—an unfortunate country with a painful past, a tumultuous present, and an uncertain future.

At the end of 2022, the situation was looking grim, as if many Ukrainians would not survive the snow and subzero temperatures settling in across the country. According to my calculations, we had to hold on for about 120 cold days while Russia did everything possible to ensure that we would not live until spring. This was Russia's objective: to inflict the maximum pain on our people as we were going through a bitter winter.

By November 24, 2022, half of Ukraine's energy infrastructure was crippled after a series of massive Russian missile strikes. About 70 percent of Kyiv residents woke up without power or drinking water, cutting off their ability to cook food or make phone calls. The internet was either unstable or dead. ATMs were unable to dispense cash. Supermarkets were rejecting credit card transactions.

Blackouts rolled across the country one after another like storm waves trying to upend the flimsy ship of the Ukrainian economy. Kyiv officials urged citizens to prepare for a "worst-case scenario," including a complete shutdown. We woke up in the middle of the night to alarms, got up in the morning to the sound of sirens, and spent our days anticipating the next air raid. We read that Kyiv's power engineers had done their best to restore electricity in the capital, but their heroic efforts had been in vain. Russian missiles and drones gave us no respite. At night, the darkness echoed our feelings of abandonment and uncertainty.

And now it was Christmas again. This year, we had a battery-operated Christmas garland on the wall of our kitchen. A large table lamp stood in the middle of the table when we ate or read. Our shadows darted across the walls, mimicking our every move. Sitting at the table, we instinctively interpreted every sound. The slamming of doors in the hallway sounded like distant explosions and kept us on our toes. Our cell phones were always in plain sight to warn us of the next air raid. We constantly made sure that the buckets were full of water. We were never able to fully relax, which would later take its toll.

Almost every day, one of us asked a rhetorical question that sounded something like this: "Do you think the West will ever give us air defense weapons to shield the skies over Ukraine?" In December, this question was modified to this: "When will the West finally give us long-range missiles to get even with Russia?" We considered this a fair question. We were a nation suffering an unprovoked attack on our survival. Surely our friends in the West would come to the rescue of a fellow democratic nation under fire. Wouldn't they?

The Ukrainian military command and President Zelensky had for months been asking NATO for more advanced air defense systems. They pointed out that under the Geneva Conventions, attacks on civilians and the infrastructure vital to their survival must be interpreted as a war crime.

The leaders of many European countries were supporting Ukraine in its quest to obtain a weapon of retaliation. This would give us the capability of effectively entering those areas within Russian territory where the Russians' missiles were being launched. But the US-led NATO alliance repeatedly ruled out supplying longer-range missiles and other such weaponry to Ukraine amid concerns that this could lead to a dangerous escalation with nuclear-armed Russia.

Many Ukrainians considered this a cowardly decision. They demanded that the Americans stand up for a European country struggling to maintain their independence from Putin and his allies.

Why did they think this was an effective argument? Had they ever taken responsibility for electing presidents who cared more about lining their own pockets than about the security of their country? Were they going to ask Volodymyr Zelensky why he hadn't equipped the Ukrainian Army against our enemy, instead of allocating the money to PR campaigns to build up favor with Zelensky's constituents? Now we needed a miracle, and we didn't understand why Uncle Sam was in no hurry to escalate a war with high risks for both Ukraine and the United States.

To many cynics' surprise, however, the United States did *not* remain indifferent to our plight. President Joseph Biden did everything possible to unite other nations in providing crucial support to Ukraine. It was slow and often subtle work because the United States had developed a novel strategy that could be described as "boiling a frog." If Vladimir Putin felt the full might of American capabilities at once, he might react suddenly and unpredictably. But as the West gradually turned up the heat, the "frog" adapted to each incremental increase. But one day, the frog would wake up and find that it was too late to jump. It was already cooked.

Unfortunately, and again, this wise strategy also prolonged the war and was paid for with the blood of the Ukrainians.

Meanwhile, the giant frog continued to wallow in boiling water, looking for a way out. In December, Kremlin propagandists started talking about Russia's next move. They were preparing some two hundred thousand fresh troops to "finish off" Ukraine. It was another effort to demoralize Ukrainians and force us to capitulate. However, the emotional blackmail failed. Instead of agreeing to peace talks, Ukraine launched a series of strikes at military targets within Russia, some of which were located hundreds of miles from its borders, deep inside the Russian territory.

Of course, Kyiv was careful not to claim responsibility for the attacks. In full accordance with the operation "Cooking the Frog," US secretary of state Antony Blinken proclaimed that Washington had neither encouraged nor enabled the Ukrainians to strike inside Russia. After a short pause, he added that the United States was determined to ensure Kyiv had received the equipment needed to defend itself.

Shortly after his comments, we learned that Blinken was referring to an advanced US-built Patriot defense missile system suitable to counter Russian missile and drone attacks. Each Patriot missile cost around $3,000,000 and provided a comprehensive level of protection against different threats—a great addition to the extremely capable and effective NASAMS (National Advanced Surface-to-Air Missile System) that had already been in operation in Ukraine for several weeks.

NASAMS and Patriots and were not a silver bullet, but every additional resource was received with gratitude. Getting back to our frog, we kept a fire under the boiling water and kept the water boiling until it started to steam and the bubbles grew. If the fire didn't go out, you'd get a good rolling boil and eventually, the frog would bob to the surface, eyes blank, legs up, dead and cooked.

Do you think this is a cruel experiment? If so, watch footage of places where Russian missiles hit the residential areas of Ukrainian cities. Or look into the eyes of parents weeping over the mangled bodies of their children. Remember, an infectious frog must be boiled. The rabid rat must be killed. This is not cruelty. This is the rule of evolutionary selection. Hygienic procedure on a historic scale. Global disinfection.

The moves taken by Putin increasingly resembled convulsions. Secluded in his underground bunkers, he rarely came into the daylight, and looked, if not insane, then out of touch with reality. One such event happened shortly before New Year's Eve in 2022.

On December 26, the Russian president gathered the leaders of the eight Kremlin-allied countries to a summit in St. Petersburg and presented them with eight golden rings engraved with the words "Happy New Year 2023" and "Russia." Putin's odd choice of gift to his puzzled allies sparked various mocking interpretations which made reference to Tolkien's trilogy *The Lord of the Rings* in which the Dark Lord Sauron gave out magical rings to the nine kings of men in order to bend them to his will and do his bidding.

We Ukrainians have long called Russian soldiers orcs, making reference to Sauron's army in the novel so Putin only confirmed our terminology. At the same time, he provided commentators with another reason to doubt his sanity. His "rings of power" were mocked as "rings of powerlessness" considering that Putin was facing increasing isolation on the international stage and had as his only allies men who were clearly unwilling to turn their states into provinces ruled by a madman.

The clumsy idea of the Kremlin celebration looked comical and desperate in comparison with the forthcoming visit of the Ukrainian president to the United States.

Moscow Vladimir and Kyiv Volodymyr made their moves almost simultaneously and clearly demonstrated their potential to the entire world.

CHAPTER 19

Ballistic Trajectories

VLADIMIR PUTIN COULD NOT HELP BUT ENVY HIS ALTER EGO, VOLODY-myr Zelensky. For two decades, the Russian president had basked in the rays of glory, first domestic, then international. Year after year, he created his image of a courageous macho leader, enjoying the adoration of millions of people. But after February 2022, everything went to hell. Unexpectedly, Putin returned to the psychological state in which he had lived during his youth when he was a frail, bony teenager, vulnerable to bullying and victimization by his peers.

At the same time, Zelensky underwent a reverse transformation, from a slapdash comedian to a hero of the world media. Putin looked old-fashioned and simply *old* compared with his young, successful rival. He had become a loser. He lost the respect of world leaders and forfeited the right to pose and shake hands with them in front of cameras. To some extent, it was more terrible for him than death. He had unexpectedly entered political oblivion.

The champion's pedestal, which Putin considered his own, was now being occupied by someone else. His sworn enemy. His entire antipode. That man was Volodymyr Zelensky, whom the Russian president had so long despised and abused. Suddenly, they had switched roles—and as a professional actor, Zelensky did it easily and naturally.

The real gift of acting is the ability to captivate an audience. Although not an outstanding actor, Zelensky nevertheless possessed all the necessary skills to become one. He knew how to change his voice intonations and facial expressions. He had the tried and tested set of poses and gestures. Moreover, they did not look feigned, because quite often Zelensky allowed himself to be sincere. It wasn't purely a sham—it came rather naturally to him. And it worked—well and effectively.

Before his ascent to the political Olympus, Volodymyr Zelensky starred in the television series, *Servant of the People*, where he played the role of an honest, simple-minded, decent person fighting Ukrainian corruption and bureaucracy. Without ceasing to play this winning role, he won the 2019 presidential election. Three years later, he was forced to change his image. He had grown a belligerent beard and built up his biceps, emphasizing this with his extra short-sleeved T-shirts. His clothes were either camouflage or black, a reminder that Zelensky was the leader of a country at war.

It wasn't hypocrisy but a completely natural choice. Zelensky did not look like a sham— he really showed courage, appearing on the front lines among soldiers and officers, where he could have become a target for sniper bullets and enemy shells. He blended seamlessly into his new role and was greeted with applause from a grateful worldwide audience.

Zelensky had become a popular figure. His former transgressions were forgotten for a while. He was not asked uncomfortable questions at press conferences and received large-scale publicity and the friendly attention of world celebrities. Western leaders welcomed him with open arms.

Finally, the day came when Joseph Biden forgot his previous grievances and invited Zelensky to the United States for an official visit. It was the finest hour for Ukraine and its leader. When Zelensky appeared on Capitol Hill in Washington on December 21, 2022, he was greeted by America's political elite with a standing ovation.

Claire, my literary agent, was watching this on TV and couldn't resist commenting admiringly. I, too, was touched to the core. Zelensky's address to the US Congress has since been compared to the speech Winston Churchill gave eighty-one years earlier, nearly to the day, in December 1941, when the British prime minister appealed for American support with his country under relentless attack from Hitler's Germany. These parallels were not accidental. Zelensky's speechwriters had done an excellent job. When Zelensky told Congress that "Ukraine holds its lines and will never surrender," echoing one of Churchill's most famous phrases, he earned a storm of applause.

That day I buried the skepticism lurking deep in my mind. It would remain there until Ukraine's victory. Volodymyr Zelensky had turned out to be the best possible figure in the presidency. I couldn't imagine another leader who personified Ukraine so vividly. Like all men, he had his faults, but his virtues far outweighed them on the scales of history.

Above all, Zelensky was a man who strove for self-improvement. He learned and quickly changed for the better. This alone earned him my respect. Zelensky was flexible in contrast to the stubborn, entrenched Putin. He was our David fighting Goliath. And his dark past was no more significant than the impressive new shadow he cast. In December 2022, while I did not become an unrestrained fan of Zelensky, I did shift away from being his critic.

I tried not to think about the war on the eves of Christmas and New Year. Christmas trees installed in our homes and twinkling garlands helped elevate our spirits and put us in a festive mood. Running around the apartment, Erica would break some glass ball every now and then, but no one scolded her. I looked at her and remembered how Severine used to drop New Year's toys on the floor, and I felt the threat of sudden tears. I asked myself if the war would end in 2023 and convinced myself that yes, it probably would. We all thought so. We dreamed that after the New Year, the lights would turn on in Ukraine and the air sirens would go silent.

We humans are accustomed to counting our lives according to the dates on the calendar. It seems to us that on December 26 or January 1, everything will change for the better. We will start a new life and cross out the old one. A few days pass, and we find ourselves in the same place we were before. Santa Claus does not bring us the magic key to the door to a better future.

The Ukrainian Santa Claus is named "Father Frost." He wears a long red coat lined with white fur and is accompanied by the Snow Maiden, a blue-eyed girl with a long blonde braid over her shoulder. I don't remember ever liking this couple. I always knew that my parents had delivered my New Year's gifts, not Father Frost. Early in the morning, barely opening my eyes, I would run to the festive tree and eat chocolates hung from the spruce branches. Since then, I have always associated the New Year with the taste of chocolate, the aroma of tangerines, and the rustle of wrapping paper hiding gifts. Those were unforgettable moments!

As an adult, I had forgotten how to enjoy such trifles, and yet I looked forward to the New Year holidays.

Putin could not allow Ukrainians to have even the slightest reason to rejoice. Russia shelled us on Christmas Day. Russia shelled us on New Year's Eve. They blew up several houses and killed several people, but failed to ruin our holidays. Kyiv's electricians made superhuman efforts to provide the city's arteries with power and heat. For two or three days we enjoyed hot water, warm radiators, and light. After the blackouts, this seemed like a heavenly life.

However, our family decided not to celebrate the New Year together. There were several reasons for this. First, Putin could order a particularly heavy bombardment of Kyiv. Second, it was embarrassing for us to gather at a festive table when people were dying every day in Ukraine. And, finally, Luba felt unwell.

Repeated sessions of radiation therapy had severely damaged her body. With each day she moved more slowly and became weaker. When she left the house, she did not know if she would be strong enough to walk back upstairs if the elevators were stopped. Svitlana or I had to accompany her during walks just in case. Most of the housework now fell on my shoulders. My personal time was reduced.

My wife's illness continued to alarm me. Sergiy and Svitlana were also worried. We did not know for sure what had caused the sharp deterioration in Luba's health. She tried not to show her weakness and refused to undergo a medical examination. I understood. She was afraid to hear a terrible verdict.

I was very worried about my Luba. I often had strong feelings of tenderness for her and wanted to hug her, but I showed my emotions with restraint. If my wife noticed a change in my behavior, she might think that I did not believe in her recovery, and my love was mixed with sadness. This would make her feel even worse.

That winter, Sveta and I often walked together in the morning, discussing Luba's health and the war. Usually, our route ran between the high-rise buildings in our area to McDonald's, where we got coffee and cocoa in paper cups covered with brown plastic lids. We were going to walk on Saturday morning, January 14. But we never got to McDonald's that day. Something else happened that morning—something that made us forget about our desire for coffee.

It was unusually warm for January. The sun shone through the low clouds. We discussed the recent shelling and dreamed of the day when this nightmare would end. Svitlana believed that this would happen in the spring or summer. It sounded too good to be true to me, but I didn't mind dreaming a little. We drew pictures of our joint vacation on the sea coast, and this alone was enough to make us feel quite happy. Svitlana's husband had gradually developed his business, and I was hoping for an advance payment for my book, so our plans looked feasible.

We narrowed our choice to Bulgaria or Spain when a deafening blow shocked us. A mighty sound, a heavy reverberation louder than the sound of thunder forced us into stunned silence. We looked around for a threat. The sky above was serene. Buildings blocked our view. We stood in place, confused, not knowing where to run.

Another explosion sounded. This time, it didn't sound like thunder at all. It was like a blow of a giant hammer very close to us. The ground trembled under our feet. The antitheft sirens of cars turned on. Passersby ran in different directions.

Svitlana and I, without saying a word, rushed to the nearest building, looking for protection against its wall. It would have been a mistake because in the event of a hit, we could be buried under the rubble. But more and more peals of a terrific roar left no space in our brains for rational thinking. We were driven by the instinct of self-preservation. It was ancient and therefore erroneous. Our distant ancestors did not know how to behave during a bombing.

Crouching in a nook near the basement of the building, we counted four or five nearby explosions. Only then did the air-raid alarm sound. This meant that the Russian missiles had arrived too quickly for the radar to catch them.

"It looks like they were ballistic things," I told Svitlana when it became quiet and we rushed home.

"Hypersonic?" she asked on the run.

Svitlana has long learned to understand the characteristics of missiles that were aimed at us almost every day. And she remembered the threats of Putin, who claimed that there was no salvation against Russian ballistic missiles or S-300 antiaircraft missiles that fly on a ballistic trajectory.

Our assumption turned out to be correct. According to Ukrainian official sources, the missile hazard alert came late due to a lack of radar data. "Unfortunately, we are not able to detect and shoot down ballistics," said the representative of the military department.

We never found out where those damn things ended up. We saw no smoke, no fire, no destruction. Information about the impact was vague. Two dozen people were injured and some industrial facilities were impacted. Judging by the evasiveness of the authorities, the missiles caused severe damage to military logistics, and this information had to be classified.

Meanwhile, another tragedy occurred the very same day, 250 miles from the capital in the Ukrainian city of Dnipro. That afternoon, Russian Tu-22m3 long-range bombers launched five Kh-22 cruise missiles at the territory of Ukraine. One of them reached Dnipro about 4 p.m. and hit a local high-rise building. Two entrances on the ninth and second floors were smashed by the blow and at least seventy-five people were injured. Some forty were killed, including small children. Thirty-five people were missing.

Millions of Ukrainians mourned this loss, and YouTube was flooded with videos from the crash site. The smoking ruins of the Dnipro apartment building showed us what could happen to our own apartments. Any day. Any night. Any time.

In the instant before the explosion, hundreds of people were living their normal lives. Just like in Kyiv before, Dnipro's alarms did not have time to work, when the explosive package of the Moscow assassins took off into the skies and then swiftly flew down on the citizens' innocent heads. What were they doing, what were they thinking, what were they talking about? Someone was sitting at the kitchen table, someone was watching TV, or playing with the children, or reading the latest news, not suspecting that they were about to be the subject of this news.

The Kh-22 rocket flew right at them, choosing a target at random. It could have hit another part of the building or any other building in the neighborhood. The Kh-22 was a rather old cruise missile that was less accurate than most modern missiles.

However, the Russians deliberately chose a residential area as their target. There were no military installations or infrastructure facilities. These were ordinary apartment buildings inhabited by Ukrainians. *They* were Putin's target. Special military operation? No. Special mass murder.

Every serial maniac has his favorite murder weapon. For Putin and his generals, it was a Kh-22 rocket because the armed forces of Ukraine didn't have weapons capable of shooting down this type of missile. Since the beginning of the war, more than two hundred Russian missiles of this type had been fired at the territory of Ukraine. The mass of the warhead of a Kh-22 is about 2,100 lbs. its maximum range is 370 miles. When applied from long distances, the deviation from the target can be hundreds of meters. When it explodes, it destroys all living things in its target area. Boys and girls playing in their playrooms. Young men and women in their bedrooms. Old women with their knitting. Old men solving their crossword puzzles. Suddenly, they have all become one continuous bloody mess, littered with piles of concrete, and rescuers had to pull them out one by one or in parts.

And at the same time, tens of millions of Russians were enjoying watching this on their TV. And Russian representatives sat on the United Nations Security Council talking about human rights. And a new flow of weapons was sailing to Russia through the Bosporus, a strait controlled by Turkey, a full member of NATO. Don't you think that history should be written not by politicians but by psychiatrists?

The tragedy in the Dnipro shocked me so much that I again tried to convince my daughter to take Erica and go somewhere far away.

"Where?" Svitlana asked. "There's not a single safe place left in Ukraine."

"You could go back to Poland," I said.

"No way, Dad. Can't you see? I will never be a refugee again."

"Even for Erica?"

"Patriots will protect her," Svitlana said firmly. "And everyone else."

She was not talking about Ukrainian patriots who fought in the war. She meant the US antiaircraft missile systems, able to intercept Kh-22s and any other air targets. Western partners hesitated for a long time before starting to supply Patriot PAC-3 systems to Ukraine, but the tragedy in Dnipro dispelled their last doubts. Putin once again failed to foresee the result of his actions, achieving the opposite result. On January 17, 2023, the United States and Germany each announced they were sending a Patriot defense battery for Ukraine. The next day the Netherlands joined them, and it was only the start.

We were all happy to know this, but I couldn't shake the thought that the Russian "military frog" was being boiled for too long. According to very cautious (if not timid) estimates by UN officials, more than eight thousand civilians died in Ukraine during the year of the war, and almost fourteen thousand were injured.

I have met people whose religion was lost during this terrible year. It is said that soldiers in war begin to believe in God, even if they were atheists before. I don't know. I haven't been able to verify this claim. As for me, God has not disappeared from my life. He just became different—completely different for me.

Among my close relatives, Svitlana was the only one I could talk to about this. Sergiy rejected everything that was connected with mysticism. Alexander was too absorbed in his business to think about such things. Luba's religiosity began and ended with Orthodox holidays. Svitlana and I walked the same spiritual path and understood each other perfectly.

One day I presented to her my renewed conception of God, which had come to me after frequent painful reflection.

"Where do we get the idea that God is merciful?" I asked her while walking. "Who came up with this? Didn't He create a world in which some living beings feed on others? And doesn't a hare feel pain when a fox eats it? Why do people decide that they are in a special position? Everyone in this world suffers and dies. Is this mercy? The ancient Greeks and Romans feared their gods for a reason. God can be gentle, but He can also be cruel. Otherwise, He would not be omnipotent. He must have all the qualities that we have. He created us, didn't he? How could He make us brutal without being brutal Himself?"

Svitlana listened to me and asked a counter question: "Dad, why did you exclude Satan from your concept?"

"Satan was invented by people so that they can be saved by a beautiful, all-merciful Lord," I said. "Otherwise, they would be too scared to live in this world without hope, without faith in justice."

Svitlana thought a little more and said: "Do you think Putin is doing the will of God?"

My perfect logical construction collapsed at once. I muttered something unintelligible. For some time, we walked in silence.

I can't explain how it was connected, but I returned home that day with the firm resolve that I must write the book you hold in your hands. My memoirs about the Donetsk mafia were about halfway completed. Claire was preparing a mailing list to query American publishers. Rationally, I should have focused on the true-crime book, but I was now driven by an irrational impulse.

War! What could be more important?

There are things that inspire us. No, this word is not quite the right choice. I'm talking rather about those events that bow down like a springboard beneath our feet, ready to push us with a ton of force out of our safe, familiar world into a space much more dangerous but at the same time more significant and extraordinary. Only in moments like this are we fully able to experience the feelings that accompany a freefall. Blood retreats from our faces and our hearts skip a feverish beat, leaving us gasping and shocked.

Wow! I'm here! I see it! I should definitely tell everyone about this if I ever survive the landing. What we learn about ourselves and others, in the moments when the ground has slipped from under our feet, can be vital for those who are not yet on the springboard or do not realize that they're already there.

I couldn't help but write this book. I understood that not every person would want to read it because some things in my book might upset the reader. There would be talk of pain and death, tears and discomfort, and violence of all kinds, from cruelty to real abuse. But there will be kindness, too, I thought, and even hope for a happy ending. Wouldn't God, who wants to see us as human beings and not animals, help us reach a happy ending to this brutal war?

CHAPTER 20

True Crime versus True War

IN FEBRUARY 2023, BLACKOUTS WERE BECOMING LESS AND LESS FRE-
quent, until they at last ceased—a happy event for my family and all the
inhabitants of Kyiv. The flow of Russian missiles and drones had dried
up. We guessed that Russia needed a break to replenish its arsenal, but we
tried not to think about it. The war taught us not to look too far ahead.
You cannot make long-term plans without knowing what awaits you
tomorrow or even today, in an hour, in a minute, in a second.

The Ukrainian troops gradually grew stronger, gaining invaluable
military experience and receiving the latest models of Western weapons.
Belarusian President Lukashenko, Putin's closest ally, did not dare repeat
the unsuccessful Russian thrust toward Kyiv at the start of the war nearly
a year ago. Ukrainian units were reliably protecting the 650-mile frontier
of marsh and woodland for a possible offensive from the north.

The fighting in the east and south continued, but Russia did not
have enough strength to break through. Its troops were dwindling and
exhausted. The hastily carried out mobilization calls did not bring the
desired results, nor did the recruitment of prisoners for military service.
The Russian army was replenished by bringing in more than three hundred thousand inexperienced, unequipped, disorganized men, fit only to
be killed in the first battle. Newcomers were sent into minefields and
under Ukrainian shelling as "trial balloons." Many more of them did not
even have time to receive the promised monetary reward that was offered
to tempt them to go to war. Ukrainian soldiers called such attacks "meat
assaults." The fields and groves were littered with rotting bodies.

On Valentine's Day, February 14, 2023, the internet was flooded with reports about the defeat of the entire Russian brigade of the elite 155th naval infantry while storming Vuhledar. This was a coal-mining town in the Donetsk region, where some five thousand members of the brigade had been killed, wounded, or taken prisoner.

After a year at war, Russia had suffered a military defeat, while Ukraine achieved a major strategic and moral victory that few had expected. Nevertheless, the war continued with no end in sight. Neither side was ready to negotiate. Ukrainians, inspired by their victories on the battlefield and filled with a desire for justice and revenge, could not accept even a hint of a land-for-peace compromise. For Russia, compromise was out of the question as long as the country was run by Putin, whose presidency was entirely dependent on military success or failure. Both sides were preparing for a long war.

Looking at the situation dispassionately, you saw only one possible outcome of this confrontation. In a protracted war, the clear advantage was to Russia, whose population was three times larger than that of Ukraine's. Though Russia has suffered massive casualties of about two hundred thousand dead and wounded, and Ukraine's losses were twice as small, Ukraine suffered a bigger loss than its eastern neighbor.

Russia's giant territory was intact and not under the constant threat of shelling. In 2021, Russia's GDP was nine times larger than Ukraine's GDP, and in spite of Western sanctions, Russia was selling record-breaking volumes of oil to China and India, so Putin had a lot more money to equip his army.

And he had a trump card. Defeat or its prospect would likely prompt him to resort to nuclear strikes.

On February 18, when US vice president Kamala Harris told the Munich Security Conference that Russia had committed crimes against humanity during its war in Ukraine, Vladimir Putin immediately responded by announcing that he conducted exercises for a massive nuclear strike, and the entire world froze in anxious anticipation.

That left the United States and its allies without any good options, except to ramp up military support and hope for the best.

Such was the situation at the beginning of the second year of Russia's full-scale invasion of Ukraine. Psychologically, this was a tough challenge for all parties to the conflict. The frog was boiling. The pressure of the steam in the seething cauldron increased. Everyone in the vicinity risked receiving fatal burns.

Amazingly, the expectation of the Apocalypse had no effect on people's behavior. Walking around Kyiv, I didn't see frightened faces or alarmed eyes directed up at the sky. Life went on. Even though people were talking about the likelihood of a nuclear war, TV presenters did not forget to put on makeup and style their hair properly. Athletes set records, dealers traded cars, and café customers made the difficult choice between cakes and pastries.

Alexander and I would go to the market and see crowds of people there, concerned not with the war but with prices and the freshness of greens and fish. In the mornings, schoolchildren with backpacks walked to their schools, laughing and chatting cheerfully with each other. Vehicles drove through the streets in a continuous stream. Billboards rose above the city barricades.

It was wild, it was unnatural, but it was true. For the most part, people did not think about war or the nuclear threat. Was it stupidity or psychological self-defense? Watching these carefree people, I thought that the end of the world might not be the way it was portrayed in apocalyptic novels and movies. Everything will happen very quickly and routinely—an unimpressive end to a turbulent world history.

I remember walking down the street on a winter day when an air raid siren sounded. Nobody hastened their pace, nobody showed alarm. Each of us continued to go his own way. People looked at their phones, walked their dogs, picked up their kids from school, chatted, and ate snacks on the go.

Out of curiosity, I went down to the subway, which served as a bomb shelter during the rocket attacks. There were no more than a hundred people there. Some of them simply waited for the resumption of train traffic. I thought that if there was an atomic explosion upstairs now, we would have survived down here. But I realized that I wouldn't want to stay alive, wandering among the radioactive ruins in search of my loved ones. Life as I knew it would be much worse than death.

I went upstairs. I understood why we Ukrainians had stopped feeling fearful. Every feeling has its own upper limit. Happiness, grief, horror, fun, sadness, hatred . . . Only love has no limits. We are capable of loving people and things throughout our lives. Maybe that's why they say that "God is love." Nowadays, we think about God in the underground, not so much in the church.

The next time I went down to the subway was the morning of February 20, 2023, as I traveled to the center of Kyiv to take a walk and visit some bookstores. When you live in a remote residential area, you sometimes need to expose yourself to the capital's noise and din, huddle in the crowd or sit in a crowded café. It was the Day of the Heavenly Hundred, and I intended to visit the Maidan, where our heroes had died during the 2014 Revolution of Dignity.

Disappointment awaited me. All my familiar walking routes were now blocked by the police. I tried to get to the center by subway, but the station I needed was closed. While I was on the train, I heard Joe Biden's name several times. What happened to him? The advanced age of the American president made me fear the worst.

The day before, when I'd called my parents in Donetsk, my mother told me at length how weak and forgetful my ninety-three-year-old father had become. It hurt me to listen to this. Then suddenly my mother said:

"But your dad looks and acts much better than this American geezer."

"Do you mean Biden?" I asked, mechanically.

"Who else?" She laughed sarcastically. "What do Americans think? Do they really hope that their good-for-nothing old man could cope with our Putin?"

"They're not gonna fight in a boxing ring," I said.

"Well, of course! Biden can barely move his legs."

I didn't respond to this outburst. My mother, as usual, echoed everything reported by the Kremlin propaganda and refused to hear counterarguments. I understood this very well, and yet I could not help worrying about "our good old Joe." US President Biden was one of the most consistent, loyal, and reliable allies of Ukraine in this war. And, what was more important, he had power and influence that no one else had in the entire world.

What would happen to Ukraine without the support of the United States?

Ukrainians fought to the death, that's right. But can you win at the cost of your own death?

President Joseph Biden did not let us down this time, either. He did not get sick and did not get into a plane crash. Instead, he made a surprise trip to the capital of our embattled country to demonstrate what he called America's "unwavering support" for Ukraine in its war with Russia.

His forty-hour journey into and out of a war zone was conducted under the cloak of secrecy. Mr. Biden slipped out of Washington in the dark of night without notice, landed in Poland, and continued by train, invisible to anyone behind the drawn shades of the presidential car. It was a long and arduous journey for an eighty-year-old man, but at 8 a.m., when Joseph Biden stepped off the train at the platform of Kyiv station, he looked as energetic and fresh as his tie of blue and yellow—the colors of the Ukrainian flag.

Half an hour later, Volodymir Zelensky greeted him at Mariinsky Palace, wearing his signature black sweatshirt with green "militarized" pants, and a black beard, which made him look a little like an Afghan mujahideen. Praising him and the Ukrainian people, the US president said that their "sacrifices have been far too great," but "Putin's war of conquest is failing."

"He's counting on us not sticking together," Biden said. "He thought he could outlast us . . . but he's just been plain wrong. *Plain* wrong."

I am sure that Putin, having heard these words, turned green with envy and impotent rage. He, who was going to take over Ukraine in three days, had to sit in an underground bunker somewhere in the Moscow suburbs while the American leader walked freely around Kyiv, accepting the applause of the Ukrainians.

When Biden and Zelensky left the palace for a visit to Saint Michael's monastery in downtown Kyiv, crowds gathered at barricades erected outside it in the hopes of catching a glimpse of the two leaders.

They didn't have time to admire the sun glittering off the monastery's golden domes, as an air raid alarm suddenly wailed, adding a dramatic touch to the excitement of the moment. The blare of the siren was triggered by a Russian MIG fighter jet taking off in Belarus, whose missile could hit the square in front of St. Michael's monastery in under twenty minutes. Biden's face remained impenetrable behind the sunglasses, although I think at that moment he had a keen sense of what Ukrainians have been dealing with for twelve months of the war.

The very next day, back in Poland, he firmly stated, "Ukraine will never be a victory for Russia." After a short pause, he added, "Never."

His categorical statement, uttered in a quiet, old, almost faint voice, meant a lot to all of us and to me personally. Whoever held the post of President of the United States of America was the most powerful and influential person on the planet. Joseph Biden advocated an unconditional victory for Ukraine in the war with Russia. It was a clear signal to the whole world. Those leaders who had so far hesitated have now rallied definitively around the United States in their quest to prevent Russia from swallowing up Ukraine.

America has once again confirmed its leadership and readiness to uphold the principles of democracy at any cost. And the world was finally divided into two halves. The progressive part of humanity united under the United States and its allies. Countries with dictatorial, barbaric regimes openly or tacitly continued to support the aggressive policies of Russia and China.

History has placed Ukraine at the forefront of an epic battle between good and evil, no matter how pompous it may sound. In fact, it is the Third World War. Call it cold, although for us Ukrainians it was hot—piping hot!

Putin's response to a direct challenge from Joseph Biden sounded like the grunt of a dog backing away at the sight of a whip in a man's hand. On February 21, only a few days ahead of the first anniversary of Russia's invasion, in a rather frustrating state-of-the-nation address, he mumbled that he was going to pull out of a nuclear treaty and blamed—who else?—Ukraine and the West for the war he had started!

These absurd words were spoken in front of a crowd of fourteen hundred people in Moscow, addressing military commanders and members of both houses of parliament, while video screens were also put up across the country. And what do you think? The Russians listened to their leader without batting an eyelid. They believed (or pretended to believe) his every word. However, the rest of the world took Putin's speech with skepticism. The Kremlin recluse had resorted to nuclear blackmail too often for his threats to have an intimidating effect. He looked like a card shark throwing the same marked card on the table. It was monotonous and primitive.

It is not that world leaders have prevented the use of tactical nuclear weapons by Russia. But it has ceased to be a red line. By this point, the Pentagon had warned the Kremlin that if nuclear missiles were launched, the Russian army would be destroyed with high-precision conventional weapons of war.

Was it a counter-bluff? Putin had to guess when the United States and NATO invited him to play Russian roulette, leaving him to make the first move. The revolver was pointed at his temple—was there a lethal cartridge in the barrel? To find out, Putin had only to pull the trigger. He was in no hurry to do this, realizing that the wrong decision could be fatal—for him.

Similar situations were often described in old Westerns, which have long been my favorite genre. One gunfighter invites another to a competition of strength. Which of them will be faster and more accurate? The shooter, not confident in himself, remains motionless, not daring to draw against his rival. Both gunfighters keep their hands hovering above their guns for a while. They look sharply at everyone, just waiting for a move. If the rival's hand goes down to his holster, the lucky gunfighter is ready. Quick as a bolt of lightning, he drops his hand, whips out his gun, and blasts the rival before he even knows what hit him. Zap!

It was a purely American contest in which Joseph Robinette Biden had an undeniable advantage over Vladimir Vladimirovich Putin. The Russian army was outdated, corroded by the rust of corruption, and clumsy. Besides, Putin was not a gunfighter. He was raised on Soviet war films, not Westerns. He lacked the guts to reach for the weapon.

Almost all my life I have been convinced of the superiority of the United States over the Soviet Union, and then over Russia. It wasn't just about money, power, or scientific progress. It was about morality and intelligence.

Back in my early school years, I was taught that the West would rot while the USSR flourished. My teachers, the press, radio, and television told me that American mass culture was cheap and miserable. I was just nine years old when I realized it was a lie. That was the day I saw my first comic, then strictly forbidden. After discovering American books, movies, and music, I was hooked. It was often cheap pulp fiction, rock'n'roll, and films like *King Kong*, but that was enough. This was a *different* culture. Free, bright, full of imagination. Superman was closer to me than the heroes of the Soviet Union with their boring, monotonous exploits. I didn't want to die for my country. I wanted to listen to rock music, watch movies about the Magnificent Seven, and read about the amazing adventures of Tarzan.

It probably sounds naive, but back then, I was a naive teenager who dreamed of finding myself in New York City and seeing a *real* car, like a Cadillac or a Chrysler. Many years later, my childhood dream took me to the United States as a writer. Was it actually a miracle? When my literary agent told me the news, I didn't believe her. It was so unexpected.

On February 3, 2023, Claire wrote to me: "Hi, Sergey. Today I sent out twenty-five proposals! Five immediate responses were positive . . . I think we're off to a good start . . . " A week later, her enthusiasm for my true-crime book became more subdued: "I have heard back from a few with various reasons to pass . . . It's still early days, Sergey. And I know how hard it is to wait."

She was right. The wait was difficult, more so than I had expected. Behind me were ten months of endless edits, rewrites, discussions, and genre changes. I felt like Sisyphus who pushed the huge boulder almost to the top of the mountain. But the stone was unstable, ready to fall back down to the bottom, and I had no strength left to keep it from rolling down.

Another week passed, during which we received rejection after rejection. Claire encouraged me as much as she could. I saw her in the position of a guide who may have led her tourist in the wrong direction and suddenly realized her error. Claire didn't say it directly, but I saw the concern in her eyes in our Zoom meeting, and I thought I felt it in the tone of her emails.

For two long weeks, I hid my dismay from my family. Over the past year, I had worked hard to be flexible and invest my hopes in American publishers. Yet, no acceptances had arrived at my doorstep. Was it time to give up on my ephemeral dream? *Stop fooling yourself, Sergey! You'll never break into the Western book market. You should stay where you belong. Forget your hope.*

Finally, I decided to talk about it with my children. Luba was too absorbed in her struggle with her illness to worry about my creative problems. Sergiy and Svitlana could understand me much better.

"Keep writing, Dad," Sergiy said. "Long ago, I used to send hundreds of emails a week to art directors and never get a response. Now they write to me themselves. Just do not give up. If you work with your heart, it will definitely lead you somewhere. Don't worry about the outcome, Dad. Focus on what you are doing."

My next personal coach was Svitlana.

"Dad, look at me," she said. "I made about twenty unsuccessful attempts and I keep going. Will you quit when you've almost reached your goal? Maybe you just have to take the last step. It was a long distance and it's stupid to stop near the finish line. Go on, Dad. Just keep going."

My adult children didn't tell me anything I didn't know, but their encouragement helped restore my determination. I opened the file with the first chapter of my war book and reread it with a sense of detachment. After a long break, it was like reading a text by an unknown author. To my surprise, I actually liked it!

Now, I had to find out if Claire would like it. Would she be willing to submit my second book when the first was still unfinished? I hated the prospect of looking for a new agent. I was very comfortable working with Claire and didn't want to swap her for some unknown. I decided that what would happen next was up to her.

On February 17, Claire fed me another batch of rejections from publishers. She had no reassuring news for me, although she tried to sweeten the bitter pill:

> *So far, the few who have responded are claiming "I don't know how to position this" or "I'm not sure how to handle this," which means they don't see an audience for your Mafia book, since it isn't about the current war. In addition, you are (as yet) an unknown personality. However, we have yet to hear from most of the editors.*

In response, I wrote her the following:

> *My friend,*
> *Thanks for the detailed report. Be sure, I do not doubt your perseverance and professional skill. I doubt only the readiness of publishers to accept the crime theme during the war. (This idea flashed in your letter.) Claire, I mentioned to you at the very beginning of our acquaintance that I began my promotion to the Western market with a book about the current war . . . Look at this, please, with your experienced eyes. If we reach a dead end, this may be a new solution.*
> *It is very important for me to know your opinion. Please be not just soothing, but be extremely frank about it.*

And Claire replied:

> *First of all, I'm always straight with you, Sergey. I will never lead you on or soft-pedal the truth. You and I have too much respect for each other and too little time to waste. So let me read your two documents and think about the prospect of sending the new proposal out. I know there are already a couple of books on the subject out there, but yours may have something irresistible to offer. Back to you soon . . .*

And Claire didn't let me down. Far from it! She came back very soon—with stunning news! She had managed to connect with two editors—one for each book—who were intrigued by my concepts! One was Becca Rohde Beurer, a managing editor specializing in criminology and criminal justice, who liked the idea of exploring the early years of the Ukrainian mafia from an insider's perspective.

The other editor was Ashley Dodge, executive editor in the area of world history, who praised my proposal about my family's true story of survival in the current Ukraine war.

What was most surprising was that both of these luminaries of literature worked in the same publishing house, Rowman & Littlefield! They had chosen me independently of each other. So three American women whom I had never met in person had possibly granted me my greatest wish (as a writer)!

It was unbelievable, but it was true! I spent two or three weeks in agonized expectation, waiting for the editors' final decision.

In the spring of 2023, Claire sent me two contracts and I found myself in the position of being an author with *two* deadlines drawn in front of him at once. But I didn't care—I knew that I would do everything on time. When you get two chances out of two thousand, you will never miss them.

My first book for Rowman & Littlefield was to be my wartime memoir, *Life on the Run*. When I signed the contract, I had already completed the first part. The next two parts were to be completed by June 15, 2023, one part per month. I checked the calendar, counted the days, and sat down to work.

The war in Ukraine was in full swing, but my thoughts were on my twin objectives—making my deadlines and joining the ranks of successful published authors!

Chapter 21

Raid of the Valkyries

At the beginning of his "blitzkrieg," Putin thought it would last a few weeks at most, and he failed to prepare for a real, long-term war. He believed his military advisers and intelligence agencies who told him exactly what he wanted to hear. They promised him that Russian troops would actually be "welcomed" by the Ukrainians as liberators, thus leading to the collapse of the Ukrainian army.

While Putin was pacing in front of a military map using his red marker to show the directions of the main strikes, his generals were mercilessly plundering the budget. At the same time, they were keeping the Russian army on half-starvation rations. Is it any wonder that, from the very start, the scheduled blitzkrieg failed miserably on all fronts?

It took Putin many months of deadly battles to recognize the staggering reality he had created: this war to conquer Ukraine was not the quickie operation he had envisioned. Russia's penchant for boasting, self-praise, and underestimating the enemy had produced failures across the board. Russian troops were ill-supplied and lacked an established chain of command. As a result, troops were competing with each other for resources.

The world's most advanced rocket artillery systems, HIMARS, supplied by the United States, allowed Ukraine to hit dozens of Russian ammunition depots. Unable to properly supply their frontline troops, Putin's generals were confused. Their military doctrine was based on the overwhelming superiority of artillery and aircraft. Without this, the Russian troops were simply marking time and stagnating, suffering colossal losses in manpower. These losses had to be replenished. Urgently.

In the year since the Russian invasion of Ukraine, Putin was close to panic. He could not call for a general mobilization for fear of an explosion of social discontent, and he could not continue the war without an influx of fresh forces for his weakened army.

Then Yevgeny Prigozhin came to Putin's aid. He was a hoarse-voiced guy with a big shaved head, big mouth, and protruding ears—an appearance that would have given him a brilliant career in the horror films of the forties. Thanks to his private army's victories in Syria, this tough-talking ex-con had transformed himself into a powerful Russian oligarch and a trusted warlord to the Russian president.

He had at his disposal an army of approximately five thousand highly paid mercenaries who had gained military experience in Africa and other hot spots in the world. At their core, they were professional cold-blooded assassins who took pride in the motto on their arm-patches which read: "Death is our business—and business is good." Almost all of these commandos had served in elite military units or in security services and were equipped with a variety of modern weapons.

Prigozhin had no intention of sacrificing his personal guard by throwing it into the fighting in Ukraine. He found another solution to the problem, a very simple and effective one. For several weeks, Yevgeny Prigozhin traveled to Russian prisons and colonies of strict regimes, addressing the prisoners with the same speech. He offered criminals a pardon in exchange for six months of service with the company in Ukraine. "It's going to be very dangerous and difficult," Prigozhin would tell them. "If you try to run away, my guys will shoot you. But if you go to the war and manage to survive, then you're all free."

It was an unprecedented and absolutely illegal campaign that freed rapists and murderers in contravention of the Russian Criminal Code. Of course, neither Putin nor Prigozhin cared about such a blatant violation of the law.

About forty thousand inmates (of the fifty thousand new mercenary soldiers) joined the Wagner Group—roughly 10 percent of Russia's prison population. But in contrast to original Wagnerites, these newcomers had just a few days of training, which barely gave them enough time to familiarize themselves with a weapon. In the next few months, as many as 80 percent of them had been killed, had deserted, or surrendered in Ukraine. However, thanks to so many obedient human masses, the Wagner Group had started collecting a growing number of victories.

In the meantime, Ukraine was preparing its soldiers for counteroffensives that were likely to launch in the spring. Ahead of that offensive, Bakhmut, a city in Donetsk in eastern Ukraine, remained the flaming epicenter of battles in which about five to six thousand Russian occupants have been killed every month.

My brave and restless Sergiy visited Bakhmut before it was destroyed. He spent a sleepless night there among the Ukrainian soldiers who were serenely snoring under the incessant cannonade. He returned from there with a pile of sketches and a vivid memory of how the car he was in had come under mortar fire.

"You know, Dad," he told me, "When mines go off nearby, you completely lose your head. We ran back to our car to get out and couldn't find the keys. Each of us had forgotten where the damn keys were. These were moments of panic. Finally, someone opened the door and we rushed away. It was something."

"It was recklessness," I said, turning on my stern fatherly voice. "Was it worth the risk?"

"Of course, Dad," Sergiy said. "You can't draw war if you haven't seen it with your own eyes."

I thought about my book. It was a story about a war that surrounded me, but I had not experienced it as a fighter. But to a greater extent, it had inhabited the hearts and souls of me and my family. We were literally wrapped up inside this war; it affected each breath we took, each move we made. I did not pretend to be a military observer or analyst. I just talked to people about what I saw, heard, read, thought, and experienced. And I hoped that this nightmare would be over by the time I finished the book.

In March, my work on the book progressed without much hindrance. Our incredible engineers had kept the power in our homes flowing *without interruption* across the country, despite losing scores of power lines, transformers, and other key components of Ukraine's infrastructure. Due to their dedicated work, we had not been brought to our knees and most of us have long since become accustomed to power cuts and lack of heating.

And we, the residents of Kyiv, had experienced daily shelling. Western war experts wrote that this indicated a shortage of precision-guided missiles in Russia needed to carry out effective attacks on Ukrainian infrastructure facilities. Our defenders had also become quite adept at shooting down incoming missiles and drones.

In the dead of night on Wednesday, March 9, 2023, I woke up with a vague anxiety. It was dark and quiet.

"Are you awake?" Luba asked in a whisper.

"Uh-huh," I said.

"Me, too," she said.

The next moment, our mobile phones turned on at the same time, alerting us to the start of an air raid alert.

This turned out to be the first big, coordinated wave of Russian attacks on Ukraine's power infrastructure since last October. They showered Kyiv, Lviv, and other major cities across the country with an unprecedented array of eighty-one missiles, including six Kh-22 air-launched cruise missiles plus six ballistic rockets that have the ability to elude our air defenses. The name of those ballistic "parcels" was the Kinzhal, which meant "dagger" in Russian.

Vladimir Putin has repeatedly boasted that his hypersonic Kinzhal missiles, capable of carrying conventional or nuclear warheads up to fifteen hundred miles, have no equal in the world and cannot be destroyed by any air defense systems. Five months before the start of the war, Russian state TV simulated a nuclear strike on three European capitals as presenters claimed the missiles would obliterate Paris, Berlin, and London in around two hundred seconds and there would be "no survivors."

Having no victories on the battlefields, Putin decided to compensate for his military weakness by throwing "daggers." Western journalists often wrote that he was indifferent to human lives and suffering. It was a delusion. Indeed, the Russian president was inspired by the death of civilians. Throughout the spring of 2023, the shelling of Ukrainian cities again became his favorite pastime.

The air raid alert on March 9 lasted for almost seven hours overnight and into the next day, and this was an attack unlike any I had seen before. The darkness outside the windows was occasionally lit up by flames. Volleys of antiaircraft systems alternated with explosions. Every time I tried to go to the window to look outside, Luba screamed at me not to dare get closer. I returned to my half of the bed and lay down.

"Maybe we should hide in the bathroom?" my wife asked.

"If I am destined to die, then let it happen in bed," I muttered and closed my eyes.

There was a break in the air raid and we fell asleep. In the morning we read that ten regions across Ukraine had been shelled. The attacks had hit residential buildings and critical infrastructure. At least a dozen people were killed and more than twenty injured, so the night was not in vain for Putin.

If I were to put together all the opinions of the people of Kyiv that I heard the next day, we would get the following: "Those sons of bitches can only terrorize us. That's all they can do. But it won't help them. And they won't get away with it. The bastards will get payback for everything they've done."

The Russians were of the exact opposite opinion. Over the past year, propaganda had managed to convince them that it was the Ukrainians who had started the war. Or, at the very least, Putin was forced to launch a preemptive strike to prevent "Ukrainian fascists" from attacking peaceful Russia. It was like the Land of Crooked Mirrors—any truth was turned inside out there, distorted beyond recognition and acquiring the opposite meaning. For example, my parents still believed that Russia had the right to own Ukraine and its people. For them, we were rebels who dared to challenge the master.

On March 11, when I called my mother in Donetsk to congratulate her on her eighty-eighth birthday, she asked me how bad things had been in Kyiv the day before. I cautiously replied that it had been a difficult night.

"I prayed for you, Son," my mother said. "And for all of you. Trust me, I know how bad it can be. Not a week here goes by without shelling. All winter we froze and saved water. Now it's become a little easier, but Ukrainian troops are constantly destroying the water canal and do not allow it to be repaired. I'm tired. I'm so tired, my son."

Hearing this from my aged mother was painful. Suddenly, I had discovered a new truth about the war, the truth that no one wanted to hear in the warring Ukraine.

I told Svitlana about the shelling of Donetsk. She shook her head and said: "Impossible! This is a lie. We're not at war with civilians."

Then, without realizing it, she literally repeated the formula of the Russian officials, which they uttered in response to accusations of terrorism. "We are not at war with civilians. We only strike at strategic targets."

In part, this was true. The Kyiv railway station was a strategic target. And the Donetsk water arteries were also of strategic importance. But did this mean that the military had the right to destroy the lives of unarmed persons? Was the suffering of *all* children and *all* old people equal, or were we supposed to prioritize "ours" while ignoring "theirs?"

I shared my doubts with Sergiy. He logically explained to me that the so-called People's Republics of Donbas were to blame for their own fate. But he failed to prove to me that the hardships of my parents were the results of "justice."

Were the bombings of Hamburg and Dresden in 1943 and 1945 justified? Can the destruction of Hiroshima and Nagasaki be considered just? They could be the *right* decisions. They might even be *necessary* decisions. But these actions were about rationality, not about justice.

An eye for an eye, a tooth for a tooth? Arithmetically, there is no flaw in this commandment. But this can be very inhumane under certain circumstances. Here's the main truth about the war: Yes, it can be liberating, defensive, patriotic, sacred, whatever. But it cannot ever be humane because any war is directed *against* people.

Thou shalt not kill. Remember that Commandment? The worst thing about war is that it forces us to go against this truth. Russian President Putin cannot be prosecuted for bringing millions of people to an animal, bestial state. But the world will find ways to punish him as a warning to other dictators.

The first legal charge has already been brought against him. This happened on March 17, 2023, when the International Criminal Court (ICC) in The Hague issued an arrest warrant for Vladimir Putin on allegations of war crimes. The Russian president together with his administration's commissioner for children's rights, Maria Lvova-Belova, were accused of organizing a government campaign to remove Ukrainian kids from their own families and home country. At this point, roughly six thousand children have been taken from Ukraine and sent to Russia, many of whom were then adopted by Russian families, or given to special camps for military training.

All over the world, such activities have always been considered "kidnapping," one of the most heinous criminal offenses. This accusation alone would be enough to lock up Putin for the rest of his life. But Russia refused to recognize the legitimacy of The Hague. Dmitry Medvedev, deputy chairman of the Security Council of the Russian Federation and former president, went even further, suggesting firing a hypersonic missile at The Hague after Putin's ICC arrest warrant. "Look carefully into the sky," he pointedly wrote in his Telegram blog. It wasn't the threat of an alcoholic whose face was swollen from constant drinking. It was a statement by a Russian official.

World leaders winced in disgust. Only one of them found it possible to visit Moscow to shake hands with the child abductor and call him "dear friend" publicly. It was Chinese President Xi Jinping, who also invited Putin to visit Beijing in a demonstrative show of support after The Hague's arrest warrant restricted the Russian leader's travel options.

The reaction of Mr. Xi and Mr. Pu was rather sour. Shaking hands in front of the reporters' cameras, both dictators tried to smile as confidently as possible, but the facial muscles of the two leaders showed their tension.

I remember looking at one of those photos on my laptop screen while Erica played with Lego pieces behind me. Putin and Xi stood in front of their flags, dressed in dark suits, and carefully stretching their lips into semblances of smiles. The Russian president's tie was the color of clotted blood. The Chinese leader opted for a bright red tie, which I also associated with blood, only fresh.

"Why are they angry, Grandpa?" Erica asked.

I looked over my shoulder. She looked at the photograph with unusual attention for a child. She was only four and a half years old, and a quarter of her life had been spent escaping from war zones. I wanted to believe that this would not affect her psyche in any way in the future.

"Why are they angry?" Erica repeated her question. "Someone piss them off?"

I looked back at the photo. My little granddaughter had just described the status of Putin and Xi Jinping: they were really "pissed off." Their three-day political circus on the Kremlin stage had turned out to be a failure. It was driving them mad.

"They're just always angry," I said and closed the laptop.

I didn't want Erica to remember the images of these two men. When she grows up, they should no longer exist in the world.

Sometimes, I feel that God was prudent when he didn't endow us humans with immortality.

CHAPTER 22

Awaiting the Victory

FROM APRIL TO MAY WE WERE WAITING FOR THE UKRAINIAN COUN-teroffensive. All the bloggers, reporters, and reviewers talked about nothing else. When I woke up, I scrolled through the news feeds and did this till the end of the day, and then, in the middle of the night, I turned on the phone again so as not to miss the event.

Everyone discussed the upcoming offensive, naming the dates and directions of the main attacks. And everyone was wrong. The final truth was known only to President Zelensky, Commander-in-Chief Zaluzhnyi, and maybe two or three of the most reliable people from their entourage.

The date of the offensive was the strictest state secret in Ukraine. Any information leaked to the media was false—either intentionally or through incompetence. The truth was shrouded in "the fog of war," as the military calls it. The enemy had to be misled and disoriented as much as possible before someone inflicted a stunning blow on him. Or two. Or three. One by one or at the same time. On the forehead or from the back. There were many options. Zaluzhnyi had to choose the only correct one. Throughout the spring of 2023, he kept a mysterious silence. Other people spoke instead.

When it became clear that the offensive would not take place in April as announced, the commentators switched from giving statements to asking questions. The primary one had no answer and sounded like this: "Is the Ukrainian army capable of dislodging Russian troops from land they are occupying?" The answers were both positive and negative.

My family and I were supporters of the "we win" scenario. It seemed to me that we had every reason to achieve this objective.

An influx of powerful Western weapons has been vital in strengthening Ukraine's army and shaping the course of the war. Now, Kyiv could seize the battlefield initiative with new batches of Leopard and Abrams tanks, howitzers, a million rounds of artillery ammunition, and troops trained in the West. US officials had already held tabletop exercises with Ukrainian military leaders.

As far as I understood, our troops were waiting only for favorable weather conditions to move forward, but this was my amateur's opinion. As I later realized, General Zaluzhnyi had paused to mentally exhaust the enemy. He did the same thing that Russia had done before the start of a full-scale invasion of Ukraine. The raised iron fist did not strike, creating an atmosphere of constant threat and uncertainty. Undoubtedly, this got on the nerves of both Putin and the Russian military leadership. The soldiers in the trenches and the townsfolk were under constant stress, maintaining a continuing state of depression in the country.

In Kyiv, everyone I met was waiting for the offensive and talking about it. Ukrainians were tired of the war. It had already been about 450 days and nights. On the one hand, everyone was used to martial law, curfews, and air raids (as much as possible). On the other hand, we wanted to experience a sense of security and alleviate, if not end, the constant state of uncertainty. Life without air sirens and closed borders seemed almost too good to be true.

One day, I met an old mate from Donetsk on the street. Valery was my age and, starting in 2014, had traveled a path identical to mine. He left the family apartment, moved to Kyiv with one suitcase, and was forced to build a new life from scratch. His granddaughter was six years old and his wife had undergone major surgery. For a while, we discussed the prospects of returning to our hometown, but both of us decided that this would hardly be possible.

During the last several years of the war, Donetsk had become a habitat for embittered, itinerant, and poorly educated people. The intellectual and business elite had left the city long ago when it became clear that it would be turned into a Russian military outpost for raids into Ukraine.

Young men were forcibly mobilized and sent to war, where they faced being crippled or killed. Who would want to live among unbalanced people who had spent long years in isolation from the civilized world? The cost of a three-room apartment in Donetsk had already fallen to several thousand dollars.

"They'll never accept Ukraine," Valery said. "They'll always look at us as enemies."

"And so we are," I said. " . . . until a new generation grows up that won't remember the war."

"We won't see it," Valery said with a sigh.

"Our grandchildren will see it," I replied.

"Let's hope."

But Putin did everything possible to ensure that this war would never be forgotten by Ukrainians for generations to come. On Friday, April 28, around 4 a.m., a barrage of long-range cruise missiles was launched from Russian aircraft in the Caspian Sea area. Almost all of the twenty-three missiles were intercepted by the Ukrainian air defense system. However, one steel cigar filled with explosives hit the target—a residential building in Uman—accurately, killing seven people, including a child, and injuring seventeen more.

"The strike has achieved its goal," Lieutenant General Konashenkov, the Russian defense ministry's spokesperson, solemnly proclaimed. "All the designated facilities have been hit."

Meanwhile, Putin, the organizer of this massacre, was completely shielded in Moscow or Sochi. His two daughters lived in luxury and comfort under false names, as did his grandchildren, whom Putin carefully hid from the public. A man ready to unleash a nuclear was reliably protected by all Russian air defense systems and had every chance of living another ten or even twenty years, ruling a country that threatens the whole world.

Ukraine was the first, and so far the only, country in the world to openly and selflessly fight this monster. Our Western allies armed and supported us, of course, but Ukraine felt the brunt of the Russian blows. And Ukraine could no longer put up with this state of affairs, when the war was being fought only on its territory.

Tactically and strategically, we were on a road to nowhere. How can you defeat an enemy who destroys your life while he himself is unpunished and out of reach for retaliatory strikes? For a long time, the United States and its allies kept Ukraine from using long-range weapons on Russian soil. In the spring of 2023, this became impossible.

The inhabitants of the Kremlin could no longer feel completely safe. While issuing his criminal orders, Putin could not help but fear that retribution might one day follow. He understood that Ukraine might attempt to carry out aerial attacks on him or his residence. For that reason, an impressive number of antiaircraft systems were spotted on Moscow rooftops in the vicinity of key government buildings.

However, in the very early hours of Wednesday, May 3, the "irresistible" ring of security that surrounds Moscow's Kremlin, a large historical and government complex, was penetrated by what appeared to be two attempted drone attacks.

The first one caused a minor fire in the dome of the Senate building, causing smoke to rise over the Kremlin. The second one exploded in an intense burst of light near the same dome, while two men were climbing up there to extinguish the fire.

The attack on the Kremlin looked rather amateurish and did not cause much damage. Nevertheless, the Russian presidency claimed that Ukraine had attempted a strike on Vladimir Putin's residence and described it as "a planned terrorist act."

For all the seeming insignificance of the event, it made a strong impression on Russia's president. In fact, the drone attack took place a week before the main Russian holiday: the so-called Victory Day. By tradition, on May 9, the whole country celebrates the Soviet Union's victory over Nazi Germany in World War II. This victory has long been privatized by Russia, which renamed it the "great patriotic war."

The event held more and more significance for Russians every year, even to the point of absurdity when the whole country fell into a frenzy and threatened Germany (and the rest of the world). The warlike dances on May 9 were held under the slogan "We can do it again" and gradually developed into the centerpiece of a theory of Russian racial superiority since Vladimir Putin's twenty-three years in office.

The carefully orchestrated victory parades across the country became an obligatory part of the mass hysteria. For Putin, it was the most important event of the year, presenting him with an opportunity to flaunt his military might and status as the nation's leader. Over the years he derived his entire legitimacy from Victory Day, framing himself as the direct successor of Joseph Stalin who defeated Adolf Hitler.

Traditionally, the May 9 celebration included military parades in Moscow and more than two dozen Russian cities. It would involve thousands of troops, hundreds of types of weapons, and months of nightly rehearsals. Usually, the main parade started at 10:00 a.m., when military men and vehicles passed through the famous Red Square, where they were inspected by Putin personally, his senior army figures, and foreign leaders.

After a spectacular flight of supersonic fighters and strategic bombers over the Kremlin, the theatrical Immortal Regiment entered the stage—a colorful procession of people with portraits of relatives who died in the war. Putin could also join the march, positioning himself as "part of the nation," but still his place was on Lenin's Mausoleum podium, from where he would proclaim in fiery speeches the greatness of Russia and its great victories.

The year 2023 was different for Putin and "his people." On the eve of May 9, the country looked far from triumphant in its current war. A nervousness close to paranoia hit Moscow before Victory Day parades. The drone attack on the Kremlin revealed the inconsistency of its defense against other possible air strikes.

To add to Putin's worries, Ukraine increasingly and resolutely shelled targets on Russian territory. A few days prior, several fuel storage facilities had been attacked in Russia, not to mention freight trains derailed, and power lines destroyed by explosions. Although none of these attacks were claimed by Kyiv, it was clear that undermining Russia's logistics formed part of the preparations for Ukraine's long-expected (and long-suspected) counteroffensive.

Standing out against this menacing backdrop was the shady figure of Putin's favorite warlord, Yevgeny Prigozhin, owner of a private mercenary army known as the Wagner Group. Abandoning subordination and decency, Prigozhin recorded a remarkable profanity-laced video series blaming the top Russian military chiefs for mediocrity and inability to fight. In a separate message, he also hinted at a certain "happy old guy" who sits on Red Square and thinks that he is fine. "But what should the country do if this old guy turns out to be a complete asshole?" Prigozhin exclaimed at the end of the tirade.

No one in Russia has ever dared to insult Putin with such frankness. It was a public humiliation timed to coincide with the president's favorite holiday. Putin was losing power and influence. Would the decrepit tiger turn tail and run?

The May streak of rocket launches had not yet begun when my father's ninety-fourth birthday arrived. I did not congratulate my parents on Victory Day, which was my usual practice before the start of the war.

In previous years, I had managed to squeeze out a few words of greeting because my mother always asked me to. World War II was the backdrop to my parents' childhood and youth, and they considered themselves part of this tragedy. I understood them and continued to call them every May 9 even after Russia seized Donbas and Crimea. Now those times was over. Victory Day was actually a purely Russian holiday. The Russians didn't mourn the dead and didn't pray for peace. They remembered their victory in 1945 only to declare their greatness and determination to fight for more victories. They turned May 9 into a festival of war. I hated the very thought of it.

So I was going to skip congratulating my parents on Victory Day this year. However, I had to call my mother on May 9 because she expected my call every day—it was an obligatory and unchanging ritual. I remained the only thread connecting her with the rest of her family in Ukraine, where she had lived all her adult life until Russia attacked. Now she was a citizen of Russia, but she still remained my mother.

I spent a week preparing for this conversation, wondering what I should say if she said something like "Happy VE Day, Son." My concerns turned out to be unfounded. When I called Donetsk, my mother didn't have time for me. She and my father were watching Putin's speech in Red Square, and I had interrupted their main entertainment of the year. TV meant more to them than a son.

Believe me when I say I didn't take offense. I understood them. They heard and saw on television what they wanted to hear and see. There, on the screen, Russia was still great, and Vladimir Putin was deciding the fate of the world. It was an illusion, but who among us does not have illusions? Do we really want to lose the imaginary shell that protects us from cruel reality?

Even such a strong, hard, and independent man like my father needed to hang onto an illusion. He could do without God, but he was unable to live without Putin. Faith in the Russian president had replaced religion for my parents. It became the meaning of their life. They might have died if he was gone. And that moment is getting closer every day.

Their inevitable death scared me more than all of Putin's cruise missiles. The war had deprived me of the opportunity to be with them in the last days of their lives. Only the victory of Ukraine and the liberation of Donetsk could give me a chance to see my parents again.

Would I ever be able to return to my hometown in time to hug my parents while both of them are still alive?

Military experts gave encouraging forecasts, but I didn't believe them. No matter how much I yearned for the end of the war, I understood intuitively that this was still very far away. When I called my father on May 13, I had the feeling that I was talking to a man in a sunken submarine that was not destined to rise to the surface again.

His voice was weak, and he could not hear me very well.

"Happy birthday, Dad," I said. "I love you. I have always loved you."

The last time I had seen my father was nine years ago when his eighty-fifth birthday ended in a family quarrel. If I had the opportunity to fix just one day of my life, it would be May 13, 2014.

"I wish you happiness and health, Dad," I said. "Don't be sick, okay? Wait for me."

"What?" he asked, his voice distant and quiet. "I can't hear you. How are you, Sonny? Everything is fine?"

"Yes," I shouted. "How are you, Dad? Is the war hard for you?"

"I can't hear you," he said weakly. "I'd rather give the phone to your mom. Thank you for remembering us, Son. I love you. Be safe. So long."

So damn long . . . So unbearably long!

I walked for an hour or two in the drizzling rain, remembering the good and bad moments with my father. There were more good things. I wished I knew what *his* memories of me were. Did he consider me a good son? Hardly. He was a very demanding and picky man. I rarely lived up to his expectations—just as I'd failed to live up to my mom's illusions. They would both have preferred I live in Donetsk next to them and share their destiny. But I had my own destiny, so my path led me away. It was both fair and sad to realize this—but I couldn't turn back. I didn't want to. The Russian world belonged to yesterday. I was longing for tomorrow.

Ukraine, also, had no way back. Putin's war had cut us off from Russia forever. The Russians became for us one huge terrorist organization with whom it was impossible to negotiate anything. There were militants, their ardent supporters, and tens of millions of people who either approved of Russian aggression or did not oppose it. Putin spoke on their behalf and enjoyed their support. They could be Buryats, Yakuts, Russians, Tatars, Chechens, Ingush, whatever. It was not a question of nationality. It was a question of belonging to a criminal state called the Russian Federation.

On May 16, Russia bombarded Kyiv with nine Kalibr missiles and three ballistic rockets, as well as dozens of drones. The furious attack came at 2:30 a.m. Emergency sirens woke us. Luba and I stayed in our beds, listening attentively to the sounds outside.

"Seems quiet," she said after a few minutes.

I was about to reply when loud booms sounded and car alarms went off outside the window. The windows trembled, and the floor beneath me shuddered. Luba yelled out a short curse, and I rushed to help her get out of bed.

The surgery and radiation had severely damaged her delicate body. Since the beginning of spring, she had experienced such great pain in her lower back that she couldn't stand up, lie down, bend over, or pick up anything heavier than a plate of food. The doctors had offered an unpronounceable diagnosis that sounded like gibberish to my ears: *vertebrogenic lumboischialgia*, abbreviated as lumbago, or *lumbalgia*. Any tension in her back caused her agonizing pain. She was not able to go down into the bomb shelter, so all we could do was wait out the shelling in the bathroom or hallway where there were no windows. While there, we could be sure that we wouldn't be hit by pieces of broken glass. Unfortunately, the concrete walls of our apartment could not protect us from a direct hit by a missile or drone.

We spent about fifteen minutes hiding in the bathroom until the explosions stopped. We returned to our beds, but within seconds the cacophony of war brought us back to our feet. I saw a bright flash outside the window, illuminating the predawn sky.

"The explosions are very close," Luba warned me, her voice shaking.

"Those are shots," I said. "We are hearing the work of the American Patriots. Don't be afraid, dear. The Russian Kinzhals are not so scary anymore."

To tell the truth, I didn't know if we were protected by these super-powerful air defense systems, donated to Ukraine by the United States and Germany. However, my guess was confirmed in the morning when we read that six out of six Kinzhal missiles launched at Kyiv had been shot down. Spokespersons for the Ukrainian army did not speak directly about the use of US Patriots, but a day later, history repeated itself when a new powerful air raid by Russia failed. The Kremlin's most potent hypersonic weapon no longer worked in Kyiv.

Of course, the fragments of the downed Kinzhals had fallen on residential areas, causing destruction, fires, and even death, but these were smaller losses compared to the many thousands of victims that the missiles filled with tons of explosives could have caused.

After such a powerful demonstration of the effectiveness of the newly deployed Ukrainian air defenses, Putin's response was to stubbornly fire his beloved Kinzhals and Iskanders again and again.

Throughout May, Kyiv was subjected to systematic shelling on an almost daily basis. Sometimes people died. Sometimes there were children among them. But the general mood of the citizens in the capital was much more optimistic than in other Ukrainian cities where there were no Patriots.

The discussion of nighttime shelling became the topic of casual social conversations, like the weather or something like that. You went to a café and chatted with the bartender: "Hi, how are you? Did you manage to sleep today?" Kyivans had ceased to perceive ballistic missiles as a threat to their lives. But this was premature.

On the night of May 31, Russia struck a Kyiv hospital, killing two children. It was the most brutal attack in my memory. The explosions sounded so close, I braced myself for the worst.

I didn't feel anything like panic. It was more like apathy when you say to yourself: "Come what may, I don't care." This is a dangerous state to be in when the instinct for self-preservation no longer works.

I remember how, during one of the early morning raids, I went out to the balcony to look at the sky. It was a reckless and stupid idea, but I did it. I wanted to see where the danger was coming from. And I saw. A black dot was moving in the gray sky above and between the two twenty-five-story buildings. At first, I took it for a flying bird. Then I heard a lingering sound like the buzzing of an old electric razor and I realized that I was looking at an enemy drone. It was about a mile away, as far as I could tell. This might be wrong. It is usually difficult for people to determine the distance between objects flying high in the air.

When I saw the drone, I should have immediately left the balcony and warned my wife of the danger. I didn't. I watched the drone fly as if I were mesmerized.

It seemed to me that it had slightly turned around and was flying straight at me. My feet were rooted to the floor. I just stood frozen, watching. Instead of running away, I thought about Death and what it would bring. I imagined that my book would not be written, and Luba would be left alone without my support. I wouldn't see my granddaughters grow up. I wouldn't see the end of the war. There would be nothing else for me, except for the last dying flight to nowhere.

All this happened much faster than I can describe. I watched the drone for four or five seconds, I think. Then, in its place, there was a flash, small and bright orange in the predawn twilight, like a flame at the end of a match. I didn't hear the shots. I didn't even hear the explosion. I was lost in thought about The End.

On a gray background, a small, black, round cloud appeared, carried by the wind. As I watched, the smoke stretched into a sinuous line that turned into a question mark. I ran to get my phone and turn on the camera, but only a neat black dot remained in the sky. I wish I knew what that meant, but the universe rarely gives us definite answers. We have to discover them for ourselves.

CHAPTER 23

Making the Deadline

THERE WAS EVENING, AND THERE WAS MORNING—AND IT WAS NOW MY last day to finish my first book for my new publisher.

The contract said I was to deliver it on June 15, 2023, Thursday, the 472nd day of the war, but I intended to complete my work a few days earlier. I never cross over deadlines. There is something ominous about the word. I like the word "lifelines" better.

I pick up my cell phone from the floor and look at the timer. It's 3:45 a.m. An air raid warning symbol pops up on the screen. It started an hour and a half ago. I yawn. Could I have thought a year ago that I'd be yawning and stretching in bed when my phone warned me about an air raid? But I am absolutely calm, if not serene.

I've heard no explosions so far. This means that Russia launched low-speed Shahid drones. They'll fly up to Kyiv in about half an hour. Or they will not reach us at all, as has happened before. In any case, I have time to wash, brush my teeth, and make tea.

I sit down on a mattress spread out on the bare floor. My wife often has to turn around at night to find the right position for her poor spine, so I now sleep alone. Until 2014, when we were still living in Donetsk, we had a wide double bed, where we slept side by side and there was enough space for two of us. Now we don't have a bedroom. We live in a one-room apartment with a fold-out sofa.

The living room, study, and bedroom all fit in one room, ten paces long, and seven paces wide. When Erica comes to visit us, it also becomes a children's room, with toys, books, and all sorts of things strewn about the floor at random. She is our guest every day. It is a great joy to see your grandchildren grow up. But I miss Severine's sweet presence beside me. She and her mother are still in France. Perhaps complete happiness is not possible, especially during the war.

When I leave the bathroom, the air raid alert has already been canceled. Good news. As long as Russian missiles and kamikaze planes are flying in the sky, I can't get my daily dose of music because I have to be aware of external sounds. When I work in the morning, I sit with my back to the window, and it could be fatal if I miss the start of the shelling. Now I'm perfectly safe, or I think I am.

One day the air raid alert may not work. Or the phone will be dead. There is a huge open space outside the kitchen window, except for three buildings blocking the horizon. The window faces east, where Russia stretches all the way to the Bering Sea.

The morning is so beautiful. The sky is clear, the birds are singing. The sun is about to emerge from behind the house opposite. The beginning of each new day always carries a bit of mystery. You kind of know what's coming for you, but you never really know.

I sit down at the perfectly clean white kitchen table and open my laptop. Wake up, friend. We have a lot of work to do today.

I love working more than relaxing. And I love early mornings. This is the time that belongs only to me. By managing our time, we manage our lives. What could be more valuable than this? Our life span *is* our time.

I put on my headphones and get to work. Music doesn't bother me—I hardly notice it when I write. It's just a sound wall between me and the outside world. Music helps me not to be distracted.

At one time I became addicted to Ukrainian songs, but I had to give them up. There were too many emotions in these songs, too much anger and pain. I don't need it because I have enough of my own anger and pain. Sometimes I have to restrain my emotions. The writer's job is to tell, not scream. So I listen to meditative music. New Age. Ethnic. Classic melodies. They don't interfere with my thoughts.

In the middle of work, I jump up from my chair. The low sound of an explosion breaks through the musical curtain. Another muffled boom immediately follows. Through my headphones, it sounds like the drummer has knocked over his kit.

I turn on the phone. Oh, my gosh, I just missed the start of the second raid. This time, Kyiv is being attacked by missiles, either cruise or ballistic. One of these is capable of smashing several floors of a building even after it's been knocked down.

"Sergey!" Luba calls me from the room, her voice plaintive and alarmed. "Sergey, haven't you heard?"

I rush to her and help her up. We spend about twenty minutes waiting for more explosions, but none occur. Our phones simultaneously show the sets of alarms. I help Luba lie back down and she moans softly, looking for a comfortable position for her spine. Those small moans remind me of Time that cannot be turned back.

"I'm so tired," she mumbles. "If you only knew, Sergey, how tired I am."

I am also tired, but my wife expects other words from me.

"Be patient, dear," I say. "It'll be over soon. You know what? As soon as you recover, we'll go to the sea."

Luba smiles. "You always say that."

"And it always comes true," I say. "My publisher has already paid me half the advance. In a month or two I will have the other half. We'll have enough money, I think, to afford it."

Actually, I don't think so. I know we're not going anywhere this year. But why not dream a little?

"I'd like to go to the sea," Luba says. "Like before the war."

"Everything that is now *before* the war will be *after* soon," I say.

"It's good," Luba mumbles, sleepy now. "Open the window a little, okay? I want a bit of fresh air."

I let a cold, wet breeze into the room. Outside, it smells of ozone and wet greenery. But the rain doesn't start. The storm is passing by, flashing and rumbling far to the side, like a war that has touched us only on its edge. We're lucky, indeed. No matter what. In spite of everything.

"Sleep, dear," I say to Luba. "It is too early."

She falls asleep obediently. I return to the table.

The kitchen smells of peonies. These are Luba's favorite flowers, so at the beginning of summer they always stand in a vase on our table. Peony season is coming to an end soon. Everything has its seasons: flowers, love, life, war. Seasons change and so do we.

The "we" of yesterday is no longer the same as the "we" of today. The former *me* doesn't exist; it was just a dream. The current me, sixty-seven-year-old Sergey Maidukov, is completely different . . .

I have been writing about this for some time. Then I reread what I wrote and deleted the last three paragraphs. The stream of consciousness must be restricted; otherwise, it may go too far. I have to concentrate on what is happening here and now. This is quite a challenge, considering I'm not a Zen Buddhist.

My work continues until half past six in the morning. Time for breakfast and tea. At 7 a.m. sharp, I go on Skype to meet Claire. It's 9 p.m. in Tucson and she looks a bit tired.

"How are you, Sergey?" she asks.

This is her traditional question. My answer is also traditional.

"I'm fine, Claire."

We talk about our work for a while. Claire is sitting at her laptop, with a bookcase in the background. I hold my cell phone out in front of me. In order not to wake Luba, I communicate with Claire on the glazed balcony, behind the closed door. The sun shines in my eyes. I lower the window shade and say it looks as if Arizona has come to Kyiv. Claire laughs. She has a great sense of humor and the patience to listen to my terrible English. These are just two positive qualities from her extensive set.

We move on to discussing our next project. As always, Claire has many ideas and her enthusiasm quickens her speech. In response, I turn on my intuition. Occasionally, I have to guess what she is saying to me, but there have never been any mistakes. Claire somehow understands me when I try to catch up, and we have developed a kind of telepathic communication. Sometimes I feel like we've known each other for a long time. And I know for sure that we will see each other one day without the use of our computers and Skype. I will come to America. It will definitely happen.

After finishing our Skype session, I change my clothes and slip out of the house, trying not to wake Luba. My morning walk is an essential part of my daily schedule. I take it in every kind of weather: rain and heat, ice and snow. I walked when the forests around Kyiv were on fire and when the ghost of COVID was waiting for me around every corner. Blackouts and disabled elevators couldn't stop me. If it weren't for my wife and daughter, I would even walk during air raid alerts. But my beloved women strictly forbid it—and they also forbade me to drink coffee, fearing my sensitive stomach would act up again.

At a nearby café, I drink my first espresso and move on. The area in which we live is called Osokorki, which means "poplars." Everything here is new, young, and fresh—half of the residents are under thirty-five, by my estimate. I never tire of walking around the area and soon reach my favorite bench in the green square. I sit down to read the news, a paper cup of coffee in my hand. This is the second "fix" today. I adore coffee, and I instinctively rebel when somebody tries to control my private life, my time, and my habits.

Drinking coffee, I look at the "likes" on my Instagram posts. Apparently, making a career as a writer in America is easier than gaining an Instagram audience! I wonder, will my book really be published in the States? Both books? And what of those that will follow?

How many years have I put into this career? I tried to sell horror novels, fantasy, and George Harrison's biography . . . but somehow, I never managed to cross a certain border, vigilantly guarded by a garrison of literary agents. They immediately recognized me as an interloper, stopped me, and turned me around in the opposite direction:

Dear Sergey,

Thank you for giving us a chance to consider your work (*Shame on you for bothering me over such trifles*). Unfortunately, (*to our great relief*) after our careful (*cursory*) consideration, we have concluded that this is not a good fit for this agency. We receive over a (*million . . . billion . . . gazillion*) submissions a week (*a day . . . an hour*) and we must be *(vigilant against newcomers*) selective, so please understand (*don't go suicidal on us—we can't afford the lawsuit*).

These monotonous, uniform letters always ended with the same consolation prize: "However, another agent may well feel different."

And as it turned out, this was true. Another agent *did* appear, and she *did* accept me and my writing, and now everything is going—and will go—in a very "different" direction.

Temporarily buoyed by my idyllic mood, things come crashing down as soon as I pick up the *Telegram* for the latest news. Damn! Russia has not left the planet! Staying in its usual geographic coordinates and in its usual hysterical state, it has committed another war crime while the complacent UN officials prepared to celebrate Russian Language Day.

When will this nightmare end?

Reading the news, I am convinced that Ukraine is experiencing a serious environmental, technological, and humanitarian catastrophe— the first in decades! Fearing a counteroffensive by the Ukrainian army, Putin's military leadership has given the order to blow up the dam at Nova Kakhovka, built by the Soviets in the middle of the last century.

Within minutes, the Dnipro River's waters cascaded through the breach and began flooding the lowlands and plains in southern Ukraine. The crossing that spanned the river was washed away like a sand castle on the beach—as if it never existed.

This manmade disaster has affected at least a hundred thousand Ukrainians, while hundreds of thousands are left without access to drinking water. Satellite images reveal widespread devastation, drowned villages, and flooded cities. The footage looks like scenes from a movie about a biblical deluge. People hang on desperately from trees and crowd onto the roofs of houses that have gone underwater. Dead animals float down the river.

I turn off my phone and am transported to a completely different reality. I am sitting on a comfortable bench, surrounded by fragrant greenery. People walking past me are hurrying to work. It's a typical summer morning. No one sprinkles ashes on their head while mourning the dead. Nobody sounds an alarm.

Panic will arise only when Putin orders someone to blow up the Zaporizhzhia nuclear power plant, which is already mined and waiting for its time to come. Then, we inhabitants of Kyiv will rush to our cars, desperate to leave the radioactive zone. And the rest of the world will live its usual life, sad for a few minutes, then going on as if nothing happened. Although we may lack sympathy for others, we ask God for sympathy and relief for ourselves. Isn't it hypocritical?

I get up from the bench and head back home. Gradually my steps quicken and I can't wait to sit down at my laptop and pour my feelings into the pages of a new book while they're fresh. I have something to say to the world. Immediately. Without delay.

I know we can make our world a much more attractive place. It depends only on us. We need to remember to be "human" for others and not tolerate any evil. Pretty simple, right? If each of us takes one small step in this direction, then all of humanity will move forward significantly.

Suddenly, a man with a dog appears ahead of me on the street. In one hand he holds a leash, and in the other a phone. He is staring down at it, most likely reading the news about the flood in southern Ukraine. He's so engrossed in this occupation that he doesn't pay any attention to his pet, running from one side of the sidewalk to the other.

It is a rather small, furry dog, and its stretched leash constantly blocks my way. It is like a line that I can never cross. The dog's master walks slowly down the middle of the sidewalk. Whenever I intend to overtake him on the left or the right, the dog runs there with its leash straight as a tight string.

I am in a similar position to a driver who's being blocked by a truck ahead of it. The dog's owner looks big in his loose T-shirt and saggy knee-length shorts. I'm irritated. He doesn't care about those around him at all. He doesn't look back, he doesn't look around, and he doesn't look aside. His eye is on the cell, allowing his stupid mutt to run where it pleases.

And I am in such a hurry! I have to finish my message to the world.

I call out to the man, but he doesn't hear. That's because his headphones are clipped over his ears. I'm getting ready to overtake him on the left and his dog immediately appears in front of me. I lift my foot to step over the leash. Oops! This is a mistake. The dog takes this as my attempt to kick it. Baring its teeth, it yips, bounces, and hangs onto my denim-covered leg.

Damn! I shake the little devil off my leg before it bites me. The man finally looks up from his phone. I yell at him to compensate for my fright from the dog's attack. I tell him everything I think about him and his furry pal. I do this in a very brusque and aggressive way, with threatening gestures accompanying my speech.

The man, confused, backs away. The dog rushes toward me, pulling on the leash. At least a dozen onlookers are watching us. I feel ashamed of my overwrought behavior, but I can't stop.

"You'd better keep your mutt away from me, or I'll have him put down!" I shout at the man, shaking my finger at him. "And you, too! Make a notch on your nose about it!"

I step back and walk away with the air of a winner. But I don't feel like a winner. I feel like a psychopathic piece of shit. Can't I cope with my negative emotions? What are all my well-meaning thoughts worth? What right do I have to talk about empathy, compassion and so on? As charity begins at home, so honesty begins in the soul.

I turn a hundred and eighty degrees and walk in the opposite direction. Maybe I'm doing it a little too fast. Both the man and his dog react to my return without any enthusiasm. The dog's master looks at me warily. His pet barks sharply, then slightly backs away.

"Hey, I'm sorry," I say. "You know, I behaved rudely. It was disgusting and unfair. Please accept my apologies."

The dog falls silent and looks inquiringly at its master, trying to see his reaction.

"I was guilty, too," the dog's owner says. "I shouldn't have gone so deep into the news."

"Kakhovka?" I ask.

"Well, that's just it," the man replies, frowning. "I couldn't believe my eyes. How could this be?"

"Our guys will go on the offensive anyway," I say. "Neither water nor fire can stop them. There is nothing in the whole world that can."

The dog carefully approaches me, stretches its neck, and sniffs at my leg, which it recently tried to bite. I squat down and extend my hand.

"Look out!" warns his owner hastily.

"Everything's fine."

I put my hand on the dog's warm head. It bares its teeth, but now it looks more like a friendly smile than a menacing grin.

"I'm sorry," I say. "I won't do it again. We're buddies now, right?"

The dog barks shortly when he hears my apologies. Its master gives me his hand. I leave with a light heart. What I just did is more important than any words I could utter. I didn't allow myself to become worse than I *am*. This means that I have become a little better than I *was*.

Stresses, catastrophes, trials, and sorrows can release very bad qualities in us—as well as very good ones. We choose who we will become.

Ukraine entered the war as a weak, divided, corrupt country, existing on the geographical map but almost invisible in the political arena. Look at us now. And look at Russia now. A striking difference, isn't it? Fateful changes. And all this happened in less than sixteen months. That is what my book is about.

About change for the better. About choosing the best. About the will to move forward, no matter what.

I return home eager to write down my thoughts to complete the book. Luba meets me with a slightly guilty look.

"Sergey," she says, "can I ask you to do something?"

I glance toward the desk with the laptop on top of it.

"Of course, dear," I answer. "What do you want?"

She asks me to buy her fresh strawberries, farm eggs, and a few other things. It's still hard for her to carry heavy objects, so that's my responsibility. I smile at my wife and leave the house. A little delay is nothing. I will finish my book and send it to America.

And it will be published—even if Putin blows up another dam or uses tactical nuclear weapons against Kyiv. I won't disappear. I *am* this book. We are all our "books" waiting to be written, following the course laid out for each of us. It's no accident, is it, that paths merge and bring us moments of hope amidst despair?

Today, I will focus on that theme. At the end of it all, I am grateful that Life continues to bring surprises and unexpected joy when least expected. Is this not enough? For me, today, the answer is "Yes."

Appendix

Below are two articles I wrote for *American Thinker* magazine two months before the first Russian troops openly attacked Ukraine in the summer of 2014, and almost eight years before the outbreak of full-scale war on February 24, 2022. These pieces will allow you to judge how accurate my opinions and forecasts about Putin and Russia turned out to be. I hope this will also convince you of the correctness of my current thesis.

Unfortunately, my voice was too lonely and weak in 2014 to wake up American officials and the public. My warnings went virtually unnoticed in the States. In Russia it was different. These two articles were translated into Russian and appeared in the press. It did not bring me any money or popularity. All I got were repeated threats on the phone and on social media platforms. As a result, I was forced to close all my web accounts and lost the opportunity to visit my parents in occupied Donetsk. I was lucky that I left this city shortly before the start of cruel repressions against the opponents of the fascist regime established by the Russian Federation.

Who doubts today that we are dealing with the bald face of real fascism, without makeup or embellishment?

March 28, 2014

The Enigmatic "Russian Soul"

By Sergey Maidukov
What makes the Russian national character so special? Is it really true that they are different from the other people?

The answer is . . . yes, definitely.

Born in the USSR
Ranked at number 155 according to the Global Peace Index, Russia is one of the most dangerous countries in the whole world. It is notorious as the lawless land, where people are assassinated every 18 minutes, averaging 84 murders per day in a nation of 143 million.

The other side of the coin is a high level of suicide. The Serbsky State Research Center in Moscow announced that Russia had reached second place in the world in suicide rates, behind only Lithuania. In the years between 1993 and 2013, about a million Russians killed themselves. Furthermore, another million die each year from alcohol- and smoking-related causes.

Russian men have an average life expectancy of just 60 years—one of the lowest in Europe. A full quarter of them die before their 55th birthday.

It seems like the whole nation, like a giant herd of lemmings, is moving in the direction of self-destruction, but that does not prevent them from being proud of themselves and their country. They believe they once lived in one of the greatest empires in the world.

A new poll, conducted by the independent Levada Center in Moscow, found that nearly 60 percent of Russians "deeply regret" the collapse of the Soviet Union. For Westerners, who grew up regarding the USSR as a menace to civilization, it is akin to the notorious mystery of the "Russian soul"—a myth that is still alive, thanks to Russian literature.

A number of similar myths exist. For example, the common legend of an ancient Slavic culture. There never was, and could not be, such a concept because the term "Slavs" in all Western European languages always referred simply to "slaves"—the pagan people who survived under the oppressive regimes of one conqueror after another.

Easy Prey
Who are the Russians and where did they come from? As long as two millennia ago, their ancestors, often referred to as "the eastern Slavic tribes," came from what is now present-day Poland and Ukraine. Those people were said to occupy the northeastern realms of the Eurasian continent. This vast territory of wild lands was considered valuable only for its forests, and with the exception of

areas near its river boundaries, the forests were rather impenetrable, without trails or even little footpaths.

"There are no roads in Russia," Napoleon once said bitterly, "only directions."

The vegetation of the country was least abundant in the southern districts; the cold region was one vast thicket. While Europe's first farmers were cutting down trees in the forest to plant fields, the Russian tribes preferred to hunt and fish. It was a less complex society—people did not have to come together to work the land. As a result, they did not have a society, and without society, no fellow-feeling, no religion, no mental development, and without trade no industry, that real source of national welfare and strength.

Very soon warlike neighbors took the occasion to seize the land from the weak natives.

First came the Vikings. They moved up and down local rivers as if they owned the place. And well . . . eventually they did. One of the cities founded by them was Kyiv. Grand Prince of Kyiv, Oleg, actually was a leader of Vikings with the good Scandinavian name of Helg, just like Vladimir was Valdemar and Igor was Ingvar.

The land of Rus' (derived from the Norse "rower") is supposed to have been a part of Sweden because the ruling class there was made up entirely of Vikings—that is Waringians, or Varangians, as they are referred to in The Primary Chronicle, *Ukraine's earliest native historical source.*

By the way, the religion, art, architecture, and language of Rus' were therefore all early Ukrainian. More northerly, proto-Russian tribes played rather a marginal or downright hostile role in history. It was they who supported the so-called Tatar-Mongol invasion.

A Barbarous Torch Relay

For the Russians of the 13th century, both "Mongols" and "Tatars" were equivalent terms. All nations to the east of Russian borders for hundreds of years were called Tatars.

The Mongols came from the east, too. On their way to Europe, they conquered dozens of various Rus' tribes, absorbing them into their forces. The bulk of the Golden Horde were Tatars who had been conquered previously by the Mongols. The Russian Princes were local collaborators, quite often sacrificing the well-being and security of their people to promote their own influence and power.

In fact, the favorite heroes of the Russian nation, Alexander Nevsky and Dmitry Donskoy, oppressed their compatriots, regarding them as brutes, as slaves of a different race. Yaroslav the Wise of Kyiv was one of these princes who later was named Tsar—which was a distorted version of the Latin title for the Roman emperors, Caesar. Before Yaroslav, the title was applied strictly to the Mongol overlords of the Rus' principalities.

The most famous Russian Tsar was Ivan IV, known as Ivan the Terrible, who rallied the Russian people around Moscow. Under him, the Muscovites conquered the Tatar khanates of Kazan' and Astrakhan, establishing Moscow's rule over a huge area of the Volga basin and the North Caucasus.

Thus was born the idea of Moscow Tsardom as "the Third Rome," although it could be better viewed as "the Second Golden Horde."

Ivan the Terrible enjoyed watching as people were burned alive or drowned in ice-holes. Peter I used to kill his servants [with] his bare hands, and taught executioners how to properly tear the nostrils of victims with pincers. Czar Paul I, known to history as the "Mad Czar," was so sensitive about his homeliness that he made mentioning of the words "pug-nosed" a crime punishable by death. Czar Nicholas I compelled his recruits to practice the goosestep while bearing upon their tall headgear a glass full of water. If a soldier spilled as much as a single drop, he was obliged to serve an additional year for every drop he spilled.

The absolute power of Russian tsars has always been brutal, oppressive, inhuman. This power was built upon a principle similar to the infamous "vertical power" that President Vladimir Putin has created in the 21st century. The principle is extremely simple. It is called a one-person tyranny, when millions of lives are worth nothing.

Stalin was not the first and not the only Russian tyrant who was ready to turn the whole nation into "camp dust." You may be interested to know that after the Crimean War of 1854–56, the government of Tsar Nicholas I sold at auction for fertilizer the bleached bones of 38,000 Russian soldiers who fell in the battle of Sevastopol.

Today the world is threatened with a second Crimean War. The troops under the command of the new tsar of Russia are on alert.

Stolen Soul

The entire history of modern Russia is nothing but a continuous cycle of tsars. Tsar Khrushchev succeeded Tsar Stalin. Brezhnev deposed Khrushchev and became the tsar himself. Weak Tsar Gorbachev ceded the throne to mighty Tsar Yeltsin, who appointed his successor, Putin . . . who appointed his successor Medvedev . . . who proposed to elect President Putin again . . .

The Russian people do not believe that they can live differently, can live better than now. In the course of many centuries, they were so pressured, so enslaved that faith was simply squeezed out of them. That is why today we see in Russia a maimed society, miserable people, utterly humbled, robbed, deceived, and full of fear of the authorities.

These people do not know what freedom is. These people used to live in an atmosphere of constant violence against the person. "Russian talk of political evil is as natural as eating," the poet Joseph Brodsky once said. They are destined to live and die in the historical Russia—the land of imperial complacency, cruel despots, and groveling before the Power.

So what about the famous Russian soul? There is no need to find it in the crowd of people who fell prostrate before the throne. The crowd has no soul. Only a hole. One giant black hole.

April 13, 2014

The Russians Came

By Sergey Maidukov

It was only 15 years ago that former U.S. president George W. Bush found permanent Russian president Vladimir Putin to be "very straightforward and trustworthy." Now, at last the mask is off, and we see a barefaced dictator with an iron hand, one finger of which is poised over the nuclear button.

Is Weakness a Sign of Strength?

Since the Crimea crisis erupted, Vladimir Putin is probably the most adored and most hated man of the 21st century. His approval rating has risen above 80 percent in his native Russia—almost as high as in foreign Syria, Venezuela, or North Korea. At the same time, the whole civilized world watches him with suspicion and nervousness. It's clear to everyone that Russia will not limit itself to the Crimea. Its historical and strategic ambitions are spread far beyond the rocky peninsula in the Black Sea.

Will Russia invade the rest of Ukraine? Moldova? Latvia? Estonia? Only Putin knows the answer.

Former secretary of state Hillary Rodham Clinton was the first noted political figure to compare his aggression in Ukraine to actions taken by Nazi leader Adolf Hitler in the runup to World War II. Very recently, German finance minister Wolfgang Schäuble said he saw parallels between the annexation of Crimea and Hitler's land grab of Sudetenland in 1938. As leader of the strongest nation on Earth politically, economically, and militarily, U.S. president Barack Obama simply could not stand aside. He declared that Russia's aggression was a sign . . . of weakness. This was the most annihilating criticism against Russia that fell from his lips.

In his recent statements, Obama has clearly signaled that the U.S. will not protect its European allies, much less Ukraine. He obstinately refuses to hear the warnings from the Pentagon and NATO that Russian military activity on Ukraine's borders could be a prelude to a military invasion. Or maybe, on the contrary, he hears them too well?

The main problem of liberal democracy is its unwillingness and inability to use force in support of its ideals. The European welfare state which cannot defend itself desperately needs an outside power to protect it. The United States has played that protective role since the end of World War II. But with Obama showing such obvious weakness in foreign affairs, America certainly cannot be considered as a dependable ally.

And Russia's president understands this very well. From the bottom of his soul he despises the West and thinks it is rotten to the core. Rather a natural point of view for the former secret policeman who has described the collapse of the USSR as "the greatest geopolitical catastrophe of the 20th century."

In the 21st century, we stand on the threshold of a much more terrible catastrophe. It is called the global rebirth of fascism.

Raised from the Ashes

In recent years, "fascism" has become a label used by anyone to discredit everything and everybody. Politics regard it as some dirty "f-word," often interpreted very emotionally and very negatively.

Today, arguments over the exact definition of fascism are not very important. After the Crimea's conquest and its inclusion in the Russian empire, you can feel it, taste it, and see it with your own eyes. It is simply here, that is all.

To verify this, it suffices to recall the fourteen typical characteristics of "Eternal Fascism," or "Ur-Fascism," from the famous essay written by well-known Italian philosopher Umberto Eco in 1995 which appeared in the New York Review of Books. According to Eco, "it is enough that one of them be present to allow fascism to coagulate around it."

The first four of the 14 properties are as follows:

1. The cult of tradition.

The central site of Moscow (and Russia) is the ancient Red Square—a huge cobblestone rectangle with its long history of public executions and military parades, its brightly colored onion-shaped domes and squat Lenin's Tomb. The first 21st-century czar of Mother Russia likes to receive foreign dignitaries at the Great Kremlin Palace glittering with gold and marble. Old and dusty heroes, from Alexander Nevsky to Peter the Great and Stalin, are more popular than pop singers and television stars. The Russians prefer to look back on their dark (they say its glorious) past, rather than forward.

2. The rejection of modernism.

In this case, modernism is the movement of progress, a general view of history in which the present is much better than the past, and the future holds everything hopeful for us. Most Russians are generally quite pessimistic and don't have much faith in a better life in the future. Sitting on the couches and watching talk show after talk show, they hear a constant and repetitive message that the modern world has degenerated due to "liberal-bourgeois fags" and "national traitors." The modernization programme launched by temporary president Medvedev in 2009 has passed into oblivion, and no one noticed.

3. The cult of action for action's sake.

"Action must be taken before, or without, reflection," Eco wrote. "Distrust of the intellectual world has always been a symptom of Ur-Fascism." In Russia, we see numerous confirmations of this statement, from Lenin's catch *phrase "The intellectual forces of the workers and peasants . . . are not its brains but its shit" to the frequent use of such expressions as "blabbing intellectuals," "foureyes" and "botanists."*

    4. Disagreement is treason.

In February, hundreds of people—along with members of the Russian punk band Pussy Riot—were arrested in Moscow for protesting against Putin. Then a number of prominent opposition leaders, including activist and blogger Aleksey Navalny and former deputy prime minister Boris Nemtsov, were sentenced to several days in prison. Last in this long list of traitors is Andrey Makarevich, whose band The Time Machine performed at the Kremlin's election event in 2008. Russian patriots started the campaign for the musician's deprivation of all state awards in connection with his critical position on events in Ukraine and in the Crimea.

    The other characteristics of the Eternal Fascism are: "Fear of difference," "Appeal to a frustrated middle class," "Nationalism," "Envy of enemies," "Denial of pacifism," "A popular elitism," "The cult of heroism," "Condemnation of nonstandard sexual habits," "Selective populism," and, finally, "[Use] of impoverished vocabulary." In fact, each one of them is perfectly fitted with the reality of Russian life.

Heil Leader!

If Umberto Eco was right, then all of the problems the world is facing in Syria, Iran, Somalia, North Korea, and all the other countries of the Third World will pale in comparison with the Ukrainian disaster.

    Russia's military forces have decayed and weakened since the Cuban crisis of 1962, but they still have sufficient numbers of nuclear warheads and are capable of destroying human civilization with no warning. Right now, tens of thousands of Russian troops are massed on the borders of Ukraine and in the direction of the Ukrainian city of Donetsk.

    Meanwhile, the pro-Russian protesters who seized the regional government building in Donetsk have declared a "people's republic." Reading from a paper, a bald, grey-bearded man acclaimed protesters would call on Russia to send in a peacekeeping force in the event of aggressive action by the authorities in Kyiv.

The big question is what happens tomorrow, or after tomorrow, or some other day? Not just in Donetsk, but in the whole eastern Ukraine, which Putin would also dearly love to snap off. The West already let him swallow the Crimea in the hope his invasion stops there. It didn't work with the Führer in 1938, and only the most naive politician would bet his best tie that it will work with the Russian leader now.

It is not known what Barack Obama thinks of it, because he keeps an enigmatic silence. So we have to settle for quoting President Richard Nixon who once said that the attitude of Russia towards Ukraine will make or break the international order established in the aftermath of the victory over Hitler and his Reich.

Indeed it is broken. Will Putin try to achieve new order—his own new order—in Europe? In the rest of the world?

We will see. Soon enough.

Index

ABC News, 47
Afghanistan war, 118
Afghan refugees, 7
Airborne Division, for US, 96–97
air defense systems: Kinzhal
  missiles shooting down, 223;
  Putin protected by, 217;
  Zelensky asking for, 180
air raids, 176; cell phones
  warning of, 180, 210, 227;
  establishments closing during,
  170; on Kyiv, 169
air raid sirens, 5, 9, 171, 197,
  210; birthday beginning with,
  168–69; in Lviv, 66; missiles
  before, 189
airspace, of Ukraine, 54
Albanians, 122
Aleppo, in Ukraine, 9
Alexander "Sashko" (son in law), 7,
  39–40, 45, 53, 58; fever suffered
  by, 73; financial difficulties
  of, 161; Kyiv returned to by,
  81; Maydukova stayed with
  by, 69–70; Ukrainian learned
  by, 160
America. *See* United States (US)

American mass culture, 202
American officials, Russian
  invasion warned of by, 53–54
American Thinker (magazine), 19,
  36, 74
ammunition depots, for Russia,
  207–8
Anna (landlord), 161
Antalya, Turkey, 36
antiaircraft batteries, 169
antiaircraft systems, 192, 211, 218
apartments, of Maidudov,
  Sergey: in Donetsk, 16; hallway
  as most protected place in,
  167–68; Ilya and Anna renting,
  161; in Kyiv, 28; Luba checking
  on, 41–42; rental rates of, 70;
  smell overpowering, 160
Arizona, in US, 116
Armed Forces of Ukraine, 124,
  177–78
Artpop! (album), 30
Assad (Syrian president), 9
Atlantic Ocean, North, 78
ATM, line at, 8
Azov Sea, 110

Miroslav (doctor), 141–42, 145
missiles, Russian: before air raid
sirens, 189; ballistic, 190;
hydroelectric dams damaged
by, 172; Javelin, 54; Kalibr,
222; Kh-22 cruise, 190, 210;
Kinzhal, 210–11; Kyiv struck
by, 167, 179–80, 229; military
training facility targeted by, 78;
S-300 antiaircraft, 190; theater
hit by, 70
Mitsubishi Crossover (car), 58–59
monasteries, 65–66, 199–200
money, 8, 36, 125, 133, 161, 175
monuments, to Russian national
heroes, 159
Morrison, Jim, 139
Moscow, in Russia, 29; antiaircraft
systems in, 218; Maidukov
sullied by association with, 25;
Putin hiding in, 199, 217; Xi
visiting, 213
mother, 30–31, 88–89; birthday of,
211; propaganda influencing,
198–99; Ukraine hated by, 40
Motława River, 105
mouse, death of, 127–28
Munich Security Conference, 196
municipal hospital, in Nowy Targ,
134–37, 139–41
Muscovite rockets, 7
music, listened to by Maidukov,
115–16

Nagasaki, in Japan, 212

National Advanced Surface-
to-Air Missile System
(NASAMS), 182
NATO. *See* North Atlantic Treaty
Alliance
Nazi Germany, 11, 218
Netherlands, the, 192
news, the, 6, 11–12, 47, 234;
addiction to, 52; Bogdana
upset by, 76–77; cell phones
propagating, 59, 62; Maidukov
reading, 62–63, 231; Malaysia
Airlines' flight MH17 displayed
on, 26–27; in Russia, 29, 57;
Ukrainian prisoners shown on,
38, 129–30; war reported on
by, 6
New Year's Eve, 53, 89, 187
New Year's tree, 89
New York City (US), Maidukov
dreaming of, 202
1984 (Orwell), 10
no-fly zone, 11
North Atlantic Ocean, 78
North Atlantic Treaty Alliance
(NATO), 11, 53–54, 95, 98–99,
180, 201; Biden, J., uniting,
171; Putin threatening, 97;
Russia confronted by, 108;
weaponry withheld by, 181
nose treatment, for Maidukov,
137–38
Nova Kakhovka, dam at, 232
Novotel hotels, 106, 115, 120–21

Nowy Targ "City of Owls," in
Poland, 125, 144; death and,
132–33; hotel in, 126, 130–31;
municipal hospital in, 134–37,
139–41
Nuclear Power Plant,
Zaporizhzhia, 76, 98, 233
nuclear weapons, Russian, 165;
Putin emphasizing, 48, 172,
196, 201; special combat
readiness of, 97–98; threat of,
96, 99, 143

Obama, Barack, 30
occupation, Putin denying,
17–18, 35
Odyssey (Homer), 80
Olenivka, penal colony in, 128
155th naval infantry (Russian
brigade), 196
Orban, Viktor, 171
Orest (Azovstal defender), 112
ortodocsal Christmas, Ukrainians
celebrating, 52–53
Orwell, George, 7, 10
osokorki. See poplars
Osokorki (area), in Kyiv, 231

pandemic, COVID-19, 8, 44, 53
Paratroopers, US, 96–97
parents, of Maidukov, 88, 198–99,
211; death and, 221; Kremlin
influencing, 20–21; Luba
boycotting, 41; TV influencing,
20, 29, 220–21; USSR

impacting, 21; war isolating,
88; World War II influencing,
220*See also* mother
partial mobilization, Russia
announcing, 165
passports, Russian, 88
Patriot PAC-3 systems, 182,
192, 223
peace, family wishing for, 53
penal colony, in Olenivka, 128
peonies, 230
People's Republics of Donbas. *See*
Donbas
Pepsi-Cola, 179
Peskov, Dmytro, 92
Peter the Great (tsar), 166
the Philippines, Devil's Sea in, 52
phones. *See* cell phones
Poland, 63–64, 67–68, 93, 95,
149, 155; Bydgoszcz in, 100;
Katowice in, 122; Krakow in,
122; Lodz in, 100; Lublin in,
85, 98; Rzeszow in, 82; Ukraine
compared with, 156; Ukrainian
refugees sheltered by, 142;
Ukrainians supported by, 108;
Warsaw in, 145; Wroclaw in,
122*See also* Gdansk; Nowy Targ
Polish salesman, family mocked
by, 82–83
poplars (*osokorki*), 231
Poroshenko, Petro, 32–34
power, electrical, 6, 169–70,
209–10

near Kyiv, 157–58; Ukrainian troops dislodged by, 215–16
Russian tsars, Ukraine invaded by, 156
Russia 1 (Russian TV channel), 58
Rzeszow, in Poland, 82

Saint Michael's monastery, 199–200
St. Mary's Church, in Gdansk, 119
St. Petersburg summit, 182–83
salesman, Polish, 82
sanatoriums, hotels functioned as by, 73
Santa Claus, Ukrainian, 187
SARS-CoV-2 virus, 44
Saul (US Paratrooper), 96
Scholz, Olaf, 171
Secretary of Defense, US, 2
secretary of state, US, 117, 157, 182
Security Council, of UN, 168
Security Council of the Russian Federation, 213
Sergiy (son), 13–15, 18, 36; Bakhmut visited by, 209; COVID-19 pandemic recovered from by, 53; Kyiv stayed in by, 26, 54–55, 60, 77–78, 86–87; Maidukov spending time with, 161–62; publications illustrated in by, 162; writing encouraged by, 203; Zelensky liked by, 44

Servant of the People (sitcom), 50, 186
Severine (granddaughter), 16, 40, 55, 62–64, 228; Erica contrasted with, 51; France left for by, 78; Lviv stayed in by, 63–64; Maidukov taking, 60–61
Shahed. *See* "kamikaze" drones
Shahid drones, 227
shame, Maidukov, struggling with, 177
Shehyni, Ukraine, 68
shelters, bomb, 5
shirts, embroidered, 32
Simonyan, Margarita, 57
Sisyphus (myth), 202
Skabeyeva, Olga, 58
Skyfall (film), 30
Skype, 40, 87, 117, 146, 148, 230–31
smoking, 104
Snow Maiden (fairy tale), 187
soldiers, Ukrainian, 61, 176–78, 209
Solovyov, Vladimir, 58
Somalia Battalion, 38
songs, Ukrainian, 228
Soviet army, Gdansk razed by, 108
Soviet train car, 25
Soviet Union (USSR), 20, 32; Nazi Germany beaten by, 218; parents impacted by, 21; US contrasted with, 91, 202
special combat readiness, of nuclear weapons, 97–98

officials from, 232; Security Council of, 168

United States (US), 201; Airborne Division for, 96–97; antiaircraft systems from, 192; Arizona in, 116; Congress of, 186–87; HIMARS supplied by, 207–8; New York City in, 202; Patriot PAC-3 systems supplied by, 192; Russia bled by, 117–18; Secretary of Defense for, 2; secretary of state for, 117, 157, 182; Ukraine supported by, 117; USSR contrasted with, 91, 202 *See also* Biden, Joseph Robinette

US elections, Russia meddling in, 47

US Paratroopers, 96–97

vacation, Maidukov hoping for, 189

Valery (old mate), 216–17

Valya (daughter of Irina), 94–95

vertebrogenic lumboischialgia (lumbago or *lumbalgia*), 222

Victory Day (Russian holiday), 218–20

Villa La Grange, in Switzerland, 47

Vitaly, 130, 133, 137

vor. See thief

Vuhledar, in Ukraine, 196

vyshyvankas. See embroidered shirts

Wagner Group, inmates joining, 208–9

walking, Maidukov prioritized by, 49, 231

war, Russia-Ukraine, 109, 147, 205, 212; boys playing at, 91; family impacted by, 40–41, 209; human life impacted by, 74; Kremlin denying, 20, 31; Kyiv ignoring, 197; Luba discussing, 175–76; Lviv bracing for, 67; the news reporting on, 6; parents isolated by, 88; personal price of, 4; prisoners of, 38, 128–30, 159; propaganda distorting, 211; Putin not preparing for, 207; rental rates impacted by, 70; Russia cut off by, 222; Solovyov supporting, 58; Ukraine destroyed by, 66; Ukrainian soldiers trying to end, 103; Ukrainians tiring of, 216; world press saturated with, 103–4; writing about, 71, 193 *See also* Russian army; Russian forces; Russian troops; Ukrainian troops

War and Peace (Tolstoy), 149

war crimes: Kremlin covering up, 123–24; Milley on, 168; by Putin, 213

Warsaw, in Poland, 145

weaponry, NATO withholding, 181

weapons. *See specific weapons*

wedding anniversary, with
Luba, 174
the West, Putin threatening, 165
Western countries, 11, 84, 168
Westerns (genre), 201
wildfires, around Kyiv, 44
winter, without heat, 172
women, resettlement of, 95
world leaders, Putin ignored by,
166–67
World War II, 75, 218; Clinton
referencing, 30; Gdansk
destroyed during, 108; parents
influenced by, 220
writing, by Maidukov, 84–85,
101, 115, 175, 230, 235; about
Devil's Sea, 52; about war, 71,
193; of *Deadly Bonds*, 176; in
English, 74; literary agents
rejecting, 231–32; process of,
112–13; Sergiy encouraging,
203; of true-crime book,
116, 193

Wroclaw, in Poland, 122

Xi Jinping, 166, 213, 214

Yanukovych, Victor, 13–14

Zaluzhnyi (Ukrainian
Commander-in-Chief), 215
Zaporizhzhia Nuclear Power
Plant, 76, 98, 143, 233
Zeit (magazine), 162
Zelensky, Volodymyr, 108, 124,
183, 199, 215; air defense
systems asked for by, 180;
Biden, J., and, 50–51, 117;
Congress addressed by, 186–87;
Kolomoisky associated with,
50; Putin infuriated by, 43–44,
55, 185; on Russian army, 157;
Sergiy liking, 44; *Servant of the
People* starred in by, 186
Zoom, 85, 96, 203